Royal
Horticultural
Society

BRITAIN'S FAVOURITE PLANTS

OVER 1,000 PLANTS CHOSEN BY THE NATION'S TOP NURSERIES

THINK
BOOKS

First published 2007 by Think Books
an imprint of Pan Macmillan Ltd
Pan Macmillan, 20 New Wharf Road, London N1 9RR
Basingstoke and Oxford
Associated companies throughout the world
www.panmacmillan.com
www.think-books.com
www.rhs.org.uk

ISBN 978-1-84525-045-4

Text Copyright: Royal Horticultural Society 2007
Design Copyright: Think Publishing and Pan Macmillan Ltd 2007

Editor: Geraldine Sweeney
Editorial Team: Tania Adams, Rica Dearman, Emma Jones, Simon Maughan,
Sonja Patel, Richard Rees, Mark Searle, Linda Stanfield, Marion Thompson
Design: Sally Laver and Lou Millward

1 3 5 7 9 8 6 4 2

A CIP catalogue record for this book is available from
the British Library.

Printed and Bound in Italy by Printer Trento

Visit www.panmacmillan.com to read more about all our books and to buy
them. You will also find features, author interviews and news of any
author events, and you can sign up for e-newsletters so that you're
always first to hear about our new releases.

Main cover image: Amanda Bunn/Flowerphotos
Additional images: Front cover, left to right: Burncoose Nurseries, Harts Nursery,
Owl's Acre Sweet Peas. Back cover, from top: Water Meadow Nursery, Shipton Bulbs,
Westcountry Lupins, www.flowerphotos.com, Halls of Heddon

Take thy plastic spade,
It is thy pencil; take thy seeds, thy plants,
They are thy colours.

William Mason, *The English Garden*, 1782

GREAT RAIL JOURNEYS

2008 Departure Dates and Prices
First Class Rail Travel

25 Mar	£1,265
1, 8, 15, 22, 29 Apr, 6 May	£1,325
13, 20, 27 May	£1,375
3, 10, 17, 24 Jun	£1,375
1, 8, 15, 22, 29 Jul	£1,375
5, 12, 19, 26 Aug	£1,325
2, 9, 16, 23 Sep	£1,375
30 Sep, 7, 14 Oct	£1,325
21, 28 Oct	£1,265

■ no of nights in hotel ◇ itinerary stops ···· by rail

What's Included

- First Class rail travel throughout.
- Swiss Travel Pass (unlimited travel on most trains, buses & steamers).
- Half board hotel accommodation.
- A full programme of excursions.
- Services of a Tour Manager.

2008 brochure out now

01904 734125

BOOK ONLINE
www.GreatRail.com

Dates and prices are subject to availability.
Prices are Per Person. Conditions apply.

  ◆ABTA
ABTA No V2170

Rail tickets are provided in co-operation with
Deutsche Bahn DB

Classic Glacier Express
— 10 DAY HOLIDAY BY TRAIN FROM LONDON —

Travel with the UK's leading specialist in holidays by rail on this sensational 10-day two-centre holiday to Switzerland. A friendly and professional Tour Manager accompanies all departures, so relax as you travel across the roof of the Alps through amazing scenery.

Days 1-2 ◆ London to Switzerland

We leave London St Pancras on *Eurostar* for Paris and travel to Dijon by *TGV* for an overnight stay. We continue into Switzerland for the scenic journey up the Rhône Valley to Brig for four nights.

Days 3-5 ◆ Brig

During our stay in Brig we take the narrow-gauge mountain railway to Zermatt, which is overlooked by the Matterhorn. We visit Interlaken where your options are endless and you have a day free to explore the region.

Day 6 ◆ The *Glacier Express*

We board the famous *Glacier Express* narrow-gauge train, probably the slowest 'express' in the world. The train climbs up the Rhône Valley before descending through woodland to the Rhine. We arrive in the historic town of Chur in the early afternoon for a three-night stay.

Days 7-8 ◆ Chur

Our stay in Switzerland's oldest town includes a fabulous journey on the *Bernina Express* across viaducts and bridges, past waterfalls and deep ravines to Poschiavo. You also have a free day to explore Chur, or alternatively you could visit the towns of Arosa or Lucerne.

Days 9-10 ◆ The journey home

We leave Chur and travel to Cologne for an overnight stay. Our journey continues to Brussels where we connect with *Eurostar* to London.

We also offer three other exciting *Glacier Express* tours including a Standard Class rail tour with prices from £825pp. Please see brochure for details.

One of over 70 escorted tours worldwide

— JOURNEYS AS GREAT AS THE DESTINATIONS —

THANK YOU

Many thanks to all the garden nurseries who contributed to this first issue of *Britain's Favourite Plants*. This book would not have been possible without your help and support.

We received an overwhelming response from all the nurseries we contacted and in order to include as many as possible, not all material supplied has made it in to the finished manuscript. We regret that we did not have room for all the nurseries who expressed an interest in the book.

A special thanks to Simon Maughan and Geraldine Sweeney for their time, patience and horticultural knowledge.

CONTENTS

Symbols key

The Royal Horticultural Society's Award of Garden Merit ♈ is given to plants that give the best all-round garden value. For more information and for a full list of plants visit www.rhs.org.uk/plants/index.asp.

This symbol ✿ shows that an NCCPG (National Collection for the Conservation of Plants and Gardens) collection exists at this nursery. Provisional collections appear in brackets. Full details of the NCCPG Plant Collections are found in the annual *National Plant Collections® Directory*, available from www.nccpg.com.

Hardiness

Hardiness ratings are shown for certain Award of Garden Merit (AGM) plants and other plants which require particular growing conditions. Plants in this book should be presumed to be hardy in most gardens in the British Isles, unless otherwise stated. Plants that require glasshouse conditions can be moved outdoors in summer.

H1 = plants requiring a heated glasshouse

H2 = plants requiring an unheated glasshouse, or very sheltered conditions outside

H3 = plants hardy outside in southern or western and sheltered inland gardens

H4 = plants hardy in most regions of the British Isles

DAVID SALISBURY®

conservatories without compromise

David Salisbury is the definition of style,
whatever your taste. We take care of everything
including design, manufacture and build.

Please call for our free brochure **0844 800 8808**
www.davidsalisbury.com

HOW TO USE THIS BOOK

Britain's Favourite Plants aims to acquaint gardeners old and new with a range of stunning plants that perfectly match their gardening needs. It presents the very best of our favourite garden plants, as chosen by those who really know them – top nurserymen and women.

Over 100 of the cream of our nurseries were specially selected by the RHS and asked to recommend their top plants. What makes *Britain's Favourite Plants* unique is that the nurseries themselves, often award-winning specialist growers or National Collection holders, have made their personal selections based on their knowledge and experience of the plants they produce. Every effort has been made to include as many as possible, yet they represent only a small proportion of the enormous number that exist.

The plants in this book are not an exhaustive list, but rather the essence of our favourite plants, enthusiastically described by those who know and grow them. Some growers, such as Cayeux Nursery, may not be based in Britain, but have been included because they are well known for growing 'British favourites'. Nurseries have focused on their best and most garden-worthy plants, so readers will find familiar favourites alongside unusual or new ones they never knew existed. For example, few may have grown *Deinanthe bifida*, but after reading Carol Klein's description of 'a class act with sage-textured pale green leaves and charming pure white flowers', many will be itching to try.

Using the book

To help readers select the best plant for their needs, *Britain's Favourite Plants* has been organised into the following categories: Interesting Mixtures, Plants for Places, Seasonal Plants, Trees, Shrubs and Climbers, Fruit, and Herbaceous Plants. Within these are nurseries'

top 10 recommendations (or top 5 for smaller species), plus invaluable advice for getting the very best from each plant, accompanied by beautiful photographs.

Readers will also find a brief profile and full contact details for each nursery, including website addresses and opening times if applicable. We believe this information is correct at the time of going to press. However, as many nurseries are small or family-run concerns, we recommend that you contact them before visiting.

Botanical names

Plant names can cause considerable difficulties for gardeners (and editors). Most would prefer to always refer to a species by its common name (rose, tulip and so on); however, common names can vary between countries – and nurseries – particularly when referring to specific subspecies or hybrids.

To avoid confusion, *Britain's Favourite Plants* orders plants by their common names, or commonly accepted botanical names (for example, asters or geraniums) in the category headings, but always uses the botanical names in the text itself (for example, *Gentiana verna* or *G. verna* where the genus is repeated in the text). Subspecies are indicated by subsp., varieties by var., synonyms by syn. (in parenthesis), form by f. and hybrids by x. Names of cultivated varieties (cultivars) are marked in quote marks (for example, *Rhododendron* 'High Summer'), but where some cultivars are known by their trade names, that name is presented without (for example, the dwarf lilac, *Syringa* Josée). Cultivar groups are also presented without quote marks, as in *T. humilis* Albocaerulea Oculta Group. For up-to-date information on plant names, we recommend the invaluable *RHS Plant Finder*.

learningcurve

www.learningcurve-uk.com

distance learning courses for gardeners

rhs horticulture
garden design
leisure gardening
organic gardening
wildlife gardening
and others...

For a free gardener's guide call:

01896 860661

or visit our website.

INTRODUCTION

CAROL KLEIN

There is an incredible richness available in today's garden plants; fleeting flashes of hot colour; fascinating textures of leaves and stems; bold statements of dramatic architectural specimens; the reliable backdrop of garden stalwarts. The current trend in modern gardening embraces the idea that a garden should be a place buzzing with vitality and a welcome habitat for wildlife. To make it happen in our own garden relies on getting the right plants in the first place, then putting the right plant in the right place!

A cursory flick through the *RHS Plant Finder* will reveal a staggering breadth of plants available from the nation's nurseries. There wasn't always this bounty. When I started gardening nearly 30 years ago, you were pretty much restricted to the range your local nursery – or the brash new Garden Centre – offered. But now you can see the fruits of how well nurseries have responded to more demanding customers and the plant aspirations of the nursery owners themselves. Backwards in time to resurrect lost treasures, forwards with wave upon wave of new strains and improved selections.

We all have much more mobility than we used to, and while I would strongly recommend we support our local nursery, in a way, all our small nurseries have become local. As well as visiting them, you can come across them at the scores of flower shows held throughout the year around the country. Proprietors and their staff are only too pleased to share their knowledge and turn an impulse buy into an informed choice. If you don't want to travel, many nurseries supply by mail order and via the internet.

Britain's Favourite Plants will certainly whet your appetite. Over 1,000 of the nation's favourite plants are unveiled here for your delectation. Here you will find a collection of some of the best nurseries trading on these shores today, many of whom are top RHS exhibitors. Each one recommends their top plants, with growing advice and useful tips. All have something different to offer, and a dip into this book is sure to introduce you to a new dimension for your gardening.

If you think your garden is already full, or, heaven forbid, you feel your gardening has become jaded, let *Britain's Favourite Plants* rekindle your desire for that special plant you must have. Discover the plant you didn't know was out there. Seek out that one nursery that holds that treasure for your garden, and bring it home.

CAROL'S CHOICE

TEN FANTASTIC PLANTS, AS RECOMMENDED BY CAROL KLEIN
OF GLEBE COTTAGE PLANTS

Eryngium bourgatii

Rudbeckia fulgida var. deamii

'm very fond of these 10 plants and wouldn't want to garden without them. They are thoroughly gardenworthy and perform reliably and beautifully in my own garden and in Glebe Cottage Plants.

1 *Eryngium bourgatii* 'Blue Form'

Spectacular! Handsome clumps of glaucous foliage marbled in white, with fabulous heads of silver-bracted flowers turning brilliant blue as summer progresses. Flourishes in any well-drained soil, but must have full sun to perform. Grows to a height of 45-60cm (18-24in).

2 *Crocosmia* 'Flame'

One of the first of these immensely useful irids to flower. Fiery blooms on 45cm (18in) stems and rich green, sword-like foliage. All crocosmia benefit from being lifted every two years and having the new corms broken off and replanted with the addition of plenty of compost.

3 *Allium beesianum*

Surely the cutest of all the ornamental onions. Grassy foliage and full heads of pendulous, vivid blue flowers. A real fairy plant, which grows to only 10cm (4in) high. Needs full sun and fares best in a rock garden or a trough. Will seed around gently.

4 *Astrantia* 'Glebe Cottage Crimson'

Selected for its exceptionally dark crimson bracts, dark stems and foliage, the small flowers that form the 'pincushion' are also deep crimson. In flower from May to October. Height 60cm (24in). Relishes heavy soil, a rich diet and plenty to drink. Very Bacchanalian!

Schizostylis coccinea

5 *Patrinia scabiosifolia*
An unusual valerian relative with umbels of acid-yellow flowers on tall stems. Russet autumn foliage, too. An accommodating plant, which combines perfectly with *Verbena bonariensis*. It can reach a height of 20-50cm (8-20in).

6 *Schizostylis coccinea* 'Major' ♔
Satiny blooms of glowing red are borne, several to a stem. One of the most handsome and long-flowering perennials. Although it starts in July, there are often a few flowers to pick at Christmas. It grows to 60cm (24in).

7 *Geranium nodosum* 'Dark Heart'
Given to us by botanist John Fielding, this outstanding cranesbill has pale-rimmed petals with a deliciously deep purple interior. Evergreen, with warm, orange-flushed foliage in the autumn, it provides excellent ground cover even in dense shade. Height 45cm (18in).

8 *Deinanthe bifida*
A herbaceous hydrangea relative, deinanthe is a class act with sage-textured pale green leaves and charming pure white flowers. Its rounded petals contain a powder-puff of white stamens and anthers. Needs shade and humus-rich soil. Height 20cm (8in).

9 *Rudbeckia fulgida* var. *deamii* ♔
Lights up the autumn garden with its brilliant yellow daisies, growing to 1m (3ft). A true plant of the prairies, at home in any good soil, it invariably gives a good show. Its black conical centres persist long after the flowers, a fine addition to the winter garden and a treat for the birds.

10 *Primula sieboldii* 'Snowflake'
Its fragile bearing and dainty flowers belie its tough, robust constitution. This enchanting Japanese primula spreads from stolons, making large clumps in damp or heavy soil, spangled with pretty, white flowers. A real shooting star, disappearing by summer. Grows to 30cm (12in).

GLEBE COTTAGE PLANTS
Pixie Lane, Warkleigh, Umberleigh,
North Devon EX37 9DH
W: www.glebecottageplants.co.uk

Carol Klein started **Glebe Cottage Plants** in 1984 to sell surplus plants she had propagated for her own garden. Most of the plants for sale in the small nursery can be seen growing in the adjacent rural cottage garden. The nursery is open Wednesdays, Thursdays and Fridays, 10am to 1pm, and 2pm to 5pm from the first week after Easter until the last week of October. Printable directions can be found on the website.

ABOUT THE RHS

The UK's leading gardening charity

The RHS believes that horticulture and gardening enrich people's lives. We are committed to bringing the personal and social benefits of growing plants to a diverse audience of all ages, to enhance understanding and appreciation of cultivated plants, and to provide contact with the natural world.

We believe that good practice in horticulture and gardening in both private and public spaces is a vital component of healthy sustainable communities and the creation of long-term environmental improvements.

The RHS has four gardens around the UK: Wisley in Surrey, Hyde Hall in Essex, Rosemoor in Devon and Harlow Carr in North Yorkshire, as well as over 100 partner gardens. It runs some of the best flower shows in the world and is a world leader in horticultural science and libraries. The RHS runs education and outreach programmes across the UK to help people realise their potential. Its charitable activities include:

- Helping over 600,000 children a year through hands-on opportunities for children to grow plants and learn about the natural environment
- Encouraging sustainable horticulture and environmental care
- Promoting biodiversity and creating wildlife habitats at its gardens
- Providing expert gardening advice
- Running the RHS Award of Garden Merit scheme to help gardeners choose plants that perform well
- Undertaking scientific research into issues affecting gardeners
- Educating and training gardeners of all levels and experience
- Maintaining the Lindley Library, the finest horticultural library in the world

The RHS relies heavily on donations and sponsorship to help enhance people's lives through gardening. For every pound received from its members' subscriptions, the charity needs to raise more than twice as much again to fund its charitable work.

While the charity receives some income from garden operations, flower shows, shops and plant centres, support from donors and sponsors is vital to its mission to bring the benefits of gardening to all.

RHS PLANT CENTRES' TOP 20 PLANTS

AS INTRODUCED BY CLARE BURGH, ADMINISTRATOR, RHS WISLEY

Lavandula angustifolia 'Hidcote'

So how did we choose our top 20 plants? We might have selected the current season's top 20 plants, popular for their newness to the market and recent promotion. Alternatively, our list could have reflected all-time bestsellers, or featured plants which are popular because they're fashionable. We've plumped for a mixture of all of these describing some absolutely must-have, great-selling plants, some new, some old, and all in demand. In this book our top 20 are broken down into herbaceous bestsellers, shrub bestsellers and Alpine bestsellers. Our staff then had no hesitation in naming our all time bestseller, *Lavandula angustifolia* 'Hidcote', which I'm sure has gently swayed into many a nurseryman/woman's list.

HERBACEOUS BESTSELLERS

Linda Dolan, Supervisor
1 *Calamagrostis* x *acutiflora* 'Overdam'
A perfect grass, so easy to grow and with such a long season of interest. It forms clumps of arching, dark green leaves with a cream margin. In summer, spikes of brown flowers appear, which last into winter. It grows to 90cm (36in) and thrives in well-drained soil in sun.

Hakonechloa macra 'Aureola'

2 *Helleborus* x *hybridus* Ashwood Garden hybrids

Developed at Ashwood Nurseries, these showy Lenten roses are wonderful heralds of spring. The cup-shaped flowers in pink, red, purple, black, green, yellow and white, produced from January onwards, are long-lasting. The plants form clumps of evergreen leaves. Height 45-60cm (18-24in).

3 *Gaura lindheimeri* 'The Bride'

I have a tiny garden, therefore plants have to earn their keep and this one certainly does, by being long-flowering and easy to grow. It forms a large plant of graceful, willowy stems carrying many flowers from July to October. Growing to 120cm (45in), it will thrive in a sunny position.

4 *Erigeron karvinskianus* ♈

A tiny plant with common names like fleabane and Mexican daisy. Tolerant of poor, dry soils, it grows well between paving stones. The daisy-like flowers open white, ageing to pink and are produced from April until October. It grows to 15cm (6in) and makes a real impact when planted *en masse*. H3

5 *Verbena bonariensis* ♈

An excellent architectural border plant which grows to 1.5m (5ft). The self-supporting stems carry long-lasting bluish-purple flowers from June to October. Our customers adore this plant. Although a short-lived perennial, it self-seeds profusely. Best grown in moist but well-drained soil in a sunny position. H3-4

6 *Hakonechloa macra* 'Aureola' ♈

A very pretty low-growing grass from Japan, it can cope well at the front of a border or in a container. The leaves are brilliant yellow with slender green lines running through them. It is non-invasive, deciduous and

Geranium 'Gerwat'

Berberis thunbergii 'Admiration'

requires little attention. Grows to 30cm (12in) and is best in semi-shade. H4

7 *Imperata cylindrica* 'Rubra'

A dramatic, showy grass which adds interest to a sunny border. It is commonly called Japanese blood grass, because it forms clumps of narrow leaves which start green and turn red through the season. It grows to 45cm (18in) and thrives in fertile soil. H3

8 *Geranium* 'Gerwat'

Hardy, reliable, long-flowering; these attributes make this one of my favourite perennials. As a bonus, it's the perfect combination of blue and white with each saucer-shaped flower having five petals, flowering from June until the frosts. This plant is tolerant of most soils, and can grow to a height of 50cm (20in) and is at its best in the sun. Its selling name is Rozanne.

Phlox divaricata
subsp. *laphamii* 'Chattahoochee'

grows to a height of 60cm (24in) and spread of 75cm (30in). H4

2 *Berberis thunbergii* 'Admiration'

This dazzling shrub suits a wide range of planting combinations. I love its small, round shape and dense habit, and its fresh bright apple-green foliage tinged brick red in spring. Later in the summer the colour becomes stronger. It produces its best colour in sun. This stunning shrub can grow to 45cm (18in).

3 *Daphne* x *transatlantica* Eternal Fragrance

What would a late winter garden be without the perfume of *Daphne* Eternal Fragrance? This neat evergreen bears dense clusters of intensely fragrant white flowers in mid-to-late spring and is still flowering in June. It thrives in sun or part shade, and can grow to a height and spread of 80cm (32in).

4 *Prunus incisa* 'Kojo-no-mai'

Diminutive form of the Fuji cherry, giving all-year-round garden interest. In winter, the slightly contorted and layered branches look splendid. Then, in spring, there are masses of pale pinkish-white blossoms. Its autumn colour is also excellent. Ideal for even the smallest garden. It has a height and spread of 90-120cm (36-45in).

5 *Cornus sanguinea* 'Midwinter Fire'

With its glowing orange and peach-pink 2m (6ft) stems, this makes a fantastic show in the RHS Garden at Wisley throughout winter. As well as winter stem colour, the leaves produce buttery autumn tints. *C. sanguinea* has white flowers in summer, which later develop into black fruits. This bestseller looks fantastic in the garden all year round.

SHRUB BESTSELLERS

Laurel Emms, Supervisor
1 *Lavandula angustifolia* 'Hidcote' ♈
No matter how many new cultivars are raised, this lavender remains the favourite. Bright purple flowers are carried above compact, silvery-grey aromatic foliage in summer. I love this plant in sunny borders or as a hedge. It

6 *Vaccinium corymbosum* 'Bluegold'

Named as one of the superfoods we should all be eating, the highbush blueberry is hugely popular. It is easy to grow, with an upright habit and mid-green leaves with rich red autumn colour. Bell-shaped white flowers appear in spring and are followed by delicious berries. Height 90-120cm (36-45in).

7 *Trachelospermum jasminoides* ♈

This twining climber is so popular we are unable to keep up with demand. An evergreen with glossy, dark green foliage, it is sometimes bronze-tinted in winter, and is complemented by fragrant white summer flowers. It thrives in sun or shade and any well-drained soil. Height 9m (28ft). H3-4

8 *Clematis armandii*

A vigorous species, sought after for its evergreen foliage, it produces fragrant saucer-shaped white flowers in early spring. The glossy, dark green leaves are pinkish-bronze when young. Best grown in full sun, on a south or west-facing wall, this climber will reach about 6m (18ft).

9 *Rosa* Gertrude Jekyll ♈

England's favourite rose, as voted by BBC viewers. Perfect scrolled buds open to large rosette-shaped rich pink flowers of beautiful old rose formation and the scent is superb. The upright, vigorous, healthy, reliable and repeat-flowering features make this a rose worth having. It grows up to 1.2m (4ft). H4

10 *Amelanchier* x *grandiflora* 'Ballerina' ♈

This *Amelanchier* is the perfect small garden tree. Upright, then slightly spreading in habit, its leaves emerge bronze, turn green in spring and then put on a show of rich red

Clematis armandii

and orange in autumn. White flowers in mid-spring are followed by juicy, blue-black fruits. Amelanchiers prefer lime-free soil, in sun or part shade and can reach 8m (27ft). H4

ALPINE BESTSELLERS

David Elliott, Manager
1 *Gentiana verna*
This is one plant which transports me straight to the Alpine mountainside. This delightful Gentian has stunning blue flowers on 5cm (2in) stems, above a carpet of green foliage in early spring. It's perfect in a trough with other alpine jewels. It will thrive in well-drained alkaline compost in a sunny position.

Rosa Gertrude Jekyll

Gentiana verna

2 *Phlox divaricata* subsp. *laphamii* 'Chattahoochee' ♈

A divine dwarf phlox, for a cool, slightly shady situation. Its lilac-blue flowers, each with a reddish-purple eye, grace its 20-30cm (8-12in) stems in late spring. It requires moist, humus-rich, but well-drained conditions, with some shade. H4

THE WISLEY PLANT CENTRE
RHS Garden, Wisley, Woking, Surrey GU23 6QB
T: 01483 211113
E: wisleyplantcentre@rhs.org.uk
W: www.rhs.org.uk/wisleyplantcentre

The **Wisley Plant Centre** at the Royal Horticultural Society's flagship garden in Surrey has been selling plants for 30 years. We specialise in reflecting the range of plants seen growing at Wisley which include many rare and unusual cultivars. With more than 10,000 different plants available there is something at **Wisley Plant Centre** for everyone. Profits from sales go towards supporting the work of the RHS. We often have plants grown specifically to meet customer demand using propagation material from the RHS Garden. Our staff are extremely knowledgeable, passionate about the plants they sell and always happy to help.

PLANTS FOR...
COTTAGE GARDENS

AS RECOMMENDED BY ROSEMARY AND ROBERT HARDY OF HARDY'S COTTAGE GARDEN PLANTS

Aster amellus 'King George'

Cottage garden plants instantly bring to mind the quintessentially English country garden. The following selection of plants is perfect for creating the feel of a cottage garden, but will also look equally at home in a more formal layout. They are plants we have either introduced ourselves, or long-standing favourites, which always perform well.

1 *Anemone* x *hybrida*
'Honorine Jobert' ♆
Commonly known as Japanese anemone,
with single white flowers in autumn. It is a
vigorous grower, reaching 1.2 x 0.6m
(4 x 2ft). Plant February to April, in well-
prepared soil with a lot of rotted garden
compost, in sun or part-shade. Definitely
a plant not to be without in a garden.

2 *Anemone nemorosa* 'Robinsoniana' ♆
This has to be one of the prettiest wood
anemones. Its large lilac flowers are
held in abundance above the dark green,
deeply divided foliage. These lovely plants
will carpet the ground in the spring
under shrubs or trees, growing to
25 x 30cm (10 x 12in).

3 *Aster amellus* 'King George' ♆
This is a very neat-growing, if sometimes
slightly woody plant, reaching 50 x 50cm
(20 x 20in). The large blue-mauve daisy
flowers have a yellow centre that attracts
butterflies. It prefers alkaline to neutral
soils. Plant in the early part of the year in
a sunny position.

4 *Campanula lactiflora*
'Prichard's Variety' ♆
This variety has vivid purple-blue
bellflowers. It is easy to grow in full sun or
part-shade, reaching 75 x 60cm (30 x 24in),
as long as there is moisture. Like most
campanulas, it grows quite fast and requires
its clumps to be split every two years.

5 *Campanula* 'Samantha'
Unusually for a campanula, the large violet
flowers are scented, making it an even more
attractive plant. It blooms for a long period in
the summer and is compact in its growth at

Campanula lactiflora 'Prichard's Variety'

Anemone x *hybrida* 'Honorine Jobert'

Campanula 'Samantha'

Cirsium rivulare 'Atropurpureum'

25 x 30cm (10 x 12in). It grows well in good soil in full sun, but tolerates dappled light.

6 *Cirsium rivulare* 'Atropurpureum'

A wonderful plant for the middle of the border, with lovely red-purple thistle flowers. It makes a large clump 90 x 80cm (35 x 31in) and grows best in moist soils. *The* plant for the last six years, used in abundance at the Chelsea Flower Show.

7 *Dicentra spectabilis* ♕

The amazing arching stems with their dark pink flowers and white tips look delicate in late spring, but the bleeding heart is a very tough plant. If cut back, it re-grows and flowers again. An invaluable plant for shady borders. Height 90cm (35in).

8 *Gaillardia* Oranges and Lemons (syn. Saint Clements)

Oranges and Lemons has large yellow and orange daisy flowers, with a long flowering season, making it excellent for cut flowers. As long as it is planted in moisture-retentive, well-prepared soil, it will grow well to 60 x 50cm (24 x 20in), in sun or part-shade.

9 *Gaura lindheimeri* 'Chiffon'

This plant has very elegant, pale-pink flowers that dance around like beautiful ballerinas on lengthy upright stems over a long flowering period. It is tall, at 50cm (20in), but also see-through. We bred this form ourselves, releasing it in 2004.

Gaura lindheimeri 'Chiffon'

Dicentra spectabilis

10 *Geranium* x *oxonianum* 'Lace Time'
The hardy geraniums have to be the most
useful plant family for cottage gardens.
This particular variety has almost yellow,
new foliage, then flowers continually through
the summer, with pale pink flowers with dark
veins, growing to 30 x 60cm (12 x 24in). Sun
or part-shade in any soil.

HARDY'S COTTAGE GARDEN PLANTS
Priory Lane Nursery, Freefolk Priors, Whitchurch,
Hampshire RG28 7NJ
T: 01256 896533 F: 01256 896572
E: info@hardys-plants.co.uk W: www.hardys-plants.co.uk

Rosemary and Robert Hardy started growing herbaceous perennials 18 years ago
and now grow over 1,200 different varieties. They moved to the present nursery
site 10 years ago, where customers are welcome to stroll around the three acres
of outdoor-grown plants. Twelve-time Gold Medal winners at Chelsea, they delight
in exhibiting at many gardening shows and events across the country. The nursery
is open daily, 10am to 5pm, March to October; Monday to Friday, 10am to 3pm,
November to February.

EASY TO GROW

AS RECOMMENDED BY ALEX BALLANCE OF BLOOMING MARVELLOUS PLANTS

Polystichum setiferum

When it comes to plants, 'easy' can be interpreted in various ways, but you should always remember that 'easy' does not need to mean 'boring'. There are plenty of interesting, unusual plants that are easy to grow. Even if you lack time or experience, that doesn't mean you can't grow something special. We have chosen 10 plants that will grow in most conditions and need little work once planted. What they all have in common is that they are perennials or hardy shrubs, which reduces work and cost compared with annual bedding.

1 *Ajuga reptans* 'Arctic Fox'
Many forms of *Ajuga* make useful ground cover, but most can be invasive. Not this one. The leaves of the variegated bugle are glossy and irregularly marked with dark green, creamy-white and even greyish-green. These are topped in spring with the characteristic spikes of bright blue flowers 10cm (4in) high.

2 *Acanthus spinosus* ♔
The flowers of this statuesque herbaceous plant, also known as bear's breeches, form impressive spikes up to 1.2m (4ft) tall, predominantly white and purple, that rise above the mound of deep green, glossy foliage. Unfortunately the flowers have vicious spines. It will grow well in full sunshine or in quite deep shade.

3 *Cephalaria gigantea*
The primrose yellow flowers of the giant scabious tower above the border from June to August. A 'see-through' giant – the plant grows to 2.4m (8ft) by 1m (3ft 3in) – use it to add height and airiness to a border. Give it lots of room and deadhead to keep the flowers going. Plant in sun or partial shade.

4 *Dicentra spectabilis* 'Alba' ♔
Arching stems of white locket-shaped flowers from April to June and bright green leaves make this a beauty for the shade garden.

Will die down in late summer, so grow it tucked in among other shade lovers. Good for lighting up a shady place. It can grow to 90cm (36in) by 45cm (18in) wide.

5 *Digitalis* x *mertonensis* ♆

Large flowers the colour of crushed strawberries rise on stems above the glossy, mid-to-dark green leaves, from late spring to midsummer. The flowers are a gentler pink than the native foxglove, and it is a short-lived perennial. Reaching 90cm (36in) by 30cm (12in), it grows in sun or light shade.

6 *Erodium pelargoniiflorum*

When this flowered in our new display beds, it sold out within days. The mound of soft, furry leaves looks like a perennial geranium, and the white flowers with dark veins look like single Pelargoniums. It flowers from April to June or July, will self-seed and grows to 45cm (18in) by 60cm (24in).

7 *Gaillardia* x *grandiflora* 'Tokajer'

The rich, dark orange, daisy-like flowers, with or without slight tips of yellow, burst into bloom in early summer and last until early autumn if you remove the dead flowers. Also known as blanket flower or the jam tart plant, it grows to 75cm (30in) by 30cm (12in) and should be planted in sun.

8 *Persicaria amplexicaulis* 'Firetail' ♆

This robust perennial has long-lasting, pinky-red flower spikes above large, leathery leaves. The flowers last all season and it's vigorous and easy to grow. The leaves turn yellow and orange in autumn before dying down. Plant in sun or partial shade. Grows to 60cm (24in).

9 *Philadelphus incanus* 'Innocence'

There are many delightful forms of the deciduous mock orange shrub. 'Innocence' not only has beautifully scented white flowers in early summer but also has gold splashes on the leaves, so it looks interesting for months. It grows to 2m (6ft 6in) by 2m (6ft 6in) and should be planted in sun or partial shade.

10 *Polystichum setiferum* ♆

A very neat evergreen fern with upright, arching, overlapping fronds, excellent for the front of a shady border or in a container. Attractive cultivars include 'Plumoso-multilobum' and 'Congestum' (the smallest of these three). They are suitable for both dry or moist soils in shade or semi-shade. Both height and spread reach 30-45cm (12-18in).

BLOOMING MARVELLOUS PLANTS
Korketts Farm, Aylesbury Road, Shipton,
Winslow, Buckinghamshire MK18 3JL
T: 01296 714714 (opening hours only) or 07963 747305
E: alex@bmplants.co.uk W: www.bmplants.co.uk
Open seven days a week, 9am to 5pm (10am to 4pm Sunday),
March to October; please phone to arrange a visit in winter.

Blooming Marvellous Plants aims to provide both keen and less experienced gardeners with a wide range of plants, most of which are easy to grow. It already grows over 1,500 varieties of perennials, shrubs, ferns, grasses, seasonal colour, herbs and veg plants. To help visitors to choose, the plants are mainly grouped into themes such as 'dry shade', 'moist shade', 'moist/boggy soil', 'tall' and so on.

EXOTIC PLANTS

AS RECOMMENDED BY ARCHITECTURAL PLANTS

Phyllostachys aureosulcata f. aureocaulis

Musa basjoo

Agave americana

An exciting collection of plants, chosen for their shapely forms, good looks and their ability to add drama and beauty to even the dullest of gardens, the exotic plants selected here are suitable for a wide variety of British gardens. Most are evergreen, many are easy to cultivate and all of them are irresistible.

1 *Phillyrea latifolia*
Green olives grows in sun or shade in any well-drained soil. Perfect as a small specimen tree, also an excellent choice for an avenue. Grows to 3m (10ft) after 15 years, reaching a maximum of 9m (30ft). Drought-resistant once established and easy to cultivate. Feed with fish, blood and bone every spring.

2 *Trachycarpus fortunei* ♈
The Chusan palm is the hardiest palm tree in the world. Very slow-growing, 7.5m (25ft) after 30 years. Grows in sun or shade in any type of soil. Hates strong winds, so avoid planting too near the seafront. Feed generously during April and May. Remove lower brown leaves as it ages. H3-4

3 *Melianthus major* ♈
Honey bush is one of the very best perennials for livening up a border. Not desperately hardy in a cold winter, but so gorgeous that it's worth the risk. Older plants produce tall crimson flowers, which are spectacular rather than pretty. Best in rich, well-drained soil in full sun or light shade. H3

4 *Yucca gloriosa* ♈
Adam's needle is a spiky addition to the garden, happy in sun or shade, and in almost any type of soil as long as it's well-drained. This one tolerates being confined to a pot for a few years. Brilliant in gravel gardens. A very low-maintenance plant. Remove older brown leaves as it ages. H4

5 Musa basjoo ♔

Fast-growing, producing huge, emerald-green leaves each season, eventually sending out bunches of tiny, inedible bananas. The Japanese banana is essential for all adventurous gardeners. Plant in a lightly-shaded spot, sheltered from the wind. For best results water frequently throughout spring and summer, and by stacking well-rotted manure around the base. H3-4

6 Agave americana

The large, succulent yet tender century plant is perfect for Mediterranean-style gardens in milder areas. The bluish leaves and shapely outline make it a bold choice. Sharply-drained soil in full sun is required, with a light feed annually in late spring. For colder gardens, wrap in fleece for the winter, or keep under glass. H1

7 Hedychium coccineum 'Tara' ♔

A simply marvellous exotic colour. Scented flowers are produced on top of 1.2m (4ft) stems at a time when most summer flowers have finished. Clumps are slow to establish, so plant in large numbers. Rich, moist soil in light shade gives the best results. H3

8 Phyllostachys aureosulcata f. aureocaulis ♔

The abundant golden-caned bamboo is fantastic for even tiny gardens providing excellent screening. The clump grows tightly instead of running amok like some bamboos. It could reach 5m (16ft) but can be kept trimmed. Requires constantly moist (but not boggy) soil and lots of food. H4

9 Hebe stenophylla

The ideal plant for difficult spots. Thrives in any type of soil, in sun or shade – even dry shade under trees. The foliage looks good all year round. It can be left as a shrub or clipped into an informal hedge. White flowers are produced in the summer.

10 Pinus patula

The orang-utan pine is a large shaggy beast of a tree, draped with long, soft foliage. Essential specimen tree for larger gardens in mild areas, needing space to fully appreciate its graceful shape. Plant in full sun in well-drained, neutral to slightly acidic soil. Keep sheltered from strong winds. Can grow to 10m (33ft) in 10 years.

EXOTIC – SOUTHERN HEMISPHERE

AS RECOMMENDED BY JOHN EDDY OF TREVENA CROSS NURSERIES

Neopanax lateus

How to arrive at my own top 10? Such a question is always difficult to answer, and the only real way to arrive at such a list is to think about the plants that have had the greatest impact on you. With so many thousands to choose from, it comes down to those that stick in your mind the most. My luxury, if I were stuck on a desert island with these plants, would be a good wheelbarrow of well-rotted farmyard manure to make sure they all grew to their best potential!

1 *Echium pininana* ♔
A triffid-like, half-hardy evergreen shrub that can cause a stir with the neighbours when the flowering spike appears in early summer. A smashing plant, adding structure and a touch of the exotic. Plant in groups of three or more. One of the best plants for the 'wow' factor. Height 3-5m (10-16ft). H2-3

2 *Calopsis paniculata*
One of the many plants Trevena Cross has been involved in introducing and promoting in the UK, a versatile plant with stems resembling bamboo, 1.5-2m (5-6ft 6in). Grows in full sun in free-draining soil and also in boggy soil in shade. A back of the border or specimen plant. H3

3 *Dicksonia fibrosa* ♔
One of the hardiest tree ferns; a splendid architectural specimen which can be grown in a large container or in the ground in a sheltered, shady site. Slow-growing with a fibrous trunk. Height 2.5m (8ft) after many years. For a more exposed spot this is the one to try. H3

4 *Protea cynaroides*
Everyone who sees this plant for the first time is just amazed – it has huge pink-crimson to cream flowers in summer. An evergreen shrub with a height 1.5-2m (5-6ft 6in). Plant in full sun in well-drained acid soil. In colder areas, plant over winter in a cool greenhouse or conservatory. H2

Protea cynaroides

5 *Leucadendron* 'Safari Sunset'

An evergreen dense, rounded shrub growing to 2m (6ft 6in), with claret flowers changing to pink as they mature. We have a few of these stems in the table decoration for Christmas Day. Plant in full sun in free-draining soil. Undoubtedly my favourite plant in my own garden. H1

6 *Rhodocoma capensis*

An elegant restio from South Africa with beautiful, 2m (6ft 6in) arching stems with fine foliage. An exotic-looking variety with a spread around 1m (3ft 3in). Who can resist the soft fluffy foliage with the very attractive seed heads on this plant? A splendid specimen plant, useful for windy sites. H3

Leucadendron 'Safari Sunset'

Rhodocoma capensis

7 *Blechnum fluviatale*

Not many ferns provide such an unusual effect in the shadier parts of the garden. The ladder-like fronds are a wonderful green and the way they radiate from the centre of the plant is most attractive. Very mature plants can form trunks up to 50cm (20in) tall. H3

8 *Dodonea viscosa* 'Purpurea'

The purple hop bush has a fascinating leaf which in the summer is either complemented by the pink flowers or clashes badly, depending on your viewpoint. I personally think the colours work well and given its height of 3m (10ft), it makes a great filler for an awkward corner. H2

9 *Neopanax lateus*

For a plant to add stature to the garden, look no further than this large-leaved, rounded shrub from New Zealand. It grows up to 3m (10ft) tall, is reasonably hardy and looks fantastic after rain with its wet glossy leaves. Will grow in sun or shade. H2

10 *Acacia verticillata* riverine form

This is without doubt the best *Acacia* we stock. It is much more compact than *A. dealbata*, reaching about 4-5m (13-16ft). In spring the foliage, which looks nothing like that of an *Acacia*, is almost covered by gorgeous yellow flowers. H2

TREVENA CROSS NURSERIES
Breage, Helston, Cornwall TR13 9PS
T: 01736 763880
F: 01736 762828
E: info@trevenacross.co.uk
W: www.trevenacross.co.uk

Trevena Cross Nurseries have been awarded Gold medals at major RHS shows including Chelsea and Hampton Court, and the Skipton award for best visiting nursery at Guernsey Flower Show 2002. Nurseryman John Eddy, who originally came from a farming background, says he finds it fascinating to be able to try so many exciting new introductions in his own garden. The garden centre is open 9am to 5pm Monday to Saturday, 10am to 4.30pm Sunday.

EXOTIC – TROPICAL

AS RECOMMENDED BY ABBOTSBURY SUBTROPICAL GARDENS

Trachycarpus fortunei

For many, the perceived image of the tropics is of hot, steamy jungles with bromeliads growing among moss-laden branches, while for others it can evoke images of sun-kissed beaches and palm trees swaying in the breeze. The very idea of creating a garden with an exotic flavour in a cool, temperate climate has been a challenge at least since the Victorian craze for big foliage plants. Plants with architectural form and shape, or bold, hot-coloured flowers and large leaves, all generate a very stylised feel and form the backbone of the exotic-looking garden when trying to mimic a jungle environment.

1 *Aloe striatula*

Aloes are mostly suited to arid or semi-arid climates. *A. striatula* seems to be the hardiest species, tolerating -5°C, given adequate drainage. The spiky, fleshy leaves are followed by yellow 'red hot poker'-like flowers hence the common name torch plant. They are drought-resistant and tolerate poor soils. Height 1m (3ft). H3

2 *Canna*

Cannas, also known as canna lilies or Indian shots are tender, rhizomatous perennial herbs with thick, fleshy roots that require a moisture-retentive soil and good drainage. *Canna iridiflora* 'Ermanii' makes a tall specimen up to 2m (7ft) with distinct nodding

Aloe striatula

rose-pink flowers. *C. indica* is a smaller plant, with dainty red and yellow flowers, followed by attractive globular seed heads. H2

3 *Chusquea gigantea*

A true giant of a bamboo that creates an immense impact once established. The culms grow in bold, vertical columns and can reach 10m (33ft). They make an impressive clump with strong arching branches, so they need an isolated site to grow, such as a lawn specimen. Sun or light shade.

4 *Trachycarpus fortunei* ♈

The Chusan palm or Chinese windmill palm is one of the hardiest palms, with fan-shaped leaves and a hairy trunk. It produces yellow flower inflorescences in early summer. It likes an open position, in full sun or partial shade, with good drainage. Good for the cool temperate exotic garden, for creating an avenue or as an architectural specimen. Height 15m (49ft). H3-4

Canna indica

Chusquea gigantea

5 *Echium pininana* ♛

The giant blue flower spikes of E. *pininana* or pride of the Canary Isles are unmistakable, and create immense stature and presence in the garden. A native of the laurel forests of La Palma, one of the seven islands which make up the Canary Islands, it can grow in full sun or shade, reaching up to 4m (13ft) in height, but really needs a frost-free environment. H2-3

6 *Tetrapanax papyrifer* ♛

Grown for its enormous, deeply-lobed leaves, this hardy plant is great for the jungle effect. Commonly known as the Chinese rice-paper plant, it also flowers in the autumn with white umbels. Annual hard pruning will encourage a bushier plant with larger leaves. Keep the roots well mulched and water regularly in summer. Height 6m (20ft). H2-3

7 *Musa basjoo* ♛

The Japanese banana makes a striking focal point and gives an instantly tropical look. It is best grown in a sheltered site in full sun or partial shade. A good mulch will keep the soil

CULTIVATION

The most important consideration for growing large-leaved exotic plants is shelter and suitable microclimates. Avoid frost pockets that trap cold air, and ensure there is sufficient shelter from hedging or trees, as this will reduce foliar scorching, heat loss and water loss through evaporation. Most subtropical bedding species can be planted out late spring to early summer. Ensure a regular fortnightly liquid feed is applied to help continue flower and leaf production. For permanent plantings it is vital to heavily mulch the roots with leaf mould or wood chip, and protect young plants with fleece for the coming winter.

Echium pininana

moisture-retentive. In colder areas, the stems and the root base will need protecting from frost. Height 2-3m (7-10ft). H3-4

8 Woodwardia radicans 🏆

This magnificent European chain fern produces graceful fronds up to 2m (7ft) long, emerging copper-coloured in spring. They are suited to moist, humid sites in partial shade. As the fronds weep to the ground, they produce rooting tips. These make new plants. Provide frost protection in colder gardens. H3

Woodwardia radicans

9 Dicksonia

Tree ferns prefer semi-shade, moisture, humidity and a sheltered site. In cold areas the crowns need protecting in winter. In dry conditions it is important to water the trunks, which are made up of their matted, fibrous roots. *Dicksonia antarctica* is the most reliable for cooler climates. Height 10m (33ft). H3

10 Neopanax laetus

This shrub grows to 3m (10ft), with superb dark green, oval, five-lobed, evergreen leaves up to 30cm (12in) long. It grows best in milder areas, succeeding in all types of well-drained soils, in sun or half shade. H2

Dicksonia

ABBOTSBURY SUBTROPICAL GARDENS
Bullers Way, Abbotsbury, nr Weymouth, Dorset DT34LA
T/F: 01305 871344   E: info@abbotsburyplantsales.co.uk
W: www.abbotsbury-tourism.co.uk
Open 17 Mar to 28 Oct, daily (except Christmas and New Year),
10am to 5/6pm (10am to 4pm/dusk in winter), but call to confirm

Abbotsbury Subtropical Gardens started life as a walled garden in 1765, providing fruit, vegetables and cut flowers for the Countess and Earl of Ilchester. Today, the nursery attached to the gardens has an unrivalled selection for plant material. The present nursery started after the restoration programme began in 1990. It specialises in tender South African succulents and perennials, together with palms, ferns, bamboos and rare species for the connoisseur.

FOLIAGE PLANTS

AS RECOMMENDED BY VANESSA COOK OF STILLINGFLEET LODGE GARDEN AND NURSERIES

Pulmonaria 'Mary Mottram'

F oliage is the backbone of the garden. It doesn't have the appeal of instant gardening or the impact of bedding plants with their bright and showy flowers. But it is what holds the garden together, allowing the gardener to paint pictures with plants. The plant relationships of colour, shape and texture are what make gardening so absorbing. See how silver foliage lifts a dark red flower, or marvel at raindrops on *Alchemilla* leaves. Here are our top 10 foliage plants.

1 *Pulmonaria* 'Mary Mottram'

Originating in Mary Mottram's nursery in Devon, the leaves are silver-edged, with silver spots. It makes excellent ground cover. The flowers open violet in early spring and become bluer with age. Grows to 30cm (12in) tall.

2 *Clematis recta* 'Purpurea'

A brilliant foliage plant in the spring. The shoots are a dark coppery-purple in mid-April. It is self-supporting until midsummer when it is covered with large, scented white flowers of the traveller's joy variety, followed by fluffy silver seed heads. Needs sun to colour well. Reaches a height of 1.1m (3ft 8in).

3 *Artemisia* 'Powis Castle' ♛

Grey foliage is a useful contrast to other colours and is often used to show other plants to advantage. Many Artemisias have drab greyish-white flowers and seed around. This form has neither problem. It has finely cut grey foliage and makes a shrubby mound, 90cm (36in) tall, needing sunny, well-drained conditions.

4 *Brunnera macrophylla* 'Jack Frost' ♛

One of the best ground-cover plants. Its large, silvery heart-shaped leaves make a weed-suppressing carpet, above which rise blue forget-me-not flowers in spring. The foliage

Brunnera macrophylla 'Jack Frost'

Clematis recta 'Purpurea'

Artemisia 'Powis Castle'

Ligularia 'Britt Marie Crawford'

lasts into autumn and is completely untouched by slugs. It's grown at Stillingfleet Lodge Nursery under a weeping pear and it survives well. Reaches a height of 45cm (18in).

5 *Alchemilla mollis* ♡

Thriving in full sun or part shade, the lady's mantle is a plant of woodland edges. The pleated, silky leaves are grey-green with a wavy margin. Above them float airy flowers of golden green. It is one of the best ground-cover plants under roses or edging paths. Grows to 40cm (16in).

6 *Euphorbia characias* 'Black Pearl'

Everyone should have one of these plants. Handsome grey foliage, looking especially good in winter, topped with huge heads of greenish-yellow flowers with black eyes. A wonderful asset to the spring garden. Needs sun and good drainage. Lower-growing than the popular *E. characias* subsp. *wulfenii* at 90cm (36in) tall.

7 *Geranium phaeum* 'Samobor'

At the nursery, this wonderful geranium is grown at the base of a hawthorn hedge, where it makes an impenetrable cover of dark-green leaves marked with a broad black-red band. The flowers, in May, are typical *phaeum* flowers with slightly reflexed burgundy petals. It can survive very dry conditions, and grows to 60cm (24in).

8 *Heuchera americana* 'Ring of Fire'
One of the best garden forms. The foliage
is heavily marked with brown, the flowers are
creamy, and in loose sprays. As the cold
weather approaches, leaves develop an orange
rim which stays all winter. Hardy in a dry,
sunny position. Grows to 45cm (18in.)

9 *Ligularia* 'Britt Marie Crawford'
In this new form the large, almost round
leaves are of a particularly good, dark
brownish-green with mahogany undersides.
The flowers in July and August are vivid
orange daisies, much loved by butterflies.

To keep the foliage colour, plant in full sun
with moisture, ideally near water. Grows to
1.1m (3ft 8in) tall.

10 *Arum italicum* 'Marmoratum' ♔
In autumn, the large spear-shaped leaves
unfurl, becoming larger throughout winter.
Heavily veined with white, they are good
in shade and excellent under shrubs.
The flowers are cream spathes followed
by spikes of scarlet berries when the
foliage has disappeared, leaving space
for summer flowers. Height reaches
15-25cm (6-10in).

Euphorbia characias 'Black Pearl'

Geranium phaeum 'Samobor'

STILLINGFLEET LODGE GARDEN AND NURSERIES
Stewart Lane, Stillingfleet, York YO19 6HP
T/F: 01904 728506
E: vanessa.cook@stillingfleetlodgenurseries.co.uk
W: www.stillingfleetlodgenurseries.co.uk

Stillingfleet Lodge Garden and Nurseries started 24 years ago to grow plants which were
not available locally. As the garden has developed, it's been used as a source of plants and to
test which varieties grow best in the soil and climate. As a result, the nursery can give
accurate help on the ideal conditions for each plant. Hardy geraniums are another speciality,
as well as grasses, climbers and, of course, many plants with variegated or coloured foliage.

FOLIAGE – SCENTED

AS RECOMMENDED BY JOHN HOLDEN OF AROMAFOLIA

Pelargonium 'Vandersea'

There is such a wide variety of scented foliage. Everyone will be familiar with the culinary herbs, but there are so many more scented plants with primarily ornamental qualities. Some have exquisite flowers, others can be grown for their attractive foliage. What most of them enjoy are warm, sunny conditions. Some are fruity, others fragrant – some are just plain peculiar! What they all do is add an extra dimension to the garden. There are few more pleasing sensations on a warm day than brushing past an aromatic plant and releasing a waft of delightful fragrance into the air.

1 *Pelargonium* 'Vandersea' ♟

It is hard to single out one scented-leaf pelargonium, but 'Vandersea' combines cerise flowers, rose aroma and compact habit. The flowers are plentiful and clear cerise-pink, with deep red veining on the upper petals. Deadhead finished blooms to ensure constant flowering through the summer months. 'Vandersea' can grow to 50cm (20in).

2 *Salvia patens* ♟

One of the most spectacular flowering plants, with large blooms of the truest blue. The triangular-shaped leaves are bristly, with a refreshingly sharp scent. It is tuberous-rooted and in colder parts of the country can be treated like a dahlia, with the tubers being dug up. It reaches 60cm (24in) in height.

3 *Agastache rugosa* 'Liquorice Blue'

Agastaches are terrific fragrant plants. Not all are hardy, however, and many sulk in damp conditions. 'Liquorice Blue' is an exception. It is very hardy, with tall, upright stems, purple-tinged aniseed-scented foliage and purple-blue flowering spikes. It can reach over 1m (3ft) and is superb in drifts.

4 *Nepeta racemosa* 'Walker's Low'

Nepetas are great for massed planting. 'Walkers Low' is a bushy variety with many sprays of soft lavender-mauve flowers over aromatic grey-green leaves. Cut it back hard after flowering to keep it tidy and encourage bushy growth and a second flush of flowers. It will reach up to 60cm (24in).

5 *Telekia speciosa*

Its aromatic leaves are extravagantly large and heart-shaped, with a rough texture, forming a substantial clump quite quickly. Over a long period in mid-to-late summer, it has yellow shaggy-petalled daisies on tall stems.

Agastache rugosa 'Liquorice Blue'

The fragrance reminds me of pines growing on a Mediterranean sand dune. It grows to a height of 1.5m (5ft).

6 *Aloysia triphylla*

One of the most deliciously fragrant aromatic plants. The slender, bright green, rough-textured leaves of lemon verbena have an unmistakable scent of lemon sherbet. It likes a sunny, sheltered spot and in colder areas may need some winter protection. It can grow to 1m (3ft), but responds well to pruning.

7 *Salvia* x *jamensis* 'Cherry Queen'

Many of the shrubby salvias have aromatic foliage with a fruity smell of blackcurrants. 'Cherry Queen' is one of the best. It has a compact habit, glossy, deep green foliage and the brightest deep red flowers. It is happiest in a well-drained spot and is very drought-tolerant. It can reach a height of 60cm (24in).

Helichrysum italicum 'Dartington'

Salvia x jamensis 'Cherry Queen'

Aloysia triphylla

Lavandula angustifolia 'Twickel Purple'

Salvia fruticosa

8 *Lavandula angustifolia* 'Twickel Purple'

There are so many lavenders to choose from, but for the depth of colour, form and fragrance I recommend 'Twickel Purple'. It is compact, reaching about 45cm (18in). Give it a sunny, well-drained spot and a severe haircut as soon as the flowers finish – don't cut into old wood.

9 *Salvia fruticosa*

An evergreen *Salvia* with pointed, pale grey-green leaves, with a sweet herby sage aroma. It makes a small, bushy shrub. A drought-tolerant plant, it is completely covered in spring with pale pinkish lavender blooms set against dark bracts. It can reach 90cm (35in) and will spread to about 1m (3ft)

10 *Helichrysum italicum* 'Dartington'

Curry plants are fun with their appetising aroma. 'Dartington' is more upright and architectural than the species. The leaves are silver-grey with dark green undersides. The button flowers are yellow, but some people trim them off. A plant for a hot, dry spot. Grows to 35cm (14in), but stays neat.

AROMAFOLIA
Barbers Farm, Leys Lane, Old Buckenham, Norfolk NR17 1NT
T: 01953 887713 E: enquiries@aromafolia.co.uk
W: www.aromafolia.co.uk
Open Apr to Oct, Fri to Sun (and Bank Holidays), 10am to 5pm

Aromafolia is a relatively new nursery, founded by John Holden in 2005, which specialises in plants with aromatic foliage, including a wide range of Salvias. It is situated just outside the Norfolk village of Old Buckenham where it propagates most of its stock from seed, cuttings and divisions. Please phone ahead if you are travelling any long distance for a specific plant. All its plants are grown in peat-free compost.

NATURALISTIC PLANTING

AS RECOMMENDED BY KIM AND STEPHEN ROGERS OF DOVE COTTAGE NURSERY & GARDEN

Hakonechloa macra

The naturalistic style of gardening can be interpreted in many ways, often with breathtaking results. We visit places with this style of planting for pleasure and inspiration. It is a style that can be tailored to suit any garden or public space. Our approach is to plant trouble-free cultivars of grasses and hardy perennials together, either in groups or randomly as in a meadow-type planting. We often plant 20% grasses and 80% hardy perennials. Our plantings have a wild appearance due to the choice of plants which are related to wild flowers or mimic them, but are easily maintained.

1 *Hakonechloa macra*
The 'little black dress' of the grass world, this variety will smartly grow anywhere. This arching, green Japanese grass is planted as a curving ribbon along the front of our hot border. It also suits pot cultivation. It can have a height and spread of 1m (3ft) after five years and grows in sun or shade.

2 *Stipa gigantea* 'Gold Fontaene'
Superior to *S. gigantea*, with finer foliage and flowering readily. The oat-like panicles are large and upright, forming a see-through screen. 'Gold Fontaene' also stands up to heavy summer rain. We grow it in gravel and rich border soil. It has an established height of 2m (6ft) and spread of 1m (3ft).

3 *Astrantia* 'Gill Richardson'
A relatively new seed strain which produces vigorous plants with large, dark red flowers May to June, repeating well. Associates well with *Sanguisorba menziesii* and *Pennisetum orientale* 'Karley Rose' and other Astrantias including 'Buckland' and 'Roma'. Its height and spread are both 60cm (2ft). It's best grown in rich soil in sun or partial shade.

4 *Foeniculum vulgare* 'Purpureum'
The bronze fennel. This plant has it all: aromatic brown foliage from spring, umbels of insect-attracting yellow flowers, good seed heads, winter structure, self-seeding and grows anywhere. A must in any naturalistic planting – perfect!

Stipa gigantea 'Gold Fontaene' foreshadowed by Eryngium

5 *Lythrum virgatum*

All purple loosestrifes suit naturalistic plantings and will even grow in waterlogged ground. This plant has a wilder look. This is because of its willowy foliage and soft mauvey flowers in July to August. Its average height is 1m (3ft), and spread 1m (3ft). We have it with *Selinum wallichianum*, *Echinacea purpurea* 'Ruby Giant' and *Stipa gigantea* 'Gold Fontaene'.

6 *Persicaria amplexicaulis* 'Rosea'

All *P. amplexicaulis* varieties suit wilder-looking plantings due to their spires, which remind us of dock and sorrel. They are easy to grow, because they are both wet and drought-tolerant. They are long-flowering and associate well with grasses and other perennials. They can grow to 1-1.5m (3-5ft) depending on the type and condition of the soil, and spread up to 1m (3ft).

7 *Phlox paniculata* 'Hesperis'

Cultivars of *P. paniculata* and *P.* x *arendsii* are often included in naturalistic plantings, due to their reliability. 'Hesperis' has small mauve-pink scented flowers and is also known as sweet rocket. It doesn't need staking and can be divided in spring. It can grow to a height of about 1.5m (5ft).

8 *Sanguisorba menziesii*

S. menziesii produces plum-red flowers in May and June. This variety coincides nicely with the Astrantias, especially 'Gill Richardson' and 'Roma'. Reaching about 60cm (24in) and preferring retentive soil in sun or partial shade, *S. menziesii* can flower twice, so remove old flowers.

CULTIVATION

Our gardening regime is enjoyable and simple. New plantings are undertaken in autumn or spring; good soil preparation is essential and we water well for the first season after planting. We recommend a 5cm (2in) mulch around plants and use a local supply made of spent mushroom compost, composted bark and sterile manure. Existing plantings are weeded and mulched in spring but the garden is alive with wildlife all year round. There is no 'autumn tidying' as we love the way summer lushness gives way to autumn colour and winter skeletons, which are cut down on a dry day in March.

9 *Selinum wallichianum*

We grow other cow parsley-type flowers in white and pink, but this is perhaps our favourite. Slightly mounded white heads are made up of many tiny flowers held above ferny foliage on pink, sturdy stems 1.5m (5ft) tall. Delightful anywhere but fabulous with *Echinacea purpurea* 'Ruby Giant', and *Veronicastrum* 'Erika'.

10 *Veronicastrum virginicum* 'Lavendelturm'

Veronicastrums are taller and sturdier than Veronicas. Whorls of leaves clothe sturdy stems topped with slim spires of many tiny flowers. 'Lavendelturm', also known as lavender tower is our favourite. It is a tall variety and can reach 2m (6ft) once established, and it comes into flower in early July, followed by good seed heads and winter structure.

Persicaria amplexicaulis 'Rosea'

DOVE COTTAGE NURSERY & GARDEN
Shibden Hall Road, Halifax, West Yorkshire HX3 9XA
T: 01422 203553
E: info@dovecottagenursery.co.uk
W: www.dovecottagenursery.co.uk

Dove Cottage Nursery & Garden opened in Easter 1997. It is situated in a rural location. The nursery and garden are generously stocked with the best hardy perennials and grasses. The nursery has a descriptive catalogue and the plants for sale are well-labelled, giving cultural advice and planting ideas. Open 10am to 5pm Wednesday to Sunday and Bank Holiday Mondays, March to October. Please phone or visit the website for directions as it is tucked away.

RARE AND UNUSUAL VARIETIES

AS RECOMMENDED BY BLEDDYN AND SUE WYNN-JONES OF
CRÛG FARM PLANTS

Schefflera taiwaniana

We live in exciting times botanically, as there are so many new plants introduced from areas that were considered remote in the past, yet are now accessible, ensuring that seed can be transported quickly to be sown while still fresh. Unusual plants do not necessarily have to be difficult to grow in gardens, though they may be difficult to obtain because they are difficult to propagate or handle in containers – hence they are not normally available from garden centres, but only from specialist nurseries. My top 10 choice has been tempered by ease of cultivation and propagation.

1 Holboellia

An invaluable group of evergreen, twining climbers related to *Akebia*, bearing similar sausage-shaped purple fruit in late summer. *Holboellia coriacea* has elegant, thick-textured foliage and small male and female flowers, which bear a sweet, heady scent from April to June. *H. chapaensis* is our latest exciting addition from Vietnam. H3

2 Beesia calthifolia

An evergreen woodlander from the buttercup family, forming tight clumps of heart-shaped glossy green leaves with conspicuous pale venation. These emerge dark bronze in early spring, contrasting with older foliage. Soon, upright, loose spikes of small white flowers, followed by pea-pod-like capsules, appear and continue through the season.

3 Schefflera taiwaniana

Schefflera is usually thought to be a group of houseplants but *S. taiwaniana* combines ornament with hardiness, forming a single-stemmed shrub 3-4m (10-13ft) tall. The lanceolate-oblong leaves are held on long purple petioles. The flowers appear in summer as slender racemes, maturing to purple fruit over winter.

4 Curculigo crassifolia

A most unusual clump-forming, tuberous evergreen perennial, with a habit more like *Phormium*. We have grown it in a container for years, where its sword-shaped, corrugated leaves attained 1.7m (5.7ft), almost hiding the curious yellow flowers at the base of the leaves, which mature to translucent berries.

Holboellia coriacea

Cardiandra formosana

5 *Veratrum formosanum*

This soon forms clumps of slender downy-textured ribbed leaves to 25cm (10in) long, thrusting flexuous upright stems to 60cm (24in) tall, bearing terminal spikes of deep mahogany-coloured flowers for weeks in early summer. Easily cultivated in good light in a moisture-retentive soil with adequate drainage.

6 *Daphniphyllum teijsmannii*

If pressed to select a single species for the average garden, *D. teijsmannii* would be my choice. It forms a small to medium-sized shrub, with leathery, elliptic leaves emerging burgundy, slowly transforming to green. Meanwhile, insignificant but scented flowers are born from the leaf axils of the new growth.

7 *Pittosporum illicioides* var. *angustifolium*

The species forms a 2m (6ft 6in) evergreen, dense shrub with elliptic, leathery, dark green leaves. It bears bell-shaped yellow flowers on slender stalks, emitting an intoxicating scent. In the variety *angustifolium* the leaf and habit differ greatly, with the leaves 20cm (8in) long and yet rarely exceeding 2cm (1in) in width.

8 *Cardiandra formosana*

This is easily mistaken for its close relative, the hydrangea. It's a herbaceous perennial standing to about 1m (3ft 3in) tall, bearing typical hydrangea-like, but thin, serrated leaves. It is crowned in late August by a wide red-stalked lace-cap purple and pink inflorescence, which persists until Christmas.

9 *Sarcococca wallichii*

Having many similarities to the well-loved Christmas box, this autumn-flowering species starts its display of bristly flowers in October and continues until January. Of a larger size than the conventional species, to 1.8m (6ft) tall, with larger elliptic long-pointed glossy, green leaves, it requires more shelter than some other species.

10 *Disporum cantoniense*

This is one of the most amenable disporum to cultivation, happy in moisture-retentive soil with adequate drainage. It has bamboo-like dark green stems to 1.5m (5ft) tall. It bears white to dark-red pendent flowers in clusters at the ends of the branches from April to July (depending on variety).

CRÛG FARM PLANTS
Griffith's Crossing, Caernarfon, Gwynedd LL55 1TU
T: 01248 670232 E: info@crug-farm.co.uk
W: www.crug-farm.co.uk (hours, events, catalogue)
W: www.mailorder.crug-farm.co.uk (shop)

❁   NCCPG National Collection holder of *Coriaria, Paris,* and *Polygonatum*
Crûg Farm Plants is well situated and signposted just north of the ancient town of Caernarfon. As well as being modern-day plant hunters, Bleddyn and Sue Wynn-Jones have established Crûg Farm Plants as one of the most respected nurseries in the world, offering a vast selection of shade plants, unusual climbers, shrubs and hardy subtropicals, and including many self-collected new introductions from all over the world.

WILDLIFE-FRIENDLY PLANTS

AS RECOMMENDED BY JOYCE MILLAR OF LADYBIRD GARDEN NURSERY

Centranthus ruber

Rudbeckia fulgida
var. sullivantii 'Goldsturm'

Echinacea purpurea

Growing plants for wildlife gives such special pleasure. Not only do you get to enjoy the plants, you also get to enjoy the countless creatures that share these plants with you. I think even the most hardened of us must feel uplifted when we see a butterfly flitting haphazardly around the garden. It is difficult to define what makes gardening for wildlife so satisfying, but I think it has to do with a quality that can be difficult to achieve otherwise – the relaxing atmosphere that is created from the drone of bees or the beautiful songs of birds.

1 *Verbena bonariensis* ♛
This exceptionally good plant is a butterfly and bee magnet, attracting many different species. What's more, by leaving the seedheads in winter, many birds will be attracted. Its lilac-purple blooms blend well with other colours and its tall 1-2m (3-7ft) wiry stems make for a wind-resistant plant.

2 *Centranthus ruber*
With its clusters of honey-scented flowers, this valerian is a rich source of nectar for many insects, including butterflies, bees and moths. Last year, we were thrilled to see hummingbird moths feeding on our valerian. We plant ours in pots as they don't need a lot of watering.

3 *Eupatorium purpureum*
Best in moister conditions, Joe Pye weed is a butterfly plant that tolerates some shade. At 2 x 1m (7 x 3ft), it is a big, majestic plant, so site at the back of a border. The first time I saw this plant it became a 'must-have' instantly, as it was absolutely alive with butterflies.

4 *Echium vulgare*
This is a plant for well-drained sunny spots. It is not a perennial, but self-seeds. It is useful for low-level interest, never getting much higher than 30cm (12in) in our garden. Bees love it and with flowers of the most enchanting shades of blue, they are definitely not alone.

5 *Miscanthus sinensis*

Grasses are an integral part of a naturalistic habitat, providing shelter for wildlife over winter. I always go to our *Miscanthus* on the first sunny days to see the ladybirds emerging. *Miscanthus* is tolerant of a wide range of conditions, but best in well-drained, moist soil in full sun.

6 *Origanum vulgare*

Better known for its use in cooking, oregano is a really easy-to-grow garden plant. Preferring well-drained soil in full sun, bees and butterflies love it and it provides food for seed-eating birds in winter. It's an ideal plant for a small garden because of its multiple uses.

7 *Dipsacus fullonum*

Teasels grow in any reasonable soil in full sun or partial shade, and attract seed-eating birds to gardens. They also have the ability to attract nectar-loving insects to their striking flowering heads. Take care though, as the backs of the leaves have thorny spines.

8 *Ajuga reptans* 'Burgundy Glow'

Best in moist, well-drained soil in sun or part-shade, *Ajuga* or bugle is a really useful evergreen carpeting plant. We are rewarded early each spring with magnificent blocks of blue flowers, absolutely buzzing with bees.

CULTIVATION

For wildlife, select plants that suit your conditions, rather than struggling with plants that have to be constantly cajoled just to survive. Limiting chemical use is of great benefit. For the past few years, we have not used pesticides or slug pellets in our garden. Having something in flower in all seasons is important as a food source. Also, when trying to attract specific species, it is more effective to plant in groups. For example, a group of plants to attract butterflies should be planted in one sheltered spot, rather than having individual plants dotted around.

---

9 *Echinacea purpurea*

Echinacea or coneflower provides a valuable source of nectar for insects preparing for hibernation. We plant ours close to other butterfly-attracting plants, and enjoy the droves of butterflies that appear.

10 *Rudbeckia fulgida* var. *sullivantii* 'Goldsturm' 🏆

This is a useful late-season butterfly and bee plant for well-drained soils in full sun or part-shade. It's said that the petals have ultraviolet markings to guide insects to the central cone. We always leave the seedheads over winter as food for birds.

LADYBIRD GARDEN NURSERY (proprietor Joyce Millar)
32 Ballykeigle Road, off Tullynagee Road, Killinchy Road, Comber, Co Down BT23 5SD
T: 028 9752 8025 E: millarjoyce@hotmail.com
W: www.ladybirdgarden.com

Joyce Millar started the nursery in 2005 with the aim of combining two passions – gardening and wildlife. She wanted to show that you could achieve a beautiful garden, with plenty of wildlife. As well as plants for wildlife, **Ladybird Garden Nursery** stocks herbaceous plants, grasses and choice annuals. The garden is open by appointment and on special days for various charities.

PLANTS FOR...
CHALKY SOILS

AS RECOMMENDED BY NICK AND LISSA HOURHAN
OF SPRING REACH NURSERY

Arbutus unedo 'Atlantic'

Chalky soils are usually 'hungry' ones, so they need plenty of farmyard manure, leafmould or garden compost to maintain the humus level in the soil. Chalky soils are alkaline and contain 20% or more of chalky material. The depth of the topsoil above the chalk is very important; if it's shallow, fill planting holes with organic matter. When there is a good depth of topsoil a variety of plants can be grown. There are many plants of all types that enjoy a chalky soil, including trees, shrubs, climbers, perennials and fruit. Here are our chalky soil top 10.

Geranium Rozanne

Agapanthus 'Midnight Star'
(syn. 'Navy Blue')

1 *Agapanthus* 'Midnight Star' (syn. 'Navy Blue')

This perennial is one of our favourites because it flowers freely from such an early age, both in pots and in the ground. It has the most wonderful vivid, dark blue flowers. It is hardy and suitable for the middle of a border, being of medium height – around 60cm (24in) – with a spread of 50cm (20in). Needs dry soil and full sun.

2 *Arbutus unedo* 'Atlantic'

This is a compact variety and has the merit of being free-flowering, with coloured strawberry-like fruits. Its dark-green foliage is evergreen, and it flowers and fruits in late autumn. It is also a great choice of shrub for attracting wildlife into the garden.

3 *Geranium* Rozanne

This geranium has everything. Its perfectly-formed flowers are a striking blue with a white eye, and its height makes it an ideal front of border plant. It begins flowering in spring and continues late in the summer, and even on into early autumn – a real winner!

4 *Campsis radicans*

A beautiful deciduous climber with large, trumpet-shaped flowers of orange-red colour. A self-clinging woody stemmed climber which is ideal for a sunny wall or fence and has the benefit of flowering in late summer and autumn. It'll certainly add a Mediterranean feel to any garden. Reaches a magnificent height of 12m (39ft). Suited to full sun and dry soil.

5 *Clematis florida* var. *sieboldiana*

One of the most striking of all the clematis we grow, it has pure white flowers with a deep violet eye, and the appearance of a passion flower. A very different clematis, hence one of our bestsellers. Ideal in a sunny situation in the garden, var. *sieboldiana* also makes a wonderful container plant. Grows to 2m (6ft 7in) tall.

6 *Cotinus* 'Grace'

Commonly known as the smoke bush, this deciduous shrub is grown for its deep-purple foliage, tiny fluffy flowerheads and excellent autumn colour, when the oval-shaped leaves turn shades of red. It is strong, fast-growing and drought-tolerant, with a height and spread of 5m (16ft). Its colour can best be appreciated in a sunny position; good in full sun, with moist soil. It's fully hardy.

7 *Buddleja* Morning Mist (syn. 'Silver Anniversary')

A new variety that is evergreen, compact and hardy. An outstanding bush with brilliant, silver foliage and pure white flowers, making this a great addition to any border, and also an excellent choice for a special celebration.

Osteopermum jucundum

Buddleja Morning Mist (syn. 'Silver Anniversary')

Cotinus 'Grace'

8 *Osteospermum jucundum* 🏆
A bestselling perennial, not only because it's evergreen, it's rabbit-proof as well. The daisy-like rose and lavender flowers, borne in profusion in late summer, make this an eye-catching sight for the front of a border. Dry soil and full sun are fine for this frost hardy plant. It grows to 30cm (12in) tall.

9 *Salvia verticillata* 'Purple Rain'
A striking plant with bold mauve pendulous-type flowers that form a shower of colour in early summer. Ideal for the front of a border. Ideal in full sun, with dry soil. Cut back after flowering to encourage a further flush of flowers. Grows to 60cm (24in) tall, with a spread of 1.5m (5ft). Frost hardy.

10 *Weigela* Wine and Roses (syn. 'Alexandra')
This has candy-pink flowers set against dark, sumptuous foliage. It's truly stunning, making it a good companion for gold or silver foliage. A desirable plant, easy to grow and will offer interest from early spring to late autumn.

SPRING REACH NURSERY
Long Reach, Ockham, Surrey GU23 6PG
T: 01483 281859
E: springreach@btinternet.com
W: www.giftaplant.com

A few miles from RHS Wisley, this family business run by Nick and Lissa Hourhan, with a small team of horticulturists, is one of Surrey's best-kept secret. Its knowledge of plants extends far and wide, with unusual, but tried-and-tested varieties, grown on the nursery. Traditional favourites are also grown, including shrubs, perennials, climbers, clematis, bamboos, grasses and plants for a purpose, including chalk, clay, hot and dry shade. Open all year, Mon to Fri, 10am to 5pm; Sat, 10am to 5.30pm; Sun, 10.30am to 4.30pm.

COASTAL PLANTS – EAST

AS RECOMMENDED BY WILLIAM AND LOUISE FRIEND OF EAST NORTHDOWN FARM AND GARDENS

Phlomis fruticosa

Cistus x Cyprius

Many parts of coastal Kent and Essex get some of the lowest rainfall in the country, resulting in a Mediterranean microclimate with a minimum winter temperature of no less than -5°C. Evergreen plants do best, they grow all winter, but lie semi-dormant in the late-summer months. They have grey-felted, dark green or glaucous waxy leaves, to avoid being scorched by drying salt-laden winds in spring and summer, or when the ground is frozen in winter.

1 *Centranthus ruber* 'Albus'
A white form of valerian, a native of rocky places around the Mediterranean. In Kent, *C. ruber* is naturalised on the sea cliffs and old walls. It has a fleshy root, and comes from seed, provided it does not cross-pollinate with the red and lilac forms.

2 *Laurus nobilis* ♔
The noble laurel or bay tree, was introduced in Roman times. It seeds itself freely from round, acorn-like purple berries. It grows in the fertile, damp chestnut woods near Amalfi in Italy. H4

3 *Phlomis fruticosa* ♔
The commonly grown form of the Jerusalem sage grows well in Kent. It is a classic Mediterranean evergreen shrub, with grey-felted leaves and golden yellow flowers from early- to mid-summer. Can grow to 1.5m (5ft). H4

4 *Cistus* x *cyprius* ♔
One of the many *Cistus* to thrive in Kent. Only roughly half the species tolerate chalk; others grow wild on the more acidic areas of shale. It has wonderfully scented, resinous leaves, and large white flowers with a red blotch on each petal. H4

5 *Acacia retinoides*

The willow or four-season mimosa from Australia. One of the best mimosas on chalk. The long, thin willow-like leaves are more resistant to the wind than the ferny varieties. It has a delicate scent and produces small yellow pompoms from July until spring.

6 *Tamarix hampeana*

An evergreen tamarisk from the eastern Mediterranean, with spikes of pink flowers in May. *Tamarix hampeana* is a wonderful plant, brought back by East Northdown Gardens from a nursery on the island of Rhodes.

7 *Cestrum elegans*

A tender South American plant that is quite happy in a sheltered spot and covered in stunning red tubular flowers in May.

8 *Oryzopsis milliacea*

A dainty evergreen grass, that flowers continuously, but is at its best in May and June, until it dries up in summer. It grows along the verges all around the Mediterranean. East Northdown Gardens brought this coastal variety back from Crete, but it has been cultivated at other nurseries ever since.

CULTIVATION

'Mediterranean' plants don't all necessarily come from the Mediterranean, but are found in areas with a similar climate, such as parts of California, Mexico and New Zealand. Some areas have acidic sandy soils, so plants like Leptospermums are best grown in containers with ericaceous compost. Plants from monsoon areas and others with high summer rainfall are less tolerant of chalk. However, these can be grown on the deeper brick-earth soils. The lack of rain in August and September is compensated for by the more heavy sea mists and dews as days shorten.

---

9 *Asphodeline lutea*

I found it growing on a cliff in Delphi, on the Greek mainland at the age of 16, while on a school excursion. I've been in love with the Mediterranean, and this plant, ever since. It has narrow grey-green leaves and dense spikes of yellow flowers.

10 *Chamaerops humilis* ♆

This small European fan palm grows in rocky places and is frequently burnt in hill fires, but regrows. It gradually suckers out into a broad, low clump. This variety is better suited to the east coast, and is wind, drought- and chalk-tolerant. H3

EAST NORTHDOWN FARM AND GARDENS
East Northdown Farm and Gardens, Margate, Kent CT9 3TS
T: 01843 862060 F: 01843 860206
E: info@botanyplants.co.uk
W: www.botanyplants.com

East Northdown Farm is on the north-east tip of the Isle of Thanet, Kent, run by William and Louise Friend. Since the earliest times, Thanet has been famed for its mild climate and fertile brick-earth soils. William took over the family farm 20 years ago, growing the traditional market garden crops in the area. For the past 15 years he and Louise have focused on establishing their nursery, specialising in coastal and chalk-loving plants.

COASTAL PLANTS – WEST

AS RECOMMENDED BY CROSS COMMON NURSERY

Fascicularia bicolor

Acca sellowiana

Echium pininana

One of the greatest assets for gardeners in western coastal areas is the Gulf Stream, which provides a temperate climate for plants to grow. The temperature in western areas is warmed by the air off of the Atlantic, giving horticulturists an extended growing season with early springs and relatively frost-free winters. Gardens in these areas also benefit from high levels of rainfall, which help keep the air mild, thus reducing the risk of hard frosts.

1 *Agapanthus*

Agapanthus is a clump-forming perennial that likes a sunny position in well-drained soil. It has long green strap-like leaves and tall flower stems, with spheres of tubular flowers from deep blue to white. Tall varieties grow to 2m (6ft), and dwarf forms reach 40-50cm (16-20in).

2 *Abutilon megapotamicum* ♕

Abutilons are semi-evergreen shrubs best grown on a south south-west facing wall in well-drained soil. They have bell-shaped flowers and flower most of the year. *A. megapotamicum* grows to 3m (10ft). H3

3 *Echium pininana* ♕

A remarkable plant that has visitors amazed at the size and beauty of its flower spire.

E. pininana grows to 4m (12ft) and produces a tall spire of small blue flowers that attract bees. It dies after flowering but brings an exotic feel to gardens. Seeds freely. H2-3

4 *Cordyline australis* ♕

Known as the Cornish palm, this tough, evergreen palm-like tree from New Zealand with strap-like leaves is popular around the coast of south-west England. This tree copes well with salt-laden winds. Cordylines produce wonderfully scented large flower heads in spring and should be grown in free draining soil. They can grow to a height of 15m (50ft). H3

5 *Fascicularia bicolor*

F. bicolor forms a clump of slender, tooth-edged leaves. In autumn the leaves turn bright red as the plants flower. The flower is made up of 30 to 40 tiny turquoise flowers. Grow in free-draining soil in full sun. Height 45cm (18in).

6 *Pittosporum crassifolium*

A tough, evergreen tree excellent for creating shelter in coastal gardens, especially those exposed to harsh, salt-laden winds. *P. crassifolium* has dark green leathery leaves, white-coated underneath and can grow to 6m (20ft). Scented red-brown flowers are produced from April to June. Grow in a sunny position in free-draining soil.

7 *Lampranthus spectablis*

A spreading, prostrate succulent with small fleshy leaves, excellent for a sunny free-draining wall or rockery, its flowers are red, mauve, white, orange, pink and yellow. An excellent drought-tolerant plant. Height 30cm (1ft).

8 *Osteospermum*

These sun loving plants flower profusely, with large daisy-like flowers through spring and early autumn. Most are low-growing, spreading plants that enjoy in a sunny site in light, well-drained soil. They are excellent

coastal plants and can grow to 30-45cm (12-18in).

9 *Metrosideros excelsa*

This large, half-hardy, evergreen tree to 15m (50ft) tall with tough, dark green leaves is a good choice for coastal planting. It produces spectacular displays with bright red bottlebrush flowers during the summer months. It will grow in dry soils and can cope with exposed coastal conditions. H2

10 *Acca sellowiana*

A. sellowiana is best grown against a warm wall or in a sunny position in well-drained soil. It is an attractive shrub with glossy green leaves, whitish undersides and white-pink flowers with red stamens and has guava-like fruits. Height 3m (10ft). H3

CROSS COMMON NURSERY
The Lizard, Helston, Cornwall TR12 7PD
T: 01326 290722/290668
W: www.crosscommonnursery.co.uk
E: info@crosscommonnursery.co.uk

Cross Common Nursery is the most southerly nursery in the UK, located in the centre of The Lizard village in Cornwall. It is a family-run nursery built up by owner Trevor Triggs, now assisted by son-in-law Kevin and daughter Suzy. The nursery specialises in plants for coastal gardens, conservatory plants, citrus, passiflora, grapevines and tropical plants. The nursery is open from March to October seven days a week April to June and six days a week June to September.

PLANTS FOR...
CONSERVATORIES

AS RECOMMENDED BY THE DUCHY OF CORNWALL NURSERY

Fuchsia 'Glenby'

Those of us lucky enough to possess a conservatory or glasshouse can grow plants from tropical jungles and arid deserts. All they need are the right conditions to flourish. Fortunately, plants are amazingly adaptable and will tolerate a variety of different environments far removed from their natural habitats. One or two large specimens will require less looking after than, for example, a collection of pelargoniums, but both will enhance our lives in so many ways. What better way to spend a rainy afternoon than gardening indoors?

Fuchsia 'Taco'

CULTIVATION

Plants generally dislike extremes of heat and cold, under- or overwatering, over- or underfeeding. In hot, sunny positions, grow plants that love those conditions. Most plants, except for cacti and succulents, benefit from some shading from the hottest sun. In a shady position, grow fuchsias or other shade-loving plants. Ventilation is essential during summer and winter. *Citrus*, for instance, will drop both leaves and fruit without adequate ventilation. Watering is often difficult as both under- and overwatering can lead to the death of a plant. Feeding should take place between March and August. Do not feed in the winter, with the exception of *Citrus*.

1 *Bougainvillea*

A reminder of holidays in warmer climates, these exotic-looking plants have fabulous flower (or rather bract) power! Available in many shades of pink, orange, yellow, magenta, purple or red, the colourful bracts are long-lasting. Tie plants onto a trellis support or bamboo canes. They grow big so are suitable for larger conservatories. H2

2 Cacti and succulents

These are wonderful and diverse groups of evergreen plants, well suited to a very hot sun-baked conservatory or glasshouse. They may be the only groups that can fend for themselves during the summer holidays. Most will need repotting every two to three years. Try *Notocactus warasii*. H1

3 *Citrus*

Oranges, lemons, limes, kumquats, mandarins and satsumas are all excellent evergreen conservatory plants. The scent from the white waxy flowers is deliciously tangy and the fruit is edible. Special *Citrus* feed,

Bougainvillea

Notocactus warasii

Plumbago 'Crystal Waters'

for both summer and winter can help ensure success. Watch out for pets near this. H1

4 *Fuchsia*

A diverse group of plants for a semi-shaded conservatory. Glenby is a typical bush variety, double flowered, free flowing and vigorous. In addition to bush and hanging basket varieties, there are many beautiful species and species hybrids. Try *Fuchsia procumbens*, from New Zealand, for unusual, small shiny purple, green and yellow flowers, or *Fuchsia* 'Taco', a species hybrid with unusual, elegant, long tubular flowers. H2

5 *Metrosideros kermadecensis* 'Red and Gold'

The dominant tree from the Kermadec Islands, north-east of New Zealand. An easy evergreen foliage plant, it makes a small, bushy tree, but can be kept under control by pruning. This form has dark green and gold leaves on bright red stems. Beautiful scarlet flowers are an early summer bonus. H2

6 *Plumbago auriculata* 🏆

Plumbago is a long-flowering evergreen wall shrub from South Africa, with flower sprays of an unusual blue from April to November. 'Crystal Waters' is a fine form. The floppy stems need supporting with wires or a framework of canes. It likes good light, but shade from the most intense sunlight. H1-2

7 *Pelargoniums*

The regals are the showiest of the bunch, with huge trusses of flowers in unbelievably vivid colours and combinations. The scented-leaved pelargoniums are aromatic and tough. They survive intense sun and heat in summer with sufficient watering from beneath the foliage. In heated conservatories, pelargoniums will flower all year round. H1

8 *Olea europaea*

The olive is easy to grow and thrives in full sun or part shade. It will not outgrow

Fuchsia procumbens

Mandevilla sanderi

its space quickly and can be hard-pruned if necessary. Clip for a more formal look. In milder parts of the country, it can be planted outside if it gets too big. H3

9 *Pseudopanax*

These evergreen shrubs from New Zealand with exotic-looking foliage are a perfect foil for flowering plants. A range of leaf shapes and purple and variegated forms can be found. Most reach 2-3m (7-10ft) but can be pruned to make bushy plants. The more you prune, the sturdier they grow. H2

10 *Mandevilla*

An evergreen, twining climber, *Mandevilla*, or *Dipladenia* as it is also known, has exotic-looking trumpet flowers in great profusion. The colour range is from white, through many shades of pale pink, to deep reds. It is easy to grow in sun or shade and can be trained up a trellis. Try *M. sanderi*. H1

DUCHY OF CORNWALL NURSERY
Cott Road, Lostwithiel, Cornwall PL22 0HW
T: 01208 872668 F: 01208 872835
E: sales@duchyofcornwallnursery.co.uk
W: www.duchyofcornwallnursery.co.uk

This nursery is part of the Duchy of Cornwall, the institution which provides an income for the heir to the throne. It carries a huge range of plants, taking full advantage of the climatic advantages of Cornwall in offering many less-hardy varieties. Specialisms include fuchsias, camellias and conifers. It is open all year round, seven days a week. A mail order service is offered via a lavishly illustrated website.

PLANTS FOR... CONTAINERS

AS RECOMMENDED BY PETER MANFIELD OF VILLAGE NURSERIES

Arctotis Hannah

Impatiens Fiesta Pink Ruffle

Thunbergia alata 'African Sunset'

S easonal containers are great fun. The selection of plants that can be grown in them and the planting combinations are limited only by your imagination and plant knowledge. I have chosen some of my favourites below; they are all reliable flowering plants that perform well over a long period during the spring, summer and autumn.

1 *Euphorbia hypericifolia* Diamond Frost

This is incredible – it just keeps on flowering with clouds of airy white flowers from May until autumn. Its principal advantage is that it never needs deadheading and always looks the same throughout its flowering period. It has a compact habit, growing to 20cm (8in) high, spread 30cm (12in). H2

2 *Cleome* 'Senorita Rosalita'

A great plant for adding height to a large tub, it has explosions of pink flowers in clusters from May until September. Best in a mixed tub and associates well with pelargoniums, Verbenas, Argyranthemums and lavenders. It grows to about 60cm (24in) with a spread of about 40cm (16in). H1

3 *Arctotis* Hannah

This wonderful daisy has deep orange-red flowers held above the grey-green foliage from May until September. Grow it alone or with others in full sun and well-drained soil. Deadhead regularly to keep it flowering and looking good. It grows 40cm (16in) tall with a spread of 30cm (12in). H1

4 *Thunbergia alata* 'African Sunset'

If you want a climber for a smaller container, this vigorous *Thunbergia* is the perfect choice. It has burnt orange flowers from May well into autumn and will spread about 1.8m (6ft). Grow it on a trellis against a sunny wall or freestanding on a tripod. H1

5 *Ocimum* 'African Blue'

Most herbs grow well in containers but this basil excels. It is a wonderful plant; the richly aromatic dark green foliage has very distinctive dark purple veins and is topped by blue-purple flower spikes from April until October. It grows to a height of 75cm (30in) with a spread of 35cm (14in). H2

NEW PLANTS FOR CONTAINERS

See them all and lots more at –

VILLAGE NURSERIES
SINNOCKS, WEST CHILTINGTON,
PULBOROUGH, WEST SUSSEX, RH20 2JX
01798 813040

Village Nurseries is a family run retail nursery which grows all it sells at very reasonable prices. We specialise in a very wide range of seasonal plants and hardy perennials. The nurseries are situated in a beautiful part of rural West Sussex midway between the A24 and the A29 ten miles from the South coast and 12 miles from Horsham. Many of our nursery grown plants are now grown in biodegradable pots. The Nurseries are open 7 days a week throughout the year from 9am-6pm [5pm in winter].

www.village-nurseries.co.uk

6 *Impatiens walleriana* Fiesta Pink Ruffle

Expect full flower power from this salmon pink double *Impatiens* throughout summer and well into autumn. It is ideal for a tub in semi-shade and mixes well with non-stop begonias and fuchsias. It has a wonderful, compact habit growing to 25cm (10in) high with a spread of 40cm (16in). H1

7 *Argyranthemum* 'Citronelle'

'Citronelle' is one of the best new dwarf Argyranthemums. It has single sherbet lemon flowers with darker mustard centres over a long period from April until October. Best in a sunny spot, it mixes well with almost anything. The height is 30cm (12in) and spread 40cm (16in). H2

8 *Diascia* Little Dancer

A superb, free-flowering variety, with lilac pink flowers, from May until October. This compact little *Diascia* is great value in a tub in sun or semi-shade and mixes well with almost anything, growing to 15cm (6in) high with a spread of 30cm (12in). H3

9 *Plectranthus* 'Blue Spire'

A bold but not brash variegated plant, the aromatic silver foliage providing a foil for spikes of rich blue flowers all summer. Ideal for a large tub, growing to 50cm (20in) high with a spread of 35cm (14cm), and mixes well with Diascias, pelargoniums and Verbenas in sun or semi-shade. H1

10 *Nemesia* Karoo Soft Blue

This *Nemesia* is exceptional. It has wonderful soft sky-blue flowers with white eyes from May until October and a neat, compact habit growing to 25cm (10in) high with a spread of 20cm (8in). This unique colour mixes extremely well with pinks, whites and blues in a cool semi-shaded position. H2

CULTIVATION

Many plants are easy to grow in containers but it is very important to match the plant to the container. Don't expect a large vigorous plant to do well in a small container. Good quality compost containing slow release fertiliser with a well-drained open texture will give much better results than a standard multipurpose mix. Regular watering is essential, especially when the weather is hot or windy. When the plants are well established always water generously, so that the water floods though the drainage holes in the bottom of the pot.

VILLAGE NURSERIES
Sinnocks, West Chiltington, Pulborough,
West Sussex RH20 2JX
T: 01798 813040 E: villagenurseries@btconnect.com
W: www.village-nurseries.co.uk

Village Nurseries is a family run retail nursery which grows all it sells. It specialises in a very wide range of seasonal plants and hardy perennials. The nurseries are situated in a beautiful part of rural west Sussex, midway between the A24 and the A29, 10 miles from the south coast and 12 miles from Horsham. The nurseries are open seven days a week throughout the year from 9am to 6pm (5pm in winter).

DROUGHT-TOLERANT PLANTS

AS RECOMMENDED BY BETH CHATTO OF BETH CHATTO GARDENS

Echinops ritro 'Veitch's Blue'

The drought-tolerant plants chosen here all grow in Beth Chatto's Gravel Garden, three quarters of an acre of well-drained poor sand and gravel, in full sun most of the day, with very low rainfall – around 25cm (10in) in both summer and winter. It began as a horticultural experiment to see what would survive, as the garden has not been irrigated since it was planted, in 1992. These plants are chosen as much for their foliage effect as for their flowers, since leaves last much longer, and for their ability to provide interest for much of the year. Here's the top 10.

1 *Echinops ritro* 'Veitch's Blue'
Known as the 'Globe Thistle', this has silvered branching stems, up to 1m (3ft) tall, clothed in dark green, deeply-cut leaves with white backs. They carry a bouquet of indigo-blue buds which open into balls of tiny, starry-blue flowers, the colour intensified by dark calyces. A wonderfully intense colour among grey and silver plants.

2 *Zauschneria californica*
In early autumn the scarlet, trumpet-shaped flowers of the Californian fuchsia are held well above a low tangle of wiry stems hidden by narrow, silvery leaves. The plant needs very well-drained soil and full sun. Top growth may be killed by winter frost, but it retains new growth below ground which emerges in spring.

3 *Euphorbia characias* subsp. *wulfenii* ♉
This *Euphorbia* makes a remarkable feature all year round. It forms stiff clumps of upright stems clothed with narrow, blue-grey leaves. From early spring until May, it illuminates the dry garden with huge, dense pyramidal heads of small yellowish-green flowers. Few flowering plants remain effective for so long.

4 *Ballota pseudodictamnus* ♉
One of the most handsome feature plants for drought conditions. Cut back in early spring to remove old clutter and make way for fresh growth of long, curving stems valued for their pale, graceful effect. Insignificant pale-lavender flowers are buried in pale-green 'clock faces' held back-to-back along the woolly stems.

Euphorbia characias subsp. wulfenii

5 *Gypsophila* 'Rosenschleier' ♉
Intertangling wiry stems carry cloud-like displays of tiny, palest pink, double flowers which overwhelm minimal grey-green leaves. Lightly trim after flowering. It is still pretty at the border edge when sparkling with frost in winter, but cut down to the base before spring growth emerges. Grows to 30cm (12in). Also known as 'Veil of Roses' or 'Rosy Veil'.

6 *Helianthemum* 'Rhodanthe Carneum' – (syn. 'Wisley Pink')
This rock rose forms a low, spreading shrublet, ideal for border edges or falling

Ballota pseudodictamnus

Helianthemum
'Rhodanthe Carneum'
(syn. 'Wisley Pink')

Origanum laevigatum
'Hopleys'

Gypsophila 'Rosenschleier'

Helichrysum 'Schweffelicht'
(syn. 'Sulphur Light')

down a slope. Clothed in ever-grey, small leaves, it is smothered in midsummer by rose-pink flowers with yellow stamens. By late afternoon they've dropped, but fresh ones open each morning, over several weeks.

7 *Origanum laevigatum* 'Hopleys'

This marjoram is valued for its ability to remain fresh and produce contrast of colour and form throughout the dry season. Clumps of crowded, wiry stems are clothed in small, pointed leaves carrying branched heads of tiny, pink flowers accented by scaly, purple bracts. A good edge-of-border plant.

8 *Sedum telephium* subsp. *ruprechtii* 'Pink Dome'

This sedum deserves to be as well known as its relative, 'Herbstfreude'. 'Pink Dome' forms a lower, more compact plant with clusters of pink buds opening to creamy-yellow, starry flowers. These mature to reddish-brown seedheads – all stages seen on the plants for many weeks from summer to autumn. It grows to around 38cm (15in) tall.

9 *Perovskia* 'Blue Spire' ⅌

The Russian sage is found wild from Afghanistan to Tibet and has a tall graceful shape that lifts the eye and contrasts well with rounded shapes. Slender, greyish-white stems clothed in grey-green dissected leaves, carry spires of lavender-like flowers from late summer to autumn on this variety. Grows to 1.2m (4ft).

10 *Helichrysum* 'Schweffelicht' (syn. 'Sulphur Light')

A pretty plant for the edge of a sun-baked, well-drained border. It makes slowly-spreading clusters of narrow leaves, so thickly felted that they appear almost white against the soil, a lovely setting for heads of pale lemon buds which open tiny, everlasting daisy-flowers. Grows to 46cm (18in).

Perovskia 'Blue Spire'

Sedum telephium subsp. *ruprechtii* 'Pink Dome'

THE BETH CHATTO GARDENS
Elmstead Market, Colchester, Essex CO7 7DB
T: 01206 822007
W: www.bethchatto.co.uk

Beth Chatto began the gardens almost 50 years ago. The gardens were faced with extreme conditions - sun-baked gravel, a boggy meadow and dry woodland. Beth was inspired by her husband's lifelong research into the natural associations of plants – where they were found, what the conditions were like, and with what else they were growing. Now, these problem areas have been transformed by choosing plants adapted to these conditions – and the nursery is based on these principles. Within **The Beth Chatto Gardens**, pot-grown plants in the sales area are arranged alphabetically and according to the different conditions in the garden: dry, shady or damp. There is also a mail order plant service from September through to March. Gardens, Nursery and Tea Room opening times are from 1 March to end 31 October, Monday to Saturday, 9am to 5pm; 1 November to 28 February, Monday to Friday, 9am to 4pm; open on Bank Holidays; closed on Sundays.

PLANTS FOR...
ROCK GARDENS

AS RECOMMENDED BY MICHAEL AND JILL AGG OF CHOICE LANDSCAPES

Campanula isophylla

Anchusa caespitosa

Saxifraga 'Tumbling Waters'

Alpine plants have become beloved of the many enthusiasts who collect these miniature flora. Most Alpines grown in this country are the same species that grow in their wild, romantic mountain habitats all over the world, rather than cultivated varieties. Alpine plants grow in mountainous regions, in the high Alpine pastures and on rocky cliffs above the tree line. In the late 1800s and early 1900s the study and cultivation of alpines was undertaken by Reginald Farrer, writer of *The English Rock Garden*, published in 1918 and still used as a reference manual among growers today.

PROPAGATION

There are many ways of growing Alpines, from seed, cuttings and nursery-grown plants. Seed should be sown fresh where possible, in trays or pans with a thin covering of fine grit. When seedlings appear they should be transplanted and grown on in small pots 6-8cm (2-3in) in alpine compost; equal parts John Innes No 2 and horticultural grit. Cuttings should be taken from non-flowering shoots in midsummer. The cutting should be as small as possible and firmly inserted in a 50/50 mixture of peat and sharp-sand or perlite, in a shaded frame. Pot on when cuttings have a good root system.

1 *Anchusa caespitosa*
A dense, mound-forming perennial with rosettes of narrowly linear hairy dark green leaves, bearing clusters of stemless, vivid blue flowers with a white eye. 5-10cm (2-4in) high.

2 *Campanula isophylla* ♈
Ideal for containers or hanging baskets, trailing much-branched stems that become slightly woody at the base, with small, light green, toothed, heart-shaped leaves. The plant can grow to a height of 15-20cm.

3 *Calceolaria* 'Walter Shrimpton'
An evergreen perennial with rosettes of spoon-shaped to oval mid-green leaves, with two-five bronze-yellow flowers in summer, heavily

spotted chestnut brown with white between throat and pouch. It grows to 10cm (4in).

4 *Asperula lilaciflora*

An evergreen perennial with tubular and star-shaped flowers, bright pink outside, blush pink inside. The plant can grow to a height of 5cm (2in) with a spread of 30cm (12in).

5 *Hypsela reniformis*

A creeping perennial with rooting stems and rounded to kidney-shaped, mid-green leaves. Flowers are lobelia-shaped and pale pink with crimson veins. It can grow to 5-8cm (2-3in).

6 *Phlox caespitosa*

A tight hummock-forming evergreen perennial 5-10cm (2-4in) high with a spread of 15cm (6in). With small, needle-like leaves, it bears stemless pale lavender-to-white flowers.

7 *Physoplexis comosa* ♔

A deciduous perennial, with ovate to heart-shaped, mid-dark green leaves. In late summer, it bears clusters of 10-20 pale violet flowers with deep violet tips.

8 *Saxifraga* 'Tumbling Waters' ♔

A slow-growing saxifrage, with large, clustered rosettes of linear, lime-encrusted

silvery-green leaves. After several years it bears small cup-shaped white flowers in spring.

9 *Teucrium aroanium*

A low-growing evergreen subshrub with densely hairy stems and silver leaves, which are 5cm (2in) long. In summer, two-lipped soft purple flowers, 5cm (2in) long, are borne.

10 *Vitaliana primuliflora* (syn. *Douglasia vitaliana*)

An evergreen perennial with creeping stems and rosettes of lance-shaped, pale green leaves with silver margins. In spring it bears yellow flowers. The plant can grow to 7cm (2.5in).

PLANTS FOR...
WATER GARDENS

AS RECOMMENDED BY RICHARD AND JANE CAIN OF PENLAN PERENNIALS

Iris sibirica 'Silver Edge'

Nymphaea 'Escarboucle'

Primula florindae

For me, water is essential in the garden. The movement and sound it creates, the reflections on the water surface and the wildlife living in and around it add another dimension to gardening with nature. If you cannot manage space for a pond, or have young children, there are small water features available that can bring just as much pleasure. I have selected 10 plants that I grow and consider 'must haves' in my own water garden. Where I have singled out a particular cultivar, I would also recommend other members of that family and have therefore made a few alternative suggestions.

1 *Nymphaea* 'Escarboucle' ♔

'Escarboucle' is fragrant with double crimson flowers and yellow-tipped, red stamens from June to September. Leaves are round and red when they emerge, turning green in the summer. One of the most popular and reliable water lilies, enjoying full sun, it is best planted at a depth of 60cm-1.75m (2ft-5ft 6in). H4

2 *Nymphaea* 'James Brydon' ♔

Chosen because it will flower in shade, *Nymphaea* 'James Brydon' has cupped, dark pink, double flowers which are highly fragrant. The flowers have gold-tipped, red stamens and last several days. Young leaves are purple, often spotted with dark red. H4

3 *Caltha palustris* 'Flore Pleno' ♔

Flowering in April, the double-flowered marsh marigold with pom-poms of bright yellow flowers has a more compact habit and blooms for longer than the species and tolerates drier conditions, so can be planted in moist soil or used as a marginal plant. H4

4 *Carex elata* 'Aurea' ♔

Particularly effective when planted in shallow water – 5cm (2in) – but can also be grown in moist or boggy soil. Tolerant of sun or part-shade and most soil types, the bright yellow leaves are edged in green during spring. Its compact habit, 45 x 60cm (18 x 24in), makes it suitable for smaller water features. H4

5 *Iris pseudacorus* ♛

This native yellow flag has sword-like leaves which emerge in April and it flowers in May and June. The yellow petals have darker yellow zoning and brown markings on the falls. Ideal for boggy or wet ground, or medium to large ponds, planting depth 30cm (12in). Essential for attracting dragonflies and damselflies. H4

6 *Rodgersia podophylla* 'Braunlaub'

Enjoying rich, moist soil in sun or part shade, this *Rodgersia* looks superbly architectural near water. Reaching 1.25 x 1.25m (4 x 4ft) the stunning brown-bronze leaves with sharply serrated edges hold their colour through the early season, becoming dark green by midsummer in shade. June brings panicles of petal-less, cream-flushed red flowers.

7 *Ranunculus aconitifolius* 'Flore Pleno' ♛

The double-flowered fair maids of France originates from the Vosges mountains. It has dark green, dissected leaves and double white, button flowers on tall stems held clear of the foliage. It enjoys a moist to wet soil in sun or part shade. Growing to 60 x 60cm (2 x 2ft) it flowers from April to July. H4

8 *Primula florindae* ♛

The giant Himalayan cowslip is similar in habit to a candelabra primula, having drooping heads of yellow, sometimes orange to blood-red, flowers on tall stems above the foliage. It is heavily scented, will grow in shallow water, planting depth 5cm (2in), or a boggy moist soil and flowers later than other members of the primula family. Tall at 60cm (2ft), it is happy in sun or light shade. H4

9 *Iris sibirica* 'Silver Edge' ♛

At 75cm (30in) this vigorous hybrid is taller than other Siberian irises and provides a sturdy vertical accent, with blue-tinted foliage topped by ruffled, silver-edged blue petals. Flowers last for several days and are at their best in the first two weeks of June. Grow in a sunny position. H4

10 *Gunnera manicata* ♛

The giant of the streamside or bog garden, growing to its full stature of 2.5 x 2.5m (8 x 8ft) only in very moist soil. It has huge umbrella leaves up to 1m (3ft) across on prickly stems. The flowers look like giant pine cones and form at the base of the stem. H3-4

WATER GARDENS – TOP 10 FAVOURITES
AS RECOMMENDED BY SIMON HARMAN OF LILIES WATER GARDENS

Nymphaea 'Hal Miller'

Marsilea mutica

It is not easy to single out 10 water garden plants from our huge collection, so I have focused on the most popular favourites. These include three waterlilies, suitable for different water depths, an unusual iris, two tall and two low-growing marginal plants for full sun, and two beautiful tropical plants that must be overwintered in a frost-free place.

1 *Nymphaea* 'Château le Rouge'

An attractive waterlily with small, dark red blooms that appear freely through summer, from June to September. It is excellent for small ponds in partial shade, with a leaf spread of 90cm (35in). Plant so there is 30-45cm (16-18in) of water above the rhizome.

2 *Nymphaea* 'Hal Miller'

Another free-flowering waterlily, much admired for its star-like, creamy white flowers. It blooms from June to September and is suitable for ponds and lakes in partial shade or full sun. Leaf spread is 1.2-1.8m (4-6ft). When planting ensure there is 45-90cm (18-35in) of water above the rhizome.

3 *Nymphaea* 'Darwin'

'Darwin' has huge, double pink blooms fading to light pink on the outer edges. Suitable for ponds and lakes in full sun, it flowers from June to September and has a leaf spread of 1.2-1.8m (4-6ft). Plant deep, with 90-120cm (35-47in) of water above the rhizome.

4 *Iris versicolor* 'Mysterious Monique'

This iris is beautiful for its interesting and unusual flower colour – velvet-purple with white, violet and yellow markings. The plant can grow to 60-90cm (24-35in). Plant the rhizomes to a depth of 4-10cm (1.5-4in).

5 *Lythrum salicaria* 'Robert'

This pink form of purple loosestrife is a clump-forming perennial, with dense spikes of wonderfully bright pink flowers from July to September. It is suitable for moist borders and the edge of ponds and streams in full sun, and grows to a height of 60cm (24in).

6 *Butomus umbellatus* 'Rosenrot'

This variety of flowering rush is named for

its umbels of cup-shaped, fragrant, dark pink flowers that are held high above the water to 90cm (35in) during June and July. It also has rich reddish-green leaves that turn dark green as they extend. Grows well at the margins of ponds and lakes in full sun.

7 *Mazus reptans* 'Blue'

This is an excellent Alpine plant for the damp edges of streams and rockeries in full sun. It is also called the Chinese marsh flower, and carries a very attractive carpet of blue flowers above a mat of toothed leaves. It flowers from May to July and can grow to a height of 5cm (2in). H3

8 *Marsilea mutica*

Variegated water clover forms a carpet of foliage patterned with red, green and yellow, covering the water's surface to about 15cm (6in). Excellent for the edges of ponds and streams in full sun or semi-shade. Plant so there is up to 10cm (4in) of water above the crown. H1

9 *Thalia dealbata*

This is a showy tropical marginal from Mexico and the US. It bears spikes of violet-blue flowers from June to September among bluish-green leaves. This variety is suitable for ponds and lakes in full sun. It can grow to a height of 1.8m (6ft). Plant to a depth of 10-60cm (4-24in) over the crown. H2

10 *Eichhornia crassipes*

Water hyacinth is a tropical floating plant that provides excellent surface cover. In the right conditions, it forms hyacinth-like flowers to a height of 30cm (12in) above water. However, in some areas with mild winters, this plant can become invasive and in many parts of the world, it is known as an aggressive weed that can clog waterways. H2

Lythrum salicaria 'Robert'

LILIES WATER GARDENS
Broad Lane, Newdigate, Surrey RH5 5AT
T: 01306 631064
E: mail@lilieswatergardens.co.uk
W: www.lilieswatergardens.co.uk

Lilies Water Gardens specialises in water plants, plants for bog gardens, marginal plants, herbaceous plants, ferns and shrubs. Simon Harman, the proprietor, has won 15 awards at the RHS Hampton Court Palace Flower Show, including the much-coveted Tudor Rose Award (three times), six Gold Medals, one Silver Gilt Medal, four Silver Medals and one Bronze Medal. The nursery is open between 9am to 5pm Tuesday to Saturday, 1 March to 31 August, and by appointment for the rest of the year. A planting and repotting service is available.

BULBS – ALL SEASONS

RECOMMENDED BY CHRISTINE SKELMERSDALE OF BROADLEIGH GARDENS

Crocus laevigatus 'Fontenayi'

Narcissus 'Lemon Silk'

I have been gardening here at Barr House, the home of Broadleigh Gardens, for more than 30 years. During that time our private garden has evolved into a demonstration garden for the nursery where I have experimented with different bulbs. My experience here formed the basis of my choice. There is a bulb for each season and these have proved themselves over the years to be very reliable and beautiful.

1 *Narcissus* 'Jumblie' ♔

This versatile daffodil is equally at home in the front of a border, or the rock garden and is ideal for pots. The flowers are golden yellow with a deeper trumpet. Plant 10-15cm (4-6in) deep in autumn. It is a good foil for blue flowered bulbs and can grow to 20cm (8in).

2 *Narcissus* 'Lemon Silk'

'Lemon Silk' opens lemon yellow and then fades to a paler shade. It is 32cm (14in) and

very vigorous. It is at home in a border or in grass. I use it at the edge of a shrub bed.

3 *Tulipa saxatilis*

This species of tulip is 32cm (14in) tall with leaves appearing in late autumn; however, it does not flower until April. Each stem has two to three large flowers of purple-pink with prominent yellow centres. It quickly spreads to form a large patch. Plant 15cm (6in) deep in autumn in dry soil which gets winter sun.

4 *Tulipa* 'White Triumphator' ♔

These elegant creamy-white lily-flowered tulips are effective in tubs or clumps among herbaceous plants. If they are to be left in the ground, plant at least 20cm (8in) deep in October to November.

5 *Crocus laevigatus* 'Fontenayi'

This is a fascinating, rather underrated crocus, which flowers in December with well-rounded petals. The inside is lilac-purple while the outer petals are suffused with a creamy buff with deep purple-maroon feathering. Plant in a well-drained spot in maximum winter sun any time from August to October.

6 *Crocus speciosus* ♔

An autumn-flowering crocus which thrives in grass under trees, where it forms a carpet of blue from mid-September to mid-November. Each flower on its slender 15cm (6in) stem is easily toppled by rain or wind. However, *C. speciosus* pushes up more flowers to replace them. Plant in August or September.

7 *Galanthus* 'Magnet' ♔

'Magnet' is immediately recognisable, with an exceptionally long perianth and large flowers on the 18cm (7in) stem. A vigorous bulb which quickly forms good-sized clumps. Plant in the autumn, and make sure they are freshly lifted from the ground, in the spring or after flowering.

8 *Agapanthus* 'Blue Moon'

One of the best for the open garden. Large, densely-packed silver-blue flower heads on stiff 1.2m (4ft) stems. It combines the vigour of the small-flowered *campanulatus* hybrids with the stature of the large-flowered *A. praecox*. It is one of the last to flower, in late August to September.

9 *Eucomis autumnalis* ♔

This South African bulb produces a delicate 23cm (9in) spike of pure white flowers in late summer. It needs to be dry while dormant and is easiest in a pot. Plant in February to May.

10 *Lilium longiflorum* 'White American'

This dwarf hybrid is ideal for pots and has a wonderful scent. It grows to 40cm (16in) and produces white flowers in August. Choose a large container, adding plenty of drainage in the bottom. Water and feed regularly to ensure the colour of flowers don't fade over time.

BULBS – SUMMER AND AUTUMN

AS RECOMMENDED BY MARK WASH OF TRECANNA NURSERY

Crocosmia 'Harlequin'

Ask any gardener to list their favourite garden bulbs and daffodils, tulips, and crocuses would be more than likely to feature among the replies. The huge selection of spring-flowering bulbs is the bread and butter of many borders, although some of the real gems of the bulb world must surely appear somewhat later in the year, during summer and autumn. Here's a selection of 10 of the best summer- and autumn-flowering bulbs. It's a hard task to draw up such a shortlist as there are so many to be enjoyed during the second half of the year.

Allium tuberosum

1 *Eucomis vandermerwei*

A wonderful dwarf form of pineapple lily, from South Africa. Growing to just 15cm (6in) high with upright flower stems packed with star-shaped dusky-pink flowers and a crest of leafy bracts atop, it resembles a miniature pineapple. Hard to beat for a rock garden or shallow container.

2 *Crocosmia* 'Harlequin'

At the top of the list of clump-forming crocosmias. Easy to grow, and tough, it's about 75cm (30in) high, with stems bearing many small tubular bi-coloured flowers, with alternate red and yellow petals. It makes a valuable contribution to the garden during July and August.

3 *Tulbaghia violacea* 'Silver Lace' (syn. 'Variegata')

Tulbaghia are the unsung heroes of the patio, producing flowers from May through to late September. The leaves of 'Silver Lace' are narrow, upright and distinctly edged in cream, making this form as valuable for foliage as for flowers. The 45cm (18in) high flowering stems bear umbels of tubular pale-lilac flowers. H3

4 *Galtonia viridiflora*

Superb for late summer borders, Galtonias increase in the right conditions to produce an impressive display. This one is known as the green Cape hyacinth and grows to 90cm (3ft) high with wide green leaves and 20 waxy greenish-cream flowers per stem.

5 *Allium tuberosum*

This reliable *Allium* is at its best in August and September. It forms a neat, dense clump

Crinum x powellii

Eucomis vandermerwei

SUMMER AND AUTUMN FLOWERING-BULB RUNNERS UP

There are some bulbs that didn't quite make it into the top 10, but still deserve real merit, so these are some of the alternative summer- and autumn-flowering bulbs that are still well worth growing:

Allium caeruleum 🏆 and *sphaerocephalon*
Amaryllis belladonna 🏆
Canna
Crocus sativus or saffron crocus
Crocus speciosus 🏆
Cyclamen hederifolium 🏆
Dahlia

Eremurus or foxtail lily
Eucomis – including *E. bicolor* 🏆 and *E. comosa*
Iris unguicularis 🏆
Lilium – many forms
Rhodohypoxis
Sternbergia or autumn daffodil
Zantedeschia or arum lily

Tigridia pavonia

Colchicum 'Harlekijn'

of narrow edible leaves. The starry white flowers are held in flattened umbels on 45cm (18in) high stems. They carry a soft oniony fragrance and attract a plethora of butterflies, bees and hoverflies.

6 *Colchicum* 'Harlekijn'

Autumn crocuses produce leaves in early spring and flowers in autumn, hence the name naked ladies as the flowers appear without the leaves. 'Harlekijn' – pronounced 'Harlequin' – produces crocus-like, goblet-shaped blooms with white tepals that develop lilac blushes, deepening as the flowers age. A very welcome sight in autumn.

7 *Crinum* x *powellii* 🏆

A mature *Crinum* bulb is often as large as a football with an elongated 'trunk' up to 45cm (18in) long. The strap-type glossy green leaves appear in spring, forming a dense clump. Flower stems appear from summer, 1.5m (5ft) high, each bearing up to 10 fragrant pink flowers. H3

8 *Schizostylis coccinea* f. *alba*

The Kaffir lily is a rampant border perennial, with red flowers from mid-August onwards. There are many different hybrids

Nerine bowdenii

but probably the daintiest of all is this pure white form of the species, with slender petals and spidery white styles. It grows up to 45cm (18in) high.

9 *Tigridia pavonia*

One for the 'hot' border. Blooms can be 15cm (6in) across, with three petals forming a triangular flower. Forms range from yellow to rich red. Bulbs produce fresh blooms each day over a reasonably long period. Leaves are spear-shaped and pleated, and the flowering height is usually around 1.5m (5ft). H1

10 *Nerine bowdenii* ♛

Nerines are superb bulbs for a late display, flowering in September and October. *N. bowdenii* is the one to grow outdoors without any real concerns. Leaves are narrow and rich green, and the dainty flowers are normally a vivid candy pink, although there are also paler pink and white forms. H3-4

TRECANNA NURSERY
Latchley, nr Gunnislake, Cornwall PL18 9AX
T: 01822 834680 E: mark@trecanna.co.uk
W: www.trecanna.co.uk

Trecanna Nursery is a family-run nursery set on the Cornish slopes of the Tamar Valley. Mark and Karen Wash grow a range of less-usual perennials and bulbs, including over 200 forms of *Crocosmia*, plus good collections of *Eucomis*, *Tulbaghia*, *Rhodohypoxis*, *Kniphofia* and *Sempervivum*. Trecanna Nursery is open throughout the year from Wednesday to Saturday, 10am to 5pm. There is a mail-order service and a detailed website where plants and bulbs can be ordered online.

SUMMER PERENNIALS

AS RECOMMENDED BY NICK AND SUE HAMILTON OF BARNSDALE GARDENS

Eryngium variifolium

Hemerocallis 'Big Smile'

Chrysanthemum 'Cottage Apricot'

Our gardens at Barnsdale are overflowing with plants that could have gone into this list of our 10 favourites, and we omitted them for no other reason than we had reached our quota. There are so many invaluable plants, but in the end we have chosen varieties that have a long interest period and are therefore excellent value for money, and are suitable for growing in all sizes of garden.

1 *Allium wallichii*
A summer-flowering perennial onion that produces a sea of rounded purple flowerheads on slender stems. Do not cut down after flowering as they look magnificent covered in frost. It will only reach 60-90cm (2-3ft) in height, ideal for the middle-front of a bed.

2 *Campanula lactiflora* 'Loddon Anna' ♔
This upright, statuesque plant produces large massed heads of dusky-pink flowers. It is a long-flowering variety, starting in early June and continuing into late August. The sturdy stems carry the flower heads up to 1.2m (4ft), good for the middle or back of a border.

3 *Chrysanthemum* 'Cottage Apricot'
A little-known, much underused variety that gives interest at a difficult time of year. This

plant brightens any late summer and autumn with its vibrant bronze-apricot, daisy-like flowers. The yellow centre to the flowers serves to enhance and complement the bright petals.

4 *Eryngium variifolium*
As the stems begin to grow out of the basal rosette of this sea holly, the spiky, silvery leaves become evident with sturdy stems reaching about 60cm (2ft) in height. At the end of their branched tips are small, vibrant blue flowers arranged into a cone.

5 *Hemerocallis* 'Big Smile'
The delicate sunny-yellow flowers of 'Big Smile' are very special, with their ruffled edges marked with faintest blush pink. The contrasts between these three features give

this variety an elegance not seen in many daylily and make it stand out without being obvious.

6 *Hosta* 'Sum and Substance' ♆

Our hostas are not often attacked by slugs and snails because our clay soil dries out, leaving a powdery layer. This hosta's enormous, fresh green leaves require a space of 1.5-1.8m (5-6ft) to spread into. During July to August we are treated to pale lavender flowers that complement the leaves beautifully.

7 *Hydrangea arborescens* 'Annabelle' ♆

This variety will grow in the deepest of shade: if you put it in the cupboard under the stairs it would still grow well. We have many dotted about the gardens, all in deep shade, with their enormous, white flowerheads like beacons in the dark. Cut to ground level each spring.

8 *Penstemon* 'Alice Hindley' ♆

We have over 170 varieties at Barnsdale, but this one has beautified gardens since 1931 and is still worthy of a place in any border. One of the taller varieties, reaching 120cm (4ft), it produces spikes of large, tubular soft lilac and white flowers from June until the frosts.

9 *Rosa* 'Noisette Carnée'

A much underused climbing rose that has lost out to larger, blousier varieties. A pity – this variety only grows to 2.1m (7ft), but that makes it ideal for arches, pergolas or fences. The small, semi-double flowers are lilac-pink with a wonderful clove fragrance and are produced continuously from June.

10 *Rudbeckia fulgida* var. *sulivantii* 'Goldsturm' ♆

A burst of sunshine in the autumn, it starts to flower late in the summer and continues until the frosts. It brightens any border, with its large flowers of narrow, bright yellow petals and a central brown knob.

CULTIVATION

Most of these varieties can be planted at any time of year, if they have been pot-grown, but *Penstemon* need a couple of months to get established before the winter. All the plants are happy in full sun, except the hydrangea and hosta, which prefer semi or full shade. *Penstemon*, *Hemerocallis* and *Campanula* are just as happy in semi-shade as in full sun.

BARNSDALE GARDENS
The Avenue, Exton, Oakham, Rutland LE15 8AH
T: 01572 813200
E: office@barnsdalegardens.co.uk
W: www.barnsdalegardens.co.uk

Barnsdale Gardens began in 1983, from just a ploughed field. In 1989 part of the adjacent field was purchased and construction of the nursery commenced. **Barnsdale Gardens** is a small, family-run business which prides itself on growing a wide range of quality, choice and unusual garden plants. Its range has increased from the 120 varieties it started with, to over 2,000. Open Monday to Sunday all year – phone for times.

AUTUMN LEAVES

AS RECOMMENDED BY PURE PLANTS

Quercus palustris

As the long, warm days of summer turn to the shorter, cooler days of autumn there is a wonderful change in the leaf colour of many plants. We think mainly of the stunning tones of tree foliage but many shrubs and perennials give a wonderful show at this time of the year. Many of the best plants for autumn colour grow best in acid soil, but there are still plenty to suit an alkaline one. While the weather plays a key role in the intensity of autumn colour, we have tried to highlight varieties that are reliable autumn turners.

1 *Quercus palustris* ♈

The pin oak is a vigorous tree growing up to 20m (66ft) in a broadly conical shape with distinctively tiered, horizontal branches that droop gracefully at their tips. The leaves turn a spectacular scarlet in autumn, remaining on the tree until well into winter. It requires lime-free soil.

2 *Liquidambar styraciflua* 'Worplesdon' ♈

Liquidambars make beautiful trees for all

seasons. The snow gum has deeply cut, longer leaves and colours beautifully from purple-black, through orange and yellow. After the leaves have fallen there is interest in the corky bark on older stems. Avoid planting in shallow, chalky soils. It grows to 30m (98ft).

3 *Acer rubrum* 'October Glory' ♈

If we had to choose, this would be our number one for its sheer intensity and reliability of colour. It's a beautiful Canadian red maple which will grow into a large round-headed tree with dark green palmate leaves turning brilliant red for a long time through autumn. It can reach a height of 30m (98ft).

4 *Fraxinus angustifolia* 'Raywood' ♚
Something of a rarity, a tree whose leaves turn red and purple in alkaline soil. Tough and tolerant of wind, poor soil and drought, this ash forms a dense upright tree of 15-20m (50-66ft) with traditional ash-shaped leaves, but without troublesome self-seeding.

5 *Euonymus hamiltonianus* 'Indian Summer'
This large shrub – 6m (20ft) – is at its best in autumn. It produces exotic-looking dark pink fruits, and then enters overdrive with its leaves turning exquisite shades of red and purple. It tolerates most soils in sun or part shade.

6 *Hydrangea quercifolia* ♚
A wonderful shrub for shade, reaching 2m (6ft 6in) with large, lobed leaves reminiscent of an oak. White flowers are produced in large conical panicles in late summer before the leaves change to bronze-purple in autumn.

7 *Halesia carolina*
In late spring the branches are clothed with white bell-shaped flowers, hence the common name of snowdrop tree. In autumn the green leaves turn rich butter yellow and winged, oval seed heads remain on the tree. Even through winter it provides interest with striped bark. It grows to 8m (26ft) in height.

8 *Lysimachia clethroides* ♚
An easy perennial, forming large clumps of soft green foliage topped by white flowers that bend over, looking like a flock of geese marching through the border. In autumn the foliage turns a strong orange which lasts well. It grows to 1m (3ft 3in).

9 *Ceratostigma plumbaginoides* ♚
A spreading perennial that makes excellent ground cover for late summer and autumn. The electric blue flowers are borne in late summer and into the autumn as the foliage turns rich red. It is happiest in a warm, sunny spot and drier soil. It can grow to 45cm (18in).

10 *Cornus kousa* var. *chinensis* ♚
An excellent tree for the smaller garden with all-year-round interest. In June the branches are clothed with small flowers surrounded by large white bracts. In autumn it produces strawberry-like fruits and the foliage turns rich bronze. The tree forms a beautiful dense shape, reaching 7m (23ft) tall.

WINTER INTEREST

AS RECOMMENDED BY ANDREW MᶜINDOE OF HILLIER NURSERIES LIMITED

Cornus sanguinea 'Midwinter Fire'

Winter should never be considered a lifeless season in the garden. Without the diluting factor of masses of green foliage around them, plants with variegated evergreen leaves, colourful stems and beautiful bark come into their own. Some plants brave the elements and produce delicate, scented flowers in an attempt to attract scarce pollinating insects; others carry shining fruits and berries that tempt the birds. With a little careful selection, plants for winter interest can make this the most colourful season in the gardening year.

1 *Cornus sanguinea* 'Midwinter Fire'
One of the most brilliantly coloured
dogwoods for winter stems, 'Midwinter
Fire' grows to 1m (3ft) tall. The light
green leaves turn warm shades of flame
and gold in autumn before they fall.
Prune hard in early spring to encourage
stems that will colour well the
following winter.

2 *Hamamelis* x *intermedia* 'Orange Peel'
Witch hazels with their curious flowers of
ribbon-like petals and distinctive fragrance,
prefer neutral to acid soil and thrive in sun
or light shade. Cultivars of *H.* x *intermedia*

PLANTING FOR WINTER INTEREST

The garden is viewed more frequently
from the windows of the house in winter:
take this into account when positioning
plants for winter interest. A variegated
holly like *Ilex* x *altaclerensis* 'Golden
King' can make a colourful focal point,
especially when decorated with berries.
A shrub with scented flowers is a good
choice by the front door, where its
fragrance can hang on the air. The low
sun in winter enhances the appearance
of plants grown for their stems, as well
as the dried leaves and flowerheads of
perennials and grasses: plant them where
the light will catch them from behind.

Hamamelis x intermedia
'Orange Peel'

Sarcococca confusa

are most popular: 'Orange Peel' is a
stunning variety, with large orange, strongly
scented flowers and leaves turning shades of
flame in autumn.

3 *Sarcococca confusa* ♔
Christmas Box is a versatile shrub thriving
on any soil in sun or shade. It is at its most
useful under trees, where its upright stems
can form suckering clumps up to 90cm

Ilex aquifolium 'JC van Tol'

Daphne bholua 'Jacqueline Postill'

Sarcococca confusa

Erica x darleyensis 'Kramer's Rote'

(35in) tall, well clothed with shining, dark green leaves. In midwinter the tiny, thread-like flowers will scent a whole garden.

4 *Skimmia* x *confusa* 'Kew Green' ♔

One of the best Skimmias and perhaps the easiest to grow successfully. The mid-green foliage retains its colour in sun or shade. 'Kew Green' forms a mounded shrub up to 1m (3ft) tall. The creamy-green buds are attractive throughout winter, opening to clusters of creamy yellow, scented flowers in early spring.

5 *Leucothoe* Lovita

A low evergreen shrub with elegant, oval pointed leaves of dark shining green tinged with purple, Lovita, also known as Zebonard forms low, spreading mounds up

to 60cm (24in) in height on acid soil in semi-shade. In winter, the foliage turns crimson-purple, bringing rich colour to the garden.

6 *Daphne bholua* 'Jacqueline Postill' ♔

Raised at Hillier Nurseries, this is perhaps the finest plant for winter fragrance. It makes a somewhat upright shrub, up to 1.5m (5ft) high, with flexible tan-coloured stems, and emerald evergreen leaves. The flower clusters open in midwinter, from purplish-pink buds to creamy-pink flowers; richly scented and profuse.

7 *Erica* x *darleyensis* 'Kramer's Rote' ♔

Heathers are versatile plants with many uses, ranging from ground cover to winter containers. *E. carnea* and *E.* x *darleyensis*

Skimmia x *confusa* 'Kew Green'

8 *Pittosporum tenuifolium* 'Tom Thumb' ♔

Evergreens with dark purple foliage are few and far between. 'Tom Thumb' grows slowly into a broad cone 1m (3ft) tall. The small, shining, waved leaves are densely packed. The foliage is dark purple-green through summer and autumn, becoming intense black-purple in winter: a stunning partner for red-stemmed dogwoods.

9 *Ilex aquifolium* 'JC van Tol' ♔

Hollies are long-lived evergreens of great substance. 'JC van Tol' is a self-fertile holly that produces shining scarlet fruits without another plant to pollinate. The shining, dark foliage is an excellent partner for variegated shrubs and those with colourful stems, such as *Cornus alba* 'Sibirica'.

10 *Clematis cirrhosa* var. *purpurascens* 'Freckles'

This fern-leaved evergreen climber has light, pretty foliage on twining stems. It grows vigorously over a wall or through a deciduous shrub in a sunny position. The hanging, open, bell-shaped flowers appear in early winter. 'Freckles' is creamy white, heavily marked with maroon, and lightly scented.

are excellent winter-flowering dwarf shrubs that are lime-tolerant and drought-resistant. 'Kramer's Rote' is an excellent cultivar, with reddish-pink flowers with dark chocolate stamens. Trim plants after flowering to produce bushy growth.

HILLIER GARDEN CENTRES AND NURSERIES
Ampfield House, Ampfield, nr Romsey,
Hampshire SO51 9PA
T: 01794 368733 F: 01794 368813
E: reception@hillier.co.uk W: www.hillier.co.uk
Gardens open all year (except Christmas Day and Boxing Day),
10am to 6pm (or dusk if earlier)

Hillier Nurseries has an international reputation for the enormous range of hardy plants grown there. The Sir Harold Hillier Gardens contains one of the largest collections of woody plants in the world. The Winter Garden, the largest of its kind in the British Isles, is one of the highlights of the gardens. Andrew McIndoe (pictured) is Garden Centre Director and designer of the company's Gold Medal-winning Chelsea Flower Show exhibit for the past 16 years.

PLANTS FOR...
YEAR-ROUND COLOUR

AS RECOMMENDED BY ADRIAN BLOOM OF BRESSINGHAM GARDENS

Rudbeckia fulgida var. *sullivantii* 'Goldsturm'

A t Bressingham Gardens, it has always been our aim to collect and test plants which can help to achieve the goal of year-round colour. We've made our suggested selection mostly from perennials able to fit in most gardens, with the exceptions of two shrubs which we believe are indispensable – one for summer through to autumn, the other from autumn until early spring. Some on the list are fairly new, some quite old, but all can be relied on to light up your garden throughout the year. We have also included the period of interest for each plant.

1 *Cornus sanguinea* 'Midwinter Fire'
C. sanguinea is outstanding for its long
display of orange leaves in autumn, and
lighting up winter spectacularly as its stems
are bared. It thrives in the sun where not
too dry, and the stems should be cut back to
15cm (6in) in March or early April. It can be
grown in a container and reaches heights of
up to 1.2-1.5m (4-5ft). (October to April)

2 *Helleborus* x *nigercors*
A splendid hybrid between *H. niger* 'The
Christmas Rose' and *H. argutifolius*. It has
attractive, almost evergreen foliage before
the large white flowers appear profusely in
midwinter. Plant in full sun or part shade,
near *Cornus sanguinea* 'Midwinter Fire'
and *Bergenia* 'Bressingham Ruby' for a
wonderful long-lasting winter display. It
reaches heights of up to 30-45cm (12-18in).
(November to April)

3 *Bergenia* 'Bressingham Ruby'
This Bressingham raised *Bergenia* is at its
best between January and March, its large,
rounded leaves a shining ruby-red with purple
undersides. In spring, rose-red flowering
spikes appear and the leaves turn green,
changing back to ruby in autumn. It thrives in
most soils where not too dry or wet and can
grow to a height of 45-60cm (18-24in) and
widths of 30-45cm (12-18in). (All year round)

Bergenia 'Bressingham Ruby'

Cornus sanguinea 'Midwinter Fire'

Brunnera macrophylla 'Jack Frost'

Helleborus x *nigercors*

4 *Brunnera macrophylla* 'Jack Frost' ♇

This is a recent introduction from the US and already a hit with gardeners for both flowering performance and foliage. In early spring, small silvery leaves appear alongside blue flowers which last into early summer. It can reach a height of 45cm (18in) and a width of 45-60cm (18-24in). Cut flowers and foliage back after flowering for clean new growth. (March to November)

5 *Geranium* Rozanne

Rozanne, named after its discoverer in a Dorset garden, Rozanne Waterer, flowers almost non-stop from June until winter frosts. Large leafy foliage in spring, making green mounds 90cm (35in) across, develops a mass of deep blue, lighter centred flowers. This plant is good in containers and can reach a height of 60cm (24in) and a width of 90cm (35in). (June to November)

6 *Crocosmia* 'Lucifer' ♇

Raised by Alan Bloom and assistant Percy Piper in the 1960s, 'Lucifer' is the hardiest, most brilliant *Crocosmia* of all. Broad sword-like bright-green leaves contrast with arching vermillion flowers appearing in July. The plant thrives in sun where not too dry and can reach a height 1.5m (5ft) and a width of 60cm (24in). Plant in groups of three or more. (May to August)

7 *Miscanthus sinensis* 'Morning Light' ♇

Probably the most striking and useful *Miscanthus* for the average garden, with its variegated leaves and compact habit. Silver-white flower plumes arrive late in the year (or not at all in colder summers) and the leaves fade to beige in autumn. The plant can reach a height of 1.2-1.5m (4-5ft) and a width of 60-75cm (24-30in). Prune to the ground in March, and keep in moist-to-average soil. (June to March)

8 *Hakonechloa macra* 'Alboaurea' ♇

This low-growing ornamental grass with gold and green leaves provides a good contrast to this section's main summer flower, *Geranium* Rozanne, and its stunning display over a long period. *H. macra* also

Hydrangea arborescens 'Annabelle'

Geranium Rozanne

makes a good ground cover or edging plant, requiring reasonable soil retaining some moisture. Great in pots. It can grow to a height of 30-45cm (12-18in) and a width of 45-60cm (18-24in). (April to December)

9 *Hydrangea arborescens* 'Annabelle' ♟
'Annabelle' can be cut to the ground in late winter and is flowering again by June or July. With the green-turning-to-white flower heads – which develop into enormous, yet delicate balls of flower – gradually dying in late autumn, you have a dramatic focal point plant in the garden, and it can reach both a height and width of 1.2-1.5m (4-5ft). (June to February)

10 *Rudbeckia fulgida* var. *sullivantii* 'Goldsturm' ♟
In late summer for many weeks, this hardy perennial – introduced in 1936 in Germany – brightens up our gardens. Enduringly popular, 'Goldsturm' has dark-green pointed leaves and grows up to a height of 60cm (24in) with a corresponding width. August sees the beginning of a stunning display of black-centred, golden-yellow petalled flowers which go on for weeks. The plant thrives in most soils, as long as they are not too dry. (July to October)

Miscanthus sinensis 'Morning Light'

Hakonechloa macra 'Alboaurea'

BRESSINGHAM GARDENS
Bressingham, Diss, Norfolk IP22 2AB
T: 01379 688282
E: info@bressinghamgardens.com
W: www.bressinghamgardens.com

❀ NCCPG National Collection holder of *Miscanthus sinensis* (cultivars)
Managed by Jason Bloom, the nursery specialises in what the Bloom name is famous for: quality perennials, ornamental grasses and garden-worthy conifers. A wide range is offered that changes with the seasons. The main business is via the internet; plants are despatched promptly. The gardens are open early April to early November – telephone for times.

BAMBOOS

AS RECOMMENDED BY PAUL AND DIANA WHITTAKER OF PW PLANTS

Chimonobambusa tumidissinoda

Fargesia robusta

For many people, a bamboo plant is thought of as a tropical giant from a far-flung, wild equatorial jungle. But there are now more than 350 species, varieties and cultivars of these outstanding, hardy, ornamental plants on our islands. Bamboos are fast gaining in popularity on these shores, useful for quick architectural structure, screening and windbreaks, soil stabilisation, specimen planting and also, if selected wisely, for containers. The winter greenery of bamboos adds a new dimension to many a garden. The following bamboo plants are nearly all evergreen and are some of the most resilient plants to be found in our gardens. In addition, they adapt very well to the cool, temperate conditions in the UK.

1 *Chimonobambusa tumidissinoda*
A remarkable plant with pronounced
saucer-like nodes on fresh green culms.
Foliage provides a delicate canopy effect.
Not for the faint-hearted as it's admirably
aggressive! It grows to 3.5-10m (11-33ft) in
10 years and can be contained in a large pot
and thinned regularly for good effect.

2 *Chusquea culeou* ♟
A Chilean species forming a large clump,
needing space of 6m (20ft), but not invasive.
Thick yellow-green culms, often with purple
tints, hold clusters of leafy branches providing
a 'bottle brush' effect. Extremely robust in
all weather and very drought-tolerant once
established. Not good in pots as it needs
cooler soil conditions.

3 *Fargesia robusta*
As lime-red, hairy shoots emerge, the
protective sheaths turn papery white and
act like a beacon. Greenery is held on
the strong, vertical culms which form
an impenetrable clump, 4-6m (13-20ft)
high and 75cm-1.5m (2ft 6in-5ft) wide.
Needs to be in a prominent position.
Useful for screening.

Chusquea culeou

CULTIVATION

Bamboos are adaptable to most soils.
As they mature, they become tolerant
of wind, sun, shade and exposure. They
also become naturally stronger and more
resilient as they get older.
   To ensure a bamboo remains healthy
and attractive:
- Add humus or organic matter when
  planting, preferably leafmould
- Water in the first two or three summers
  as needed, drenching the roots once
  or twice a week, allowing them to
  breathe in-between
- Thin out some of the older original
  culms as new thicker ones are produced
- Prune the cultivars with ornamental
  culms to enhance the appearance.

A collection of bamboos

4 *Phyllostachys vivax* f. *aureocaulis* 🏆
Magnificent thick golden culms, randomly striped green towards the base, are produced quickly from young plants. One of the fastest bamboos to mature. Forms a good-sized grove of great stature – 8m (26ft) – although not rampant. Its colouring, height and elegance give life to any area, except deep woodland.

5 *Fargesia rufa*
Tough as old boots, with short olive culms and pink sheaths on young growth. Very bushy and tight in habit, 2.5m (8ft 3in) tall. Grows much shorter given an open aspect. Plant in drifts in woodland clearings or mid-border for winter structure. Probably the best bamboo for a container.

Phyllostachys vivax f. aureocaulis

Yushania maculata

Fargesia rufa

6 Yushania maculata

Very tough, yet delicate in appearance with arching, willowy foliage. Pale glaucous culms are sheathed dark purple-brown, turning papery with age. Forms a good-sized 3.5m (11ft 6in) stand, but is compact and useful in any aspect or exposure. Good in association with other bamboos, its unusual colouring contrasting well with most of them.

7 Hibanobambusa tranquillans 'Shiroshima'

A variegated form with striped green and cream leaves, giving a silvery effect from a distance. New growth is often pink-tinted. Brightens a dark corner or lightens woodland gloom. Good in containers. Height averages 3.5m (11.5ft), spread is around 75cm-1.5m (2ft 6in-5ft) in 10 years.

8 Phyllostachys aureosulcata f. spectabilis

The golden groove bamboo is colourful and robust, with golden culms often burnished red on new growth. Glossy foliage is held high on strong branches. Fast to mature, at an average of 6m (20ft). Tough and reliable. Stays in a tight clump early on, then forms new clumps. Spreads to 1-3m (3ft 3in-10ft) in 10 years.

9 Phyllostachys nigra

Black bamboo is the most popular ornamental bamboo in the world. Often a slow starter, but worthy of patience! Grows to an average height of 6m (20ft) and forms a tight clump arching at the top. Thin out old culms. Good in pots and anywhere except dense shade. Useful for hedging.

10 Thamnocalamus crassinodus 'Kew Beauty'

A tiny-leafed clumping bamboo with a tall 4m (13ft) slightly arching habit. Eventually, thick blue culms are produced. May need extra water in hot summers. Give prominence to ensure the blue culm colouring is visible. Excellent planted by a path so it can be admired close up.

Thamnocalamus crassinodus 'Kew Beauty'

PW PLANTS
Sunnyside, Heath Road, Kenninghall, Norfolk NR16 2DS
T: 01953 888212 E: pw@hardybamboo.com
W: www.hardybamboo.com
Open Apr to Sept, Fridays and Saturdays, 9am to 5pm; Oct to Mar, every Friday and last Saturday of the month, 9am to 5pm; or by appointment

PW Plants was founded in 1987 and is run by husband-and-wife team Paul and Diana Whittaker, also trading on the internet as www.hardybamboo.com. The nursery has one of the largest collections of bamboos in Europe. It also has a wide range of ornamental grasses, unusual shrubs and perennials, with a developing range of hardy exotics. Specimen bamboos with some at 9m (30ft) in height are the main feature of the garden.

BIRCHES

AS RECOMMENDED BY KENNETH ASHBURNER AND PAUL BARTLETT OF STONE LANE GARDENS

B. ermanii
'Mount Hakkoda'

Mention birch trees and most people think of the native silver birch. However, the *Betula* genus spans the northern hemisphere from the Arctic to the Far East. And the bark is not just white, but a multitude of soft colours – from creamy yellow, orange, pink, to crimson brown, and even purple. Together with the texture of the bark and the delicacy of leaves and branches, you have a tree of great value in the garden or park. It's not surprising that birches have been included in important landscape designs since they were first introduced to horticulture. Here are 10 of our favourite birch trees. We have included some wild origin species; these are the ones with numbered names. The number relates to the origin of the original seeding.

B. albosinensis 'Pink Champagne'

PLANTING A BIRCH

Plant in a hole slightly bigger than the root ball. Fill with a mixture of soil, compost and fertiliser. Plant at the same level as it was growing before. Firm the roots in well. Secure the tree low down the stem with an angled stake. Water regularly throughout the first season. In the following years, water during prolonged dry weather or if the tree appears stressed. Feed regularly throughout the growing season. Keep weeds and grass away from the base and ensure the soil around the tree is well mulched. Most importantly, ensure the roots do not get loose in the ground.

B. utilis H&M 1480

1 *B. albosinensis* W 4106

Originating from China, *albosinensis* is the finest of birches, with smooth, freely peeling bark, subtle colours and delicate canopy. This variety has a more distinct reddish base colour than the usual pinkish-brown, on which orange, pink and white blooms are overlain. Height reaches 10-15m (33-50ft), with a lightly spreading crown.

2 *B. albosinensis* 'Pink Champagne'

This cultivar has pale-pink bark, caused by a white blooming on the surface. The scion wood was selected from a fine specimen tree in the arboretum. This was one of several seedlings received from Ness Gardens, grown from seed collected by the Chinese Forestry Service in Gansu province, China.

3 *B. utilis* H&M 1480

The Himalayan birch is a diverse species of birch covering a large geographical area. This variety has a rich, dark-brown bark with a hint of red, overlain with striking patches of white bloom, which peels freely in sheets and scrolls; particularly effective when backlit by winter sun. Height up to 10-15m (33-50ft).

4 *B. utilis* F 19505

The original trees were grown from seed collected in the Sichuan province of China. A reddish-orange bark, overlain with a really prominent bloom of white betulin, which gives some trees an almost white-looking appearance. This is one of the paler Himalayan birches, which looks very effective in closely planted groups.

5 *B. utilis* BLM 100

This is a controlled-pollination seedling from trees in the Stone Lane Gardens arboretum. The parents were grown from seed collected in central Nepal. This form of Himalayan birch has a rich orange bark, with very noticeable banding and very little blooming. Very attractive and unusual.

6 B. utilis var. *jacquemontii* 'Grayswood Ghost' ♈

Variety jacquemontii is much sough-after form of B. *utilis* for its staring white bark, peeling in parchment-like sheets which are orange-buff beneath. The ghostly effect is impressive in winter or against a dark background. Slightly broader growth than *utilis* and generally denser shade. Grows 10-15m (33-50ft).

B. alleghaniensis

B. ermanii
'Mount Zao'

B. albosinensis
W 4106

7 B. ermanii 'Mount Hakkoda'

A controlled-pollination seedling from some splendid trees in the arboretum. The parents were grown from seed collected on the slopes of Mount Hakkoda, North Honshu, Japan. The bark is a smooth creamy orange and the autumn leaf colour is a rich orange. A lovely tree for parkland and the larger garden. Grows to 12-15m (40-50ft) tall.

8 B. ermanii 'Mount Zao'

One tree in Stone Lane Gardens' arboretum produced far more purple in its bark and this, combined with prominent bands of lenticels, created an almost striped look, so unusual that it was perpetuated as a cultivar. Apart from this, it has the same growth and leaf colour as other B. ermanii.

9 B. alleghaniensis

The yellow birch has interesting, slightly rough yellow-brown bark with a metallic sheen which seems to catch the sun, especially in winter. Grows in dry soils but prefers moister habitats. The leaves are larger than some, so shade underneath is denser. It has bright yellow autumn leaf colour and reaches 10-15m (33-50ft).

10 B. medwedewii

An attractive shrub birch, with quirky metallic stems which stand out in winter. The glossy, handsome leaves with showy, persistent, fat upright fruits are, unusually, at eye level due to its size. Autumn colour is a rich yellow. Grows to 4.5-6m (15-20ft), with multi-stemmed spreading habit.

STONE LANE GARDENS ARBORETUM AND TREE NURSERY
Stone Farm, Chagford, Devon TQ13 8JU
T: 01647 231311 E: orders@mythicgarden.eclipse.co.uk
W: www.stonelanegardens.com

❀ NCCPG National Collection holder of *Betula* and *Alnus*
Run by Kenneth Ashburner and Paul Bartlett, Stone Lane Gardens, near Chagford, Devon is a five-acre woodland and water garden containing National Collections of wild origin birch and alder. The arboretum is open all year (admission charges apply). The nursery is also open all year, but if you're making a long journey it's advisable to call first to ensure someone will be at hand to help when you arrive.

BUDDLEJAS

AS RECOMMENDED BY ANDREW BULLOCK OF THE LAVENDER GARDEN

B. davidii 'Purple Friend' *B. x weyeriana* 'Sungold' *B. lindleyana*

High summer in the cottage garden, the scent of nectar... nature's jewels feeding on the richly-scented racemes of the butterfly bush... this is my earliest memory of the *Buddleja davidii* in my grandparents' garden. I love to see butterflies flying around the nursery, so no apologies that most of the hit parade is *davidii*-based. With its rich scent and large range of colours, buddleja is the number one butterfly-attracting plant.

1 *B. globosa* ♈

This frost-hardy, orange, ball-flowered plant is best grown in a large garden, and although it flowers rather early for garden butterflies, it's highly attractive to bees. Height reaches 6m (20ft) with a similar spread. Plant in full sun, with dry soil.

2 *B. x weyeriana* 'Moonlight'

This is a deciduous shrub with ball-shaped heads of creamy apricot flushed with mauve, forming long panicles. It flowers from late summer into autumn. It keeps on flowering, giving a welcome food supply to the last butterflies of the year before they hibernate. Height reaches 4m (13ft).

3 *B. x weyeriana* 'Sungold' ♈

These plants have deep golden-yellow flowers flushed with mauve. They inherit short flowers from *globosa*, one of their parent plants, so are good for bumblebees. Prune in spring. Height reaches 1.5-2m (5-6ft). It's fully hardy, and OK in full sun and dry soil.

4 *B. davidii* 'Black Knight' ♈

This is the darkest of all buddlejas, a classic rich, deep purple. Its colour is magnificent and although the plant can eventually grow tall, I find it a fairly slow-growing cultivar, taking a few seasons to really establish itself into a mature shrub. Height and spread are both about 5m (16ft).

5 B. 'Royal Red' ♕

With its long, maroon flowers, the fully hardy 'Royal Red' needs to be well pruned to keep its shape, as it can become sprawly if left unchecked. It grows to 4.5m (15ft), with a spread of 3.5-4m (11-13ft). It's fine with full sun and dry soil. A worthy addition to any sunny garden.

6 B. davidii 'Purple Friend'

Raised at The Lavender Garden and named by Natasha Bellamy as a good 'Purple Friend' for butterflies. This slow-growing semi-dwarf buddleja easily lends itself to growing in a container. Flowering in July and August, a rich mauve-purple colour, with grey-green foliage. It has a height and spread of 1-1.5m (3ft 3in-5ft) and is good in full sun.

7 B. davidii 'Blue Horizon'

The finest blue buddleja, and stunning when in full bloom. The best example I've seen was in my parents' garden late one summer evening, radiant with sapphire-blue flowers, and covered in peacock and red admiral butterflies. Although not as readily available as it deserves to be, it's worth tracking down. It grows to 2.5-3m (8-10ft) tall, needs full sun and dry soil, and is fully hardy.

8 B. lindleyana

This buddleja is so different to all the others. Its deep green leaves are complemented in summer by long, curved racemes of beautiful, slender mauve-violet flowers. B. lindleyana reaches 2-3m (6ft 7in-10ft), enjoys full sun, needs dry soil and is fully hardy.

9 B. davidii 'Orpheus'

The first chance seedling to appear at the nursery. A large deep blue raceme, with an orange eye, but as the flower ages the white circle on the corolla enlarges, producing a paler flower.

10 B. davidii 'Shire Blue'

This fully hardy, medium-sized, highly-scented shrub has large panicles of pale blue, and attractive foliage; a grey-green upper leaf complemented by silver undersides. It's OK with full sun and dry soil.

CULTIVATION

Prune buddlejas back well into April, to guarantee plants are in flower in August, the best time for the emergence of aristocrat butterflies. Or grow several buddlejas and vary the flowering time, by staggering pruning.

THE LAVENDER GARDEN,
Ashcroft Nurseries, Kingscote, Tetbury, Gloucestershire GL8 8YF
T: 01453 860356 M: 07837 582943
E: andrewbullock@thelavenderg.co.uk
W: www.thelavenderg.co.uk

❀ NCCPG National Collection holder of Buddleja
The Lavender Garden is a specialist lavender and buddleja nursery, with plants to attract bees and butterflies. We have over 100 varieties of lavender and buddleja and have attracted 28 species of butterfly to date! We strive to breed new varieties, and advice on plants and their management is freely given. Open weekends 11am to 5pm, 1 March to end of October. Call for full opening times.

Where have all the wild flowers gone?

- *In Britain, one in five wild flowers is currently threatened with extinction*

- *98% of our flower-rich meadows have been destroyed in the last 60 years*

- *Half of our ancient woodlands have been lost since 1945*

- *On average, each county loses a species every two years*

PLANTLIFE is the only UK charity dedicated to protecting wild plants. Our work ranges from recovery projects to save more than 100 threatened plants and fungi to the management of nature reserves where wild flowers can flourish.

PLANTLIFE
our plants *our* planet *our* future

JOIN US *and you can help protect wild plants and their habitats.*

CAMELLIAS – SPRING

AS RECOMMENDED BY TREHANE NURSERY

C. x *williamsii* 'Debbie'

N ow grown and appreciated throughout the world as one of the classic flowering spring shrubs, the camellia has been cultivated for many centuries for its striking flowers and glossy, evergreen foliage. In the wild, more than 200 species are found in the mountainous woodland areas of Asia, from northern India through China to Japan, and south to Indonesia. Of these, the most important in cultivation today are *Camellia japonica*, *C. saluenensis* (from which the x *williamsii* hybrids are derived), and *C. sinensis* (the tea plant). The work of breeders in the last 200 years has now produced more than 30,000 named camellia varieties.

C. 'Fragrant Pink'

C. x *williamsii* 'ETR Carlyon'

C. *japonica* 'Ave Maria'

C. x *williamsii* 'Donation'

1 C. *japonica* 'Ave Maria' ♗

Bred in California and introduced in 1956, 'Ave Maria' has lovely, mini-sized formal double flowers in a pure, soft pink, offset by the broad-leaved, dark green, glossy foliage. Blooming from January to April, its slow-growing nature and compact, upright habit make this an ideal plant for containers.

2 C. x *williamsii* 'Debbie' ♗

Easy to grow, 'Debbie' produces masses of 10cm (4in) peony-form flowers of a deep rosy pink over a long period from late winter through to spring. Flowers tend to be shed whole and the leaf colour is pale green. The upright habit and vigorous growth make 'Debbie' good for wall training or hedges.

3 C. x *williamsii* 'Donation' ♗

This is probably the best known and most popular camellia variety in Britain. The large, semi-double flowers are light orchid-pink in colour with deeper pink veining. They appear over a long season from

February to May. Hardy and reliable, it eventually forms a tall, wide bush.

4 C. x *williamsii* 'ETR Carlyon' ♔

A medium-sized white flower, which can vary from semi-double to rose-form double. Late season, flowering from March to May, so more likely to miss the frosts and other weather damage, which can be particularly noticeable on white-flowered varieties.

5 C. 'Fragrant Pink'

This is a vigorous, spreading plant with light green leaves and bronze-coloured

C. x *williamsii* 'Jury's Yellow'

C. *japonica* 'Lavinia Maggi'

young growth. Unusually, it is scented. It produces an abundance of charming, miniature, deep-pink, peony-form flowers from January to April. Although hardy in a sheltered spot in the south, it's more tender than most camellias.

6 C. x *williamsii* 'Jury's Yellow' ♔

These 8cm (3in) diameter flowers are made up of a wide anemone centre containing 50 yellow petaloids surrounded by nine white petals, and appear between February and May. The foliage is light green, and the upright, bushy and dense growth habit makes this another variety particularly suited to container growing.

7 C. *japonica* 'Lavinia Maggi' ♔

This is an old Italian variety dating from the mid-19th century. The medium to large formal double flowers are comprised of overlapping white petals, striped and splashed with carmine rose. Pure red flowers should be cut out. Forms an upright and dense mounded bush with large, dark green rounded leaves.

8 C. *japonica* 'Margaret Davis'

This is a particularly distinctive and charming variety from Australia, popular worldwide and the recipient of many awards. The creamy-white petals of the informal double flower are edged with a brilliant carmine rose and set against bold, dark green foliage.

9 C. *japonica* 'San Dimas' 🏆

This flower is exactly how many people imagine a camellia should look. The medium to large semi-double flowers have very rich, dark red petals contrasting with brilliant yellow stamens and intensely dark green foliage. The plant is upright and moderately vigorous, with a compact bushy habit, and it flowers from February through to April.

10 C. *japonica* 'Takanini'

Bred by Neville Haydon in Auckland, 'Takanini' has medium-sized, deep plum-red anemone-form flowers with a bright sheen on the petals. It is noted for its exceptionally long flowering period. Often one of the first into flower in early December, 'Takanini' can still be going strong in late spring.

C. *japonica* 'Margaret Davis'

C. *japonica* 'San Dimas'

TREHANE NURSERY
Stapehill Road, Wimborne, Dorset BH21 7ND
T/F: 01202 873490 E: camellias@trehanenursery.co.uk
W: www.trehanenursery.co.uk

Trehane Nursery is a family-run business that has specialised in growing camellias, blueberries and other ericaceous shrubs for over 50 years. Its founder, the late David Trehane, introduced many new varieties to the UK. Today the nursery grows an extensive range of over 150 cultivars. Situated in a wooded location on acidic, sandy Dorset heathland, the nursery is open to the public on weekdays throughout the year, and at weekends in spring and autumn.

CAMELLIAS – AUTUMN

AS RECOMMENDED BY COGHURST CAMELLIAS

C. sasanqua 'Rainbow'

C. sasanqua 'Crimson King'

These little-known camellias flower from September to December, sometimes longer. Many are scented, with a delightful autumn fragrance. They prefer a sunnier position than the spring-flowering camellias. They are more open in growth, but make graceful trees with arches of flowers as they mature. They can be pruned quite hard and many have attractive red leaves in their new growth. Since they flower in autumn, frost is rarely a problem because blooms shatter when finished, and they are self-cleaning.

1 C. 'Snow Flurry'
A weeping shrub growing up to 2m (6.6ft) with an open, graceful form. Streams of medium-sized blooms are produced from October to December. The flowers are a creamy-white anemone form, and bloom profusely in autumn.

2 C. *sasanqua* 'Papaver'
'Papaver' is a bushy, upright camellia with dark green leaves and single pale pink flowers, with gold stamens in the centre. It grows to 2m (6.6ft). Blooms are highly-scented, and it is a valuable plant in the garden for its long-flowering season.

3 C. *sasanqua* 'Narumigata' ♔
A fast-growing, upright plant with large single white flowers edged with pink. It is highly scented and flowers profusely from October to December. The foliage is glossy and green. Give it a sunny and sheltered site to maximise flowering. Height 2m (6.6ft).

4 C. *sasanqua* 'Jean May' ♔
A bushy, spreading camellia growing to 2m (6.6ft) after 10 years. It has semi-double pale pink medium flowers, which are produced from October to December. Plant 'Jean May' in a warm, sunny position so you can enjoy the scented blooms.

5 C. *sasanqua* 'Rainbow'

A bushy, upright camellia with cup-shaped single white flowers blushed pink in bud. It flowers from October to December, needs a sunny spot and is a stunning container plant. Height 2m (6.6ft).

6 C. *hiemalis* 'Sparkling Burgundy'

A fragrant weeping camellia with peony pink to dark pink flowers. It is in bloom from September to December. Excellent for display in a raised pot or bed and could be trained against a wall. Height 2m (6.6ft).

7 C. *sasanqua* 'Crimson King'

One of the darkest red autumn-flowering camellias, with single rich red flowers of medium size, showing gold stamens in the centre. Flowers are produced from November to January. Its open habit lends it to training against a sunny wall. Can grow to 2m (6.6ft) after 10 years.

8 C. x *vernalis* 'Yuletide'

A bushy and upright evergreen plant, flowering from November to January. Its long flowering season makes this camellia very popular. 'Yuletide' has single red flowers with yellow stamens and can be grown in a container or in the ground with equal success.

9 C. *sasanqua* 'Winter's Snowman'

An open, spreading *sasanqua* hybrid growing to 2m (6.6ft). Its medium-sized, single pink flowers have gold stamens, with an orange tinge to the centre of the bloom. It is very long flowering, blooming profusely from November to January.

10 C. 'Winter's Snowman'

This shrub is one of the most vigorous autumn-flowering camellias. It is a bushy, upright plant with pretty, bright red new leaves. The flowers are white anemone and scented, with a boss of golden stamens. It flowers best in a sunny spot in good soil. It can grow to 2m (6.6ft).

COGHURST CAMELLIAS
Rotherview Nursery, Ivyhouse Lane, Three Oaks, Hastings TN35 4NP
T: 01424 756228
E: rotherview@btinternet.com   W: rotherview.com

Coghurst Camellias was founded in 1989 when Ray and Wendy Bates started a small half-acre nursery specialising in Alpines on a rented site. Since then they have expanded the camellia collection known as 'The Coghurst Camellia Collection' and are one of the leading nurseries in the field of camellias as well as their original Alpines. The nursery is open seven days a week all year round and welcomes visitors.

CLEMATIS – MIXED

AS RECOMMENDED BY SHEILA CHAPMAN AT SHEILA CHAPMAN CLEMATIS

C. 'Buckland Beauty'

C. 'Pastel Blue'

C. 'Violet Elizabeth'

Being passionate about clematis, I find that each one as it opens is a favourite. With over 800 varieties in the nursery it's hard to select a top 10 'couldn't-do-without' list. Today I'm as addicted to clematis in all their different shapes and forms as I was when the nursery began 13 years ago. The reasons I chose the following include the beauty of the plant (to my eyes), scent, variety of shape and value in the garden.

1 C. 'Violet Elizabeth'
This clematis, raised by Walter Pennell, has fully double delicate violet-pink flowers in May and June, followed by single flowers in the autumn. It reaches a height of 2-2.5m (6ft 6in-8ft) and gives a rose-like impression.

2 C. 'Ekstra'
This plant is a late-flowerer, with medium-sized, light blue-violet flowers from July to September, reaching 2-2.5m (6ft 6in-8ft). The centre of each tepal gradually fades to light blue, contrasting with deep blue veining.

3 C. 'Mikelite'
This cultivar with has neat, small flowers with pointed purple tepals set off by a rosy-red bar and golden anthers. Raised by Uno Kivistik in Estonia, it flowers from early summer to September and reaches a height of 2-2.5m (6ft 6in-8ft).

4 C. 'Rüütel'
A midseason cultivar which posses the most glowing red flowers which are intensified by red stamens. It flowers from July to September and reaches 2-2.5m (6ft 6in-8ft) in height. Raised by Uno Kivistik in Estonia.

5 C. 'Kathryn Chapman'
This cultivar, named after my daughter, is a seedling from 'Minuet' and thrives in a sunless but not heavily shaded position. The small flowers open lemon fading to white,

which gives an impression of vanilla ice-cream and lemon sorbet. The plant can reach a height of 3-3.5m (10-12ft).

6 C. 'Pastel Blue'

This is a herbaceous clematis, raised by Barry Fretwell, which reaches only 60cm (2ft), and in time will form a small clump of slightly scented, pale blue bell-shaped flowers which, with their pointed buds and silver seed heads, are an ethereal combination.

7 C. *heracleifolia* 'Cassandra'

This plant is a selection from Germany. Its large leaves and strongly scented, small gentian-blue tubular flowers make this a highly desirable plant. It is a herbaceous clematis that fits extremely well in the border, as the large leaves are a welcome foil to many small-leaved herbaceous plants. It can reach a height of 10m (3ft).

8 C. 'Buckland Beauty'

Raised by Everett Leeds, this clematis reaches a height of 1.5-2.5m (5-8ft) with semi-nodding pitcher-shaped pinky-mauve flowers followed by the most wonderful golden seed heads. Flowering from late spring to late summer, 'Buckland Beauty' is worthy of a place in any garden.

CULTIVATION

To obtain the best results from your clematis, purchase a two- to three-year-old plant (usually sold in 2-litre pots) with a good root system. Watering and feeding make all the difference between a 'show-stopping' clematis and a tired, weak specimen. If you have access to well-rotted manure or garden compost, put plenty in base of planting hole and cover with 10cm (4in) of soil. Large-flowered clematis should be planted with 10cm (4in) of stem below soil level and back-filled with soil mixed with two spadefuls of peat and two handfuls of bonemeal. Water in well.

---

9 C. 'Broughton Bride'

This is a home-grown variety raised by Vince and Sylvia Denny. Long, pure white nodding flowers, with the added bonus of faint lilac speckles on the outside of the tepals in April to May, are followed by an impressive display of fully double flowers late in the season. It can grow to 2-3m (6-10ft) in height.

10 C. 'Princess Diana' ♛

Another Barry Fretwell introduction. Wonderful, luminous shocking pink tulip-like flowers are displayed from midsummer to early autumn. 'Princess Diana' can grow to a height of 2-2.5m (6ft 6in-8ft).

SHEILA CHAPMAN CLEMATIS
Coveney Nursery, 160 Orngar Road,
Abridge, Essex RM4 1AA
T/F: 01708 688090 E: sheilachapman@hotmail.co.uk
W: www.sheilachapman.co.uk

Sheila Chapman runs the nursery with a small, dedicated staff ranging in age from 19-76. They spend all winter racing to clean up the nursery, and all summer trying to keep ahead of the clematis before they become tangled and have to be cut down. Each year Sheila says she wonders whether she should reduce the varieties sold in the nursery, but her heart usually wins and they increase instead. Opening hours are seasonal - phone for details.

CLEMATIS – EARLY

AS RECOMMENDED BY STUART PARKMAN OF TRISCOMBE NURSERIES

C. 'Blue Eclipse'

C. Warwickshire Rose'

C. 'Markham's Pink'

The extent and range of clematis available today is confusing for the gardener, with everything from Alpines and *Clematis macropetala* to large-flowered varieties; *C. montana* and herbaceous clematis; four to seven or eight petals; nodding, bell-shaped varieties; to ones with decorative seed heads. The colour range also varies from deep wine, through every shade of pink, blue, yellow and striped to, finally, white. The uses of clematis range from covering unsightly objects to ground cover, meandering through bushes and trees. Some can be container-grown and many are used as cut flowers for flower arranging. Here are our hardiest, earliest-flowering top 10.

1 C. 'Blue Eclipse'
Quite distinct and wonderful in colour contrast. The flowers are small with fleshy, slightly ribbed sepals, blue with a cream edge and speckled on the outside. Cream stamens fill the centre. Profuse flowering in early spring is followed by a succession in moderate numbers later in the year.

2 C. 'Purple Rain'
An outstanding new clematis. Small flowers, whose buds are dark purple, very pointed and elongated, appear in early spring. The cream stamens are purple-tipped at the ends. Profuse flowering in early spring is followed by a succession in moderate numbers later on.

3 C. *macropetala* 'Maidwell Hall'
A rich, deep colour with closely-set sepals, 'Maidwell Hall' flowers with 'Markham's Pink', and they are a perfect foil for one another. An outstanding variety. Small, semi-double, lantern-like deep-blue flowers appear in April to May. Very hardy and probably the most outstanding deep-blue flowered variety in this group. It reaches a height of 3m (10ft).

4 C. *macropetala* 'Markham's Pink' ♔
Far and beyond the best in the pink *C. macropetala* variety. Delightful both in flower form and for its remarkable shade of pink. It grows to a height of 3m (10ft).

5 C. *macropetala* 'Wesselton' 🏆

The most showy of this colour group, this plant produces generously-sized lantern-like purple-blue flowers during April and May in great abundance. Very free-flowering, 'Wesselton' reaches a height of 3m (10ft).

6 C. 'Broughton Bride'

This clematis is delightful when the branches arch with their double flowers late in the *C. montana* season. It is spectacular spring-flowering variety – small flowers with long sepals are cream in bud, opening to white, and they are covered in mauve speckles and cream on the inside. The plant grows to 2-3m (6ft 6in-10ft).

7 C. 'Mayleen' 🏆

I chose this for the sheer delight it affords. It has very broad, overlapping sepals and large, deep-pink, highly fragrant flowers with golden stamens appearing in May, set against bronze-tinged foliage. It is very vigorous in growth, reaching heights of 12m (40ft).

8 C. 'Warwickshire Rose'

Small fragrant flowers of a true shell-pink are produced in abundance here. Flowers appear during May displayed against a background of dark foliage, which intensifies during summer. Suitable for pergolas, trellis-clad walls or scrambling over small trees. It enjoys any aspect provided it is open to the sky and grows to 7-12m (23-40ft).

9 C. *montana* 'Tetrarose' 🏆

'Modern' but standing the test of over 40 years, 'Tetrarose' is distinctive, if almost architectural, in form and colour. Flowers are relatively large and of a deep mauve-pink. Of moderate vigour and slightly scented, it can grow to a height of 7-8m (23-26ft).

10 C. 'Early Sensation'

A slow-growing evergreen, with finely-cut foliage and masses of small white flowers with a green backing in March to April. Also has green stamens and attractive seed heads.

CULTIVATION

Preparing the soil is advantageous. Some good topsoil mixed with compost and some bonemeal should suffice. Clematis like to have their feet in the cool, so use a piece of slate to cover the roots once they are planted. It is also advisable to plant clematis covering more than one leaf joint under the soil, which will benefit the plant in the event of frost or clematis wilt.

TRISCOMBE NURSERIES
West Bagborough, nr Taunton, Somerset TA4 3HG
T: 01984 618267
E: triscombe.nurseries2000@virgin.net
W: www.triscombenurseries.co.uk

These plants are available from **Triscombe Nurseries**, which is a family-run traditional nursery established in 1956. Clematis is one of a wide range of plants stocked and grown on the nursery, including camellias, hollies, mixed shrubs, herbaceous plants, Alpines and fruit trees. The nursery is eight miles from Taunton situated below the Quantock hills, with stunning views, in a Victorian walled garden. Open 9am to 5.30pm, Monday to Saturday; 2pm to 5.30pm Sunday.

CLEMATIS – MID-FLOWERING

AS RECOMMENDED BY RUTH GOOCH OF THORNCROFT CLEMATIS NURSERY

C. 'Fond Memories'

C. 'Mercury'

Most visualise clematis as a climbing plant, and although the majority are, some are not. The genus covers several thousand hybrids and species: some are evergreen, others are scented and some are herbaceous non-climbers. At Thorncroft we encourage our customers to plant clematis in different situations, such as through shrubs, climbing roses and small ornamental trees, or simply allow them to scramble through other plants in the border. This underused genus can add a new dimension to gardens.

1 C. 'Fond Memories'
Our best introduction to date. The blooms, about 12-18cm (5-7in) across with a beautiful satin sheen, appear almost translucent pinky-white, due to their deep mauve-pink reverse. Reaching 2-2.5m (7-8ft) tall, they can be planted in the garden or grown in a pot.

2 C. 'Odoriba'
The open, bell-shaped flowers on this clematis are about 3-5cm (1.5-2in) long and are deep pink with a white bar inside. It blooms from early summer until late autumn and reaches a height of 2.5-3.5m (8-11ft).

3 C. 'Mercury'
One of the best white early large-flowered clematis, with star-shaped blooms that have pointed tips and very wavy margins. It has two flowering periods: from late spring to early summer, then late summer to early autumn. It grows to around 2.5-3m (8-10ft).

4 C. 'Rüütel'

Extremely hardy and produces dozens of deep red, star-shaped flowers. Requiring hard pruning in late winter, it blooms from early summer until early autumn, tolerates any aspect and is superb with white or yellow climbing roses. It reaches 2-2.5m (7-8ft).

5 C. 'Lambton Park' ♔

This Tangutica Group clematis produces hundreds of buttercup-yellow, bell-shaped flowers from early summer until early autumn, followed by silky seedheads through winter. Best planted in a sunny, free-draining position, to enhance its coconut-like perfume. Height 2-2.5m (7-8ft).

6 C. x triternata 'Rubromarginata' ♔

This wonderful clematis produces thousands of star-shaped flowers, white with dark red tips, from midsummer to autumn, and vigorously grows to 3.5-5m (11-16ft). Plant in a sunny position, where you can appreciate its gorgeous perfume. A favourite in our garden.

7 C. 'New Love'

This self-supporting subshrub, from the Heracleifolia Group, is ideal for a sunny border. The violet-blue hyacinth-shaped flowers are beautifully scented and produced in clusters, blooming from midsummer to autumn on 60-75cm (24-30in) stems.

8 C. 'Rooguchi'

Purple, bell-shaped flowers are deeply ribbed with silvery purple margins from early summer until mid autumn. The non-clinging stems grow 2-2.5m (7-8ft) and require tying in if used as a climber, or plant in a border, so it can scramble over and through other plants.

9 C. 'Arabella' ♔

What the pretty mauvy-blue flowers lack in size, they make up for in quantity. 'Arabella' requires tying-in if used as a climber. We have one in full sun and one in shade, blooming continuously on stems 1.5-2m (5-7ft) from late spring until early autumn in both situations.

10 C. macropetala 'Wesselton' ♔

More an early flowerer, but one we just had to include, 'Wesselton' produces semi-double, nodding mid-blue flowers from early to mid-spring, followed by silky seedheads. Growing 2.5-3.5m (8-11ft), it is best planted in the ground or through an ornamental tree.

CLEMATIS – LATE-FLOWERING
AS RECOMMENDED BY ROSELAND HOUSE NURSERY

C. 'Étoile Violette'

C. 'Alba Luxurians'

All the late-flowering clematis enjoy the same robust constitution and growth habit; flowering only on their new growth, they can be cut back hard during winter or early spring back to a pair of healthy buds 15-20cm (6-8in) above soil level. The window of opportunity is from November to April. The 10 plants chosen here are very reliable and will no doubt do well whatever the year throws at them. The flowering period is basically during summer and autumn and they are extremely useful for keeping the colour going in the garden during this period.

C. 'Betty Corning'

C. 'Chacewater'

C. 'Kermesina'

1 C. 'Alba Luxurians' 🏆

A wonderful, trouble-free clematis
that copes well with all garden conditions,
except perhaps deep shade. The white
flowers are tipped with green, starting
in early July and continuing until late
September, the growth reaching up to
5m (16ft) during the season. They are
perfect for brightening any dark corners
around the garden.

2 C. 'Betty Corning' 🏆

'Betty Corning' should flower profusely,
even if it's planted in a north-facing
direction. The flowering period is between
July and September. The flowers are
ice-blue with pink shades and are highly
scented. 'Betty Corning' grows to around
3m (10ft) in a season. The fragrance
is wonderful and it looks great, too.

3 C. 'Chacewater'

This has a compact habit, growing up
to 3m (10ft). Its light-coloured flowers,
which are white with a pale pinky-violet
edge, appear from July to September.
The delicate colour goes well with pastel
planting schemes. It looks beautiful on a
shrub of *Buddleja* 'Lochinch' and its growth
habit is not overwhelming.

4 C. 'Étoile Violette' 🏆

'Étoile Violette' is simply one of the
most prolific flowerers in the group. Its gold-
eyed purple flowers often obscure the foliage
completely. It tends to start flowering earlier
than others – it starts in early June and
flowers to the end of August. 'Étoile
Violette' can reach up to 4m (13ft) in height.
Its imposing stature never fails to stop
garden visitors in their tracks!

5 C. 'Kermesina' ♈

A lovely, small-flowered red. Flowering from July into October, 'Kermesina' has the height to grow into big plants and will reach 6-7m (20-23ft) when happy. This can be a useful addition to climbing hydrangeas and Schizophragmas, as the nodding red flowers show up well, even high up.

6 C. 'Little Bas'

This hasn't yet earned any accolades but surely will in time. It is very like a large-flowered *C. viticella*, and grows to around 6m (20ft). It produces its nodding purple flowers in good quantities from July through to October. They look completely stunning entangled with the yellow-flowered *C. tangutica*.

7 C. *viticella* 'Mary Rose'

A beautiful plant with a long history of cultivation, being found in English gardens back in the 16th century. A deep amethyst-coloured double. A good grower, the long

C. 'Little Bas'

C. viticella 'Mary Rose'

CULTIVATION

Although clematis like deep, fertile, moisture-retentive soils, they will cope with most garden soils and situations. The key to success is regular watering during the plant's first summer in the ground, down a tube direct to the root ball. Both tube and water can be withdrawn after the plant is established, normally around 12 months. Plants will do better with some extra feeding; try blood, fish and bone feed or horse manure, depending on what's available. If not using manure, try some other form of organic mulching around the plant bases.

C. 'Minuet'

C. 'Prince Charles'

C. 'Royal Velours'

stems can reach 4m (13ft). The flowers, while not large, last a long time on the plant. It flowers from July to September.

8 C. 'Minuet' ♔
One of Francisque Morel's many fine creations from around 1900. The two-tone wine-red and white flowers are freely born from July to September but the growth remains light enough that it can be grown over shrubs like *Cistus* without harm.

9 C. 'Prince Charles' ♔
Clouds of light blue flowers from June to October. Reaches around 3m (10ft) each season. The early flowers can be quite large, but it then settles down to produce nodding flowers. Sheer quantity and length of flowering make this plant outstanding.

10 C. 'Royal Velours' ♔
'Royal Velours' draws many 'oohs' and 'aahs' when flowering in the garden. No photograph can do justice to the velvet texture of the deep purple-red flowers. It makes good growth to 3m (10ft), is reliable and especially quick to establish. It tones beautifully with the rambling rose, Violette.

ROSELAND HOUSE NURSERY
Chacewater, Truro, Cornwall TR4 8QB
T: 01872 560451 E: plants@roselandhouse.co.uk
W: www.roselandhouse.co.uk

✿ NCCPG National Collection holder of *Clematis viticella* (cultivars)
Roseland House Nursery started in 1985 and specialises in growing climbing plants. Clematis, especially *viticellas*, are a particular interest and the nursery received National Collection status in 2002. The nursery bred and named its first clematis, 'Purple Haze', in 1997, and has named four others since. The nursery propagates its one-acre garden entirely in-house, and it opens, along with the nursery, on Tuesday and Wednesday afternoons, from April to September (and other times by appointment).

CONIFERS

AS RECOMMENDED BY EVERGREEN CONIFER CENTRE

Picea orientalis 'Aureospicata'

Pieta glauca 'Conica'

Taxus baccata 'David'

Abies pinsapo 'Horstmann's Nana'

Conifers are one of the most varied groups of plants available. They are excellent garden plants, coming in all shapes and sizes. They range from miniatures and dwarf conifers – which make excellent container plants – to the giant redwoods that can grow into enormous trees. Most conifers are evergreen, but there is a range of colours available: magical when they change with the varying climates and seasons of the year. There are conifers suitable for small town gardens to the arboretums that accommodate all sizes.

1 *Abies lasiocarpa* 'Compacta Glauca'
A very slow-growing blue fir, forming a compact, narrow column. It can be clipped to a neat shape. In 10 years it can reach 90-120cm (35-47in). It is very hardy.

2 *Abies pinsapo* 'Horstmann's Nana'
A true dwarf that will grow into a dense bush of gnarled, stiff blue foliage. It can be pruned to contain its size and does well in containers. Happy in well-drained soils, it is very hardy and it grows to 50cm (20in) in 10 years.

3 *Abies pinsapo* 'Aurea'
A very hardy rare form of the Spanish fir, a bit faster growing than 'Horstmann's Nana'.

It makes a rounded bush 90-120cm (35-47in) after 10 years. It is good in containers, with spiky golden-yellow needles in spring and summer. It can be pruned to contain its size.

4 *Cryptomeria japonica* 'Sekkan-sugi'
The Japanese cedar is a hardy conifer with creamy-yellow leaves turning to almost white in winter, with brown female cones. It makes an excellent garden focal point, growing to 1.5-1.8m (5-6ft) in 10 years. The grafted form, 'Barabits Gold', is faster-growing, and happy in most well-drained soils.

5 *Picea glauca* 'Conica'
The white spruce is a neat, cone-shaped dwarf

conifer with bright-green needle-like leaves. It makes an excellent container plant and is also very attractive in borders and on screes. It never needs trimming, unlike other upright spruces but needs protection from aphids.

6 *Picea abies* 'Little Gem' ♔

The Norway spruce is a dwarf conifer of rounded habit, forming a neat bun with needle-like dark green leaves. It is a true dwarf, reaching 30-50cm (12-20in) after 10 years. Being very hardy, it is at home in most places in the garden, but is also a very good container plant.

7 *Picea orientalis* 'Aureospicata'

This spruce has beautiful golden-yellow shoots in May, which darken during summer turning to green in winter. In spring it is decorated with tiny red cones that turn brown in autumn. It reaches a height of 2-3m (6ft 6in-9ft 10in) after 10 years, so is more suited to the medium-to-large-sized garden.

8 *Pinus cembra* 'Aureovariegata'

One of the best pines, this is a narrow pyramid with distinctive foliage. The needles have a yellow cast in summer and turn golden in winter, giving a warm glow in sunshine. It is hardy and grows to 90cm (35in) after 10 years, making it suitable for a small garden.

CULTIVATION

The traditional planting time is autumn and spring, but as plants and trees are now container-grown there is a tendency to plant all through the year. It is best to avoid very cold, very wet and very hot weather. How you plant is very important for any plant. For conifers we suggest you make a good-sized hole and incorporate bonemeal and compost, mixing it with the soil that you have dug out. Make sure you have plenty of loose soil in the bottom, put the rest of the soil round plant and firm in, and water if necessary.

---

9 *Sciadopitys verticillata* 'Richie's Cushion'

The Japanese umbrella pine is slow-growing to 15m (50ft) and requires a sheltered position from strong winds. It can withstand full sun or light shade and is happy in most well-drained soils. New growth is cream in spring and summer, turning to green in winter.

10 *Taxus baccata* 'David'

A very slim golden column, this conifer has gold-edged green needles turning to gold in midsummer. It is an excellent plant, adding colour and structure to the garden. It also makes a good container plant, is very hardy and will reach 1.2-1.5m (4-5ft) in 10 years.

EVERGREEN CONIFER CENTRE
Tenbury Road, Rock, nr Kidderminster, Worcestershire DY14 9RB
T: 01299 266581 F: 01299 266755
E: brian@evergreen-conifers.co.uk
W: www.evergreen-conifers.co.uk

Evergreen Conifer Centre was started in 1989 by Brian and Shirley Warrington, who still own it. Over the years, it has built up a fine reputation for growing conifers, but all the hard work as been worth it. They grow a lot of larger conifers, as well as dwarf and slow-growing ones, but also sell acers, heathers, and trees. Contact the nursery for opening times.

CONIFERS – DWARF

AS RECOMMENDED BY GORDON HADDOW AT KENWITH NURSERY

Pinus mugo 'Carsten'

Juniperus procumbens 'Nana'

Picea glanca Alberta Blue

Dwarf conifers are defined as those under 1m (3ft) high after 10 years, while miniature conifers are under 60cm (24in) high after the same amount of time. Both are perfect for garden sizes of today. Dwarf conifers do not produce flowers but have the advantages of keeping their foliage all year round, being available in all shapes, sizes and colours, and when planted together, make an interesting dwarf landscape. These plants also look well in raised beds and many can be used individually in troughs and in pots on paved areas or on decking.

1 *Larix kaempferi* 'Nana'

Dwarf larches are rarely available but make fine garden plants and the foliage of Japanese larch is a very attractive, soft silver-blue. The autumn leaves turn gold before dropping, leaving a twiggy bush for the winter months with dark wine-red outer branchlets.

2 *Pinus mugo* 'Carsten'

Mugo pine grows in the Alps and is very hardy. 'Carsten' is as tough as the parent tree and is good in a windy, exposed site. It forms a low, spreading bush, mid-green in summer, turning bright gold for winter.

3 *Pinus parviflora* 'Fu-shiro'

This slow-growing Japanese pine produces tiers of branches with each year's growth.

The new leaves in spring are a pale yellow, turning yellow-white in the winter; the colder the winter, the whiter the leaves become. It is easily pruned and kept to the required size.

4 *Pinus heldreichii* 'Smidtii' ♔

This is a cheery, globose but flat-topped plant with stiff, mid-green leaves, which is attractive to look at. Growth averages 5-7.5cm (2-3in) per year and the buds are red-brown and white-striped. It is a hardy plant, suitable for an exposed position in places where the soil is slightly alkaline.

5 *Cryptomeria japonica* 'Tenzan-sugi'

One of the best dwarf plants from the Japanese cedar, with juvenile light-green foliage and a cushion-like shape. Older plants are so tight that when pressed, they feel like the head of a cauliflower. It has a red tinge in the winter and it is happy growing in containers.

6 *Abies koreana* 'Blauer Eskimo'

This is a very attractive plant with new light blue spring growth turning to grey-blue late in the year. Annual growth is about 5cm (2in), but it is easily pruned if required. Very effective in troughs, rockeries and scree gardens, and good growing down rocks beside ponds.

7 *Picea glauca* Alberta Blue

A narrowly conical plant with eye-catching silver-blue new foliage in spring. Good in a bed with other plants or on its own when bigger as an accent plant or single specimen. Does best in cooler, slight shade positions, which also enhances the colour.

8 *Juniperus procumbens* 'Nana' ♔

This is the best prostrate juniper which, unlike some, is happy growing down slopes, walls and the sides of troughs, while many prefer to grow horizontal. It has light-green foliage and is reasonably fast-growing, but easily trimmed back if it spreads too far.

CULTIVATION

Dwarf conifers in general need to be planted in acid soil. If azaleas, camellias and rhododendrons are growing in your area, the soil must be acid. Alternatively, buy a soil-testing kit at your local garden centre. They need free-draining soil, but they don't like clay. Heavy soil can be improved by digging in stone chippings, which enhance drainage, or lay a drainage pipe to remove excess water if soil is wet. Finally, dig a hole larger than the pot size of your plant and work in a spadeful of peat before planting, to encourage roots to spread.

---

9 *Abies lasiocarpa* 'Compacta'

An upright, conical plant with tiered branch system and mid blue-grey leaves. The leaves are held on the plant for up to eight years, giving it a dense appearance. The white trunk makes a nice contrast. Quite hardy and reliable, doing well in exposed positions.

10 *Thuja plicata* 'Rogersii'

Around for years and still one of the best. A narrowly conical, upright plant with year-round light-gold outer foliage. It does well anywhere and can be easily produced to a reasonable size.

KENWITH NURSERY
Blinsham, Nr Torrington, Beaford, Winkleigh, Devon EX19 8NT
T: 01805 603274
E: conifers@kenwith63.freeserve.co.uk
W: www.kenwithnursery.co.uk

❁   NCCPG National Collection holder of Conifers (dwarf and slow growing)
Kenwith Nursery began as a collection of dwarf conifers 40 years ago. Some time later Gordon Haddow was encouraged to propagate his plants. This went so well that he opened a conifer nursery, wrote a catalogue and began selling plants by mail order. He is also co-author, with Humphrey Welch, of *The World Checklist of Conifers*. Open March to October, Tuesday to Saturday, and November to February, Wednesday to Saturday, 10am to 4.30pm.

CLIMBERS

RECOMMENDED BY LOUISA ARBUTHONOTT OF STONE HOUSE COTTAGE NURSERY

Clematis viticella

Besides decorating a wall, giving a vertical plant effect, or disguising an ugly shed, climbers can be used to extend the range of plants beyond what would normally grow in your area. The added heat of a sunny wall behind a plant can encourage it to flower and enhance its chances of surviving the winter. In a small garden two climbers can often be trained through each other for greater impact.

1 *Actinidia pilosula*

I find this *Actinidia* preferable to the
standard *A. kolomikta* which is almost
overpowering in its leaf variegation. In
A. pilosula the leaf colouring is a little
more subtle and the pink flowers are ahead
of its more famous relation. Excellent light
and some sun are all it requires.

2 *Clematis cirrhosa* var. *purpurascens*
'Freckles' ♔

No garden should be without some winter-
flowering climbers and this is one of the
best. An evergreen, it flowers almost
continually from autumn through the
winter. The flowers are cream coloured,
and heavily blotched with maroon spots.
A vigorous grower, it accepts harsh pruning
without a murmur. H3

3 *Clematis viticella* ♔

A robust species, clematis grows with
poise and elegance. From midsummer
onwards the blue flowers dance on short
stalks in the slightest breeze. The blooms
are shaped like Victorian lampshades. It is
easy to prune; cut it hard to the ground in
February, mulch with manure and leave
it alone. H4

4 *Decumaria sinensis*

This climber is not planted often enough.
Many people require a neat evergreen
climber like this that flowers, is fragrant,
and doesn't have the vicious thorns of
a pyracantha. It flowers in early spring,
smelling slightly of honey. In the autumn
the foliage can take on a reddish tinge. H3

5 *Desmodium elegans* ♔

Not technically a climber but a shrub that

Clematis cirrhosa
var *purpurascens*
'Freckles'

Itea ilicifolia

Decumaria sinensis

Desmodium elegans

Schisandra rubriflora

Lonicera similis var. delayavi

CULTIVATION

Anything grown in close proximity to a wall or fence is going to need a good start in life. If it is planted too close it may be in the rain shadow of an overhanging roof. If planted too far it will not reap the benefit of the extra heat. Incorporate plenty of organic matter into a large a planting hole and water well during the first season. Some wire supports will be necessary. Afterwards, train and space out growing shoots, or bring those with arial roots into direct contact with the wall.

prefers to be trained against a wall. It will reward you with a succession of pale lilac pea flowers in midsummer and beyond. It has attractive lime green foliage and attractive pink-red flattened seed pods in autumn. H4

6 *Schisandra rubriflora*
A cheerful deciduous climber for a shady wall that never gets too dry. The pillar-box red flowers in May are set off by apple-green foliage. It is a vigorous grower but can be cut back. It is very hardy.

7 *Itea ilicifolia* 🏆
Itea ilicifolia is a lax grower rather than a climber, which grows happily against a shady wall with plenty of light. It will quietly impress you with its glossy foliage and bronzy new growth. In August it throws out long, scented green catkins that carry on into autumn. H3

8 *Lonicera similis* var. *delayavi* 🏆
The scented honeysuckles are at their best in early morning or late evening. This one is semi-evergreen and will grow on any

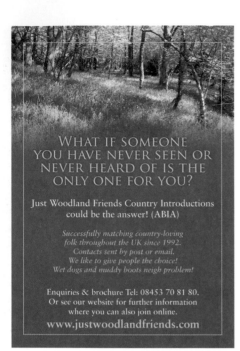

Dregea sinensis

aspect. In July and August it produces fragrant cream flowers. It is perfect for when you might be sitting outside with a glass of chilled white wine. H4

9 *Dregea sinensis*

This easy summer-flowering climber is at its best on a sunny wall and can be cut back hard during the winter. It begins to flower in late June or early July, producing panicles of white flowers with a hint of pink. The flowers have a curious scent. H3

10 *Trachelospermum jasminoides* ♆

This evergreen climber has handsome shiny leaves and fragrant flowers in July; it throws out its jasmine-like scent with gay abandon. It doesn't expect you to put your nose into its flowers to enjoy its perfume. H3-4

STONE HOUSE COTTAGE NURSERY
Near Kidderminster, Worcestershire DY10 4BG
T: 01562 69902
E: louisa@shcn.co.uk
W: www.shcn.co.uk

At **Stone House Cottage** the ¾-acre garden is the 'shop window' for the adjoining nursery. The original walled garden has been embellished with towers and follies built by James Arbuthnott and is covered with a huge range of the climbers and wall shrubs in which the nursery specialises. Louisa runs the nursery and garden single-handedly. The plants for sale, include a vast range of herbaceous, reflecting her personal choice and changing tastes.

CLIMBERS FOR SHADE
AS RECOMMENDED BY LANGTHORNS PLANTERY

Akebia quinata

Lonicera tragophylla

From the huge fig vines or *Ficus pumila* of the rainforests to more delicate specimens, such as *Aconitum hemsleyanum* or *Dicentra scandens*, there are an enormous array of climbers suitable for shade. Whatever the size of fence, wall or tree to be covered, there is a climber fit for the job. Interest can be achieved all through the seasons with either flowers or foliage. With plants being collected from around the globe, this is an exciting and educational collection of plants.

1 *Holboellia latifolia* or *H. coriacea*

These vigorous evergreen climbers can grow to 10m (33ft) and are ideal for sheltered walls. They have deep green leaves, with deliciously scented flowers in spring. Female flowers are a greeny-cream colour and male flowers have purple/pink tints at the tips. If pollinated in summer, these plants produce sausage-like fleshy fruits full of black seeds. H3

2 *Lonicera tragophylla* ♆

This is my favourite shade-loving honeysuckle. It is a hardy, deciduous climber, that can grow to 5-6m (16-20ft). Long, primrose-yellow buds open to bright-yellow flowers in June and July, followed by red fruits in late summer. They are sweetly scented in the evenings. Sometimes they are shy to flowers, but are well worth persevering with. H4

3 *Clematis patens* 'Manshuu Ki' (syn. 'Wada's Primrose')

Huge white flowers up to 20cm (8in), with primrose-yellow bars down the centre of each tepal, cover this clematis in April and May. Flowers are followed by attractive spherical seedheads. Can be slow to establish but patience rewards the grower with a show-stopping display for a shady wall.

4 *Schizophragma hydrangeoides* 'Roseum' ♆

Wonderful red stalks to the serrated dark green leaves appear from stems that climb using adhesive aerial roots. It can become huge and has stunning, sterile-pink florets that surround tiny clusters of fertile flowers in early summer. It grows in almost any soil, but really benefits from annual mulching. H4

5 *Hydrangea anomala* subsp. *petiolaris* 🏆

A fantastically reliable climber for a large, shady wall. Tolerant of most soils, this subspecies can reach 15m (49ft). It has glossy dark-green leaves, and fertile white flowers surrounded by larger white florets. This climber uses aerial roots to cover the wall.

6 *Berberidopsis corallina*

It requires fertile, humus-rich, lime-free soil, but is included here for its ability to thrive in shady conditions. Toothed, oval evergreen leaves adorn this twining plant that can reach 14m (45ft). In late summer and early autumn, dark red flowers appear at the ends of shoots on long scarlet stalks.

7 *Akebia quinata* and *A. pentaphylla*

I have included both species because they can be planted together to aid pollination and chances of fruit setting. They are vigorous, twining climbers with vanilla-scented, chocolate-coloured flowers in spring.

8 *Parthenocissus henryana* 🏆

The best form of Virginia creeper for a shady wall, it holds its tricoloured leaf colour well in the shade. This climber has sucker-like pads that stick to walls, and green leaves with white veins giving a metallic glaucous sheen,

CULTIVATION

As this is such a diverse ... it is difficult to describe how ... cultivate them. As a general guide, ... hole three times the size of the pot and mix in some well-rotted farm manure with the soil before backfilling. If planting up a tree, dig around the tree roots to create a large hole. Planting is best done in autumn or early spring for perennials and spring for seed-raised species.

and produces fiery reds in autumn. Height reaches 10m (33ft). H4

9 *Dicentra scandens* and *Aconitum hemsleyanum*

These grow well together on a shady wall. *D. scandens* has locket-shaped yellow flowers from midsummer to autumn and can grow to 2.5-3m (8-10ft). *A. hemsleyanum* has blue flowers in summer and autumn and can climb to 2.5m (8ft).

10 *Hedera colchica* 'Sulphur Heart' 🏆

I included ivy for its ability to thrive on a shady wall with little maintenance. This is my favourite of the large-leaved ivies, with its glossy, deep green leaves and streaky yellow variegation. It looks great all year, with striking foliage. Height 10m (33ft). H4

LANGTHORNS PLANTERY
High Cross Lane West, Little Canfield, Dunmow, Essex CM6 1TD
T: 01371 872611 E: info@langthorns.com
W: www.langthorns.com
Open daily, 10am to 5pm

Langthorns Plantery started in 1977, after the heatwave of 1976 when two brothers decided to make some money to buy a swimming pool. Their parents suggested they did this by selling plants from their family garden. Not only did they raise the funds for the pool, they also built a nursery business in the process. Today, Langthorns has a vast selection of herbaceous perennials, shrubs, trees, roses, grasses, clematis and climbers.

FUCHSIA BUSHES

AS RECOMMENDED BY ROUALEYN NURSERY

F. 'Rose Fantasia'

Roualeyn Nursery has been growing fuchsias for many years. Most of the varieties that we see today originated in New Zealand and South America and were discovered between the mid 18th and the late 19th century. They are popular in most of the temperate countries, with the number of cultivars running into thousands. The range of hardy, tender bush and trailing types is vast. Flowers range from the exotic-looking large doubles in various colours, to the miniatures of *encliandra* types. These are our top 10.

1 *F.* 'Rose Fantasia'

A very popular single with a rose pink corolla, blush-pink horizontal sepals and mid-green foliage. Needs to be planted separately or the effect will be lost. A must for the container garden. Grows to 45-60cm (18-24in), with a 30-45cm (12-18in) spread. H2

2 *F.* 'Anita'

An unusual combination of white sepals, a tangerine corolla and semi-erect flowers. Needs pinching back to retain a bushy shape. Ideal for containers and growing into a half-standard. Flowers from May to first frosts. Grows to 45-60cm (18-24in), with a spread of 38-45cm (15-18in). H2

3 *F.* 'Carmel Blue'

One of the best blue and whites, with exceptional flowers freely produced over summer. The tubes and long sepals are white with a hint of green on the former, and pink on the latter. The flowers have a blue, ageing to purple, corolla. Has a height and spread of 30-45cm (12-18in). H2

F. 'Anita'

F. 'Carmel Blue'

F. 'Dorothy Hanley'

CULTIVATION

Hardy fuchsias are best planted at the end of May, in a moist but well-drained soil, preferably in partial shade where they will produce flowers until first frosts. Dead-heading and regular feeding will ensure a fine display throughout the season. Pruning is best left until the following spring, so the old wood offers protection against winter weather.

Tender varieties will have to be lifted before the first frosts, at which time they need to be pruned, and kept warm for the winter. They are best grown in a good-sized container for easy removal in the autumn.

4 *F.* 'Dorothy Hanley'

Introduced in 1996, this cultivar is a first in the new aubergine colours also classed as hardy. It has striking red sepals with an aubergine-splashed red corolla. The double flowers are medium-sized, with dark-green foliage. In the garden it grows to around 40-60cm (16-24in) in height, and the width is about the same. H4

5 *F.* 'Mrs Popple' ♛

A free-flowering upright bush, suitable as a specimen plant for the hardy border. Grow it as a flowering hedge, as its spreading habit takes up a lot of space. The medium-sized flowers have scarlet tubes and sepals, and clashing violet-purple corollas. It has a 1.5m (5ft) height and spread. H4

6 *F.* 'Mrs W.P. Wood' ♛

A variety hardy enough to be planted in the garden and left out all year. It makes a wonderful shrubby plant with small, but abundant pale pink and white flowers, and

F. 'Mrs W.P. Wood'

F. 'Royal velvet'

demands a position in the border, being too vigorous for containers. Grows to 1m (3ft 3in) in both height and spread. H4

7 F. 'Patricia Hodge'

A most unusual and beautiful flower, with a tangerine corolla and salmon sepals. The small- to medium-sized leaves are light green, giving a clear background to the flower. An extremely floriferous variety, flowering continuously from April to autumn. Regular feeding is essential. Basket type. H1

F. 'Patricia Hodge'

8 F. 'Ann Howard Tripp'

A single to semi-double flower, with a short, thick white tube, and white sepals held at the horizontal, edged and tinged with palest pink. The corolla is white, lightly-veined pink, held well clear of foliage. A late flowerer, ideal for containers and the garden. Reaches approximately 30cm (12in) in both height and width. H2

9 F. 'Royal Velvet' ♛

Probably the best double in its colour range. Large double-ruffled corolla of deep purple splashed with crimson, with tube and upturned petals of crimson – much like a frilly petticoat. A great cultivar, preferring semi-shade. Grows to 45-75cm (18-30in) in height, with a 30-60cm (12-24in) spread. H2

10 F. 'Thalia' ♛

Probably the most popular of the F. triphylla hybrids. It is vigorous, upright and used for bedding. 'Thalia' has long flowers of orange-scarlet with olive-green foliage. It blooms continuously but dislikes draughts. It revels in sun, so is ideal for a sunny patio. Grows to 1m (3ft 3in) tall, with a similar spread. H1

ROUALEYN NURSERY
Trefriw, Conwy,
North Wales LL27 0SX
T: 01492 640548
E: roualeynnursery@btinternet.com

Roualeyn Nursery is situated in the Snowdonia National Park, close to the market town of Llanrwst. In 1979 the nursery began specialising in fuchsias. Today, Doug, his wife Gwyneth and son Colin run the business. Roualeyn's fuchsias are seen at most major flower shows throughout the country and have won six Chelsea Gold Medals. Visits can be arranged for gardening groups during the day or evening, with tea and coffee available.

FUCHSIAS – HARDY

AS RECOMMENDED BY KATHLEEN MUNCASTER OF
KATHLEEN MUNCASTER FUCHSIAS

F. 'Prosperity'

Hardy fuchsias are those members of the fuchsia group capable of being left in the ground all winter, growing and flowering from June until cut down by frost, giving a display when most other plants are finished. Size can vary from only about 24cm (9in) in height and spread to 2.1m (7ft) or more in height with a spread of about 90cm-1.2m (3-4ft). This range of sizes makes hardy fuchsias suitable for planting in gardens large and small.

1 F. 'Major Heaphy'
Grows to about 60cm (2ft) in our garden and spreads about 45cm (18in). Has a medium-sized flower with a short pink tube and sepals with a striking orange underside held horizontally. The petals are a bright red.

2 F. 'Nicki's Findling'
A compact mound of a plant 35cm (14in) high and wide. The flowers, formed on the top of the plant, are held horizontally or semi-erect. They are small but produced in profusion, with pink tubes and sepals.

3 F. 'Rose of Castile'
A really old fuchsia that has stood the test of time. The flowers have a white tube

and sepals with petals opening purple and maturing to dark red, contrasting beautifully with the light-green foliage. The plant grows to 60cm (2ft) in our garden and spreads to 45cm (18in).

4 F. hatschbachii
A very hardy fuchsia species with small red and purple flowers. The leaves are a beautiful shiny green, long and pointed, and set off the many flowers to perfection. This fuchsia is rarely cut down by frosts and in our garden has been trained into a pillar beside the porch.

5 F. 'Rufus' ♟
A cultivar hybridised in America which has shown remarkable hardiness in Britain.

The large single flowers are turkey-red, showing up well against the mid-green foliage. It makes a large bush about 1m (3ft 3in) high in our garden. It may need drastic pruning of branches that spread the crown of the plant.

6 F. 'President George Bartlett'

It makes a neat mound 24cm (9in) high and will spread to about 45cm (18in) if you let it. The flowers are double, with petals opening almost black, ageing to beetroot-red. Many flowers are produced on top of the dark green foliage. This plant is very popular on sight.

7 F. 'Alison Sweetman' ♛

Individually its flowers are fairly ordinary but at any time there may be up to six on each branch, so the overall effect is of a plant dripping with flowers. The flowers have red tubes and sepals and red petals with a hint of purple. Consistent and long-flowering.

8 F. 'Prosperity' ♛

One of the most popular hardy fuchsias. The flowers are large and double with many petals and are among the earliest to appear. Tubes and sepals are crimson and the petals pale pink with red veins. The plant reaches 90cm-1.2m (3-4ft) but spreads only about 45cm (18in).

CULTIVATION

Planting out is best done when all danger of frost has passed until the end of July. Plant as big a plant as you can, preferably in a 13cm (5in) or 15cm (6in) pot. Buy your hardy fuchsias early in March and grow on or buy them this size. They do not mind full sun or partial shade. In heavy clay use grit or bark mixed into the soil to help the roots spread. During the winter do not cut off old branches, which protect the plant from frost damage. Remove old growth when the plant is growing from the base in spring.

9 F. 'Whiteknights Pearl' ♛

Another vigorous, tall hardy fuchsia, superb as a centrepiece or at the back of the border. Flowers are medium but freely produced. Tubes and sepals are pale pink, the darker pink petals being set off by darkish green leaves. Height and spread 1.2m (4ft) plus.

10 F. 'Hawkshead' ♛

Probably the most popular hardy fuchsia. Flowers are small and white with green-tipped sepals but stand out among the darker flowers of other hardy fuchsias. Even when planted in full sun the flowers remain white. Growth is columnar (it doesn't spread) and reaches 1m (3ft 3in).

KATHLEEN MUNCASTER FUCHSIAS
18 Field Lane, Morton, Gainsborough, Lincolnshire DN21 3BY
T: 01427 612329
W: www.kathleenmuncasterfuchsias.co.uk

❀ NCCPG National Collection holder of *Fuchsia* (hardy)
Kathleen Muncaster Fuchsias started in 1968 and moved to Morton in 1978. It has always specialised in fuchsias, especially hardy fuchsias since 1989. It is members of the NCCPG and holds one of their collections of hardy fuchsias. It constantly tries fuchsias in the garden to test for hardiness. If a plant survives five years without any protection and flowers by the beginning of July it can be called hardy. It opens daily 10am to 5pm (except Wednesday) from February. After mid-June, the team attends shows, so it is advisable to call before visiting.

HEATHERS

AS RECOMMENDED BY KINGFISHER NURSERY

Erica carnea 'Golden Starlet'

Erica carnea 'Rosalie'

Heathers are hardy, evergreen plants which, with careful planning, can give a garden a colourful display and will require little maintenance to continue to give pleasure for many years. Colour can be achieved all year round using the different flowering seasons and foliage effects. Most heathers are low growing and suitable for all sizes of gardens. Winter and spring-flowering heathers are particularly useful, as they are easy to grow and make a stunning show when the rest of the garden is bare. There are many cultivars available, but the 10 we have chosen will make a good start for any collection.

1 *Erica carnea* 'Golden Starlet'
White flowers on golden-yellow foliage make this plant shine in the late winter and spring months. Its spreading habit creates a carpet of colour all year long. Suitable for all soil types. Height 15cm (6in), spread 40cm (16in).

2 *Erica carnea* 'Ice Princess'
Attractive long spikes of white flowers held on erect bright-green foliage from February to May. Suitable for all soil types. Height 15cm (6in), spread 35cm (14in).

3 *Erica carnea* 'Myretoun Ruby'
An outstanding plant with dark-green foliage, displaying deep-magenta flowers in late winter and early spring. Suitable for all soil types. Height 15cm (6in), spread 45cm (18in).

4 *Erica carnea* 'Rosalie'
This outstanding plant produces masses of large bright-pink flowers in the spring and has mid-green foliage. Suitable for all soil types. Height 15cm (6in), spread 35cm (14in).

5 *Erica* x *darleyensis* 'Kramer's Rote'
An outstanding heather with wine-red flowers contrasting against its blue-green foliage, brightening the darkest of winter days, flowering on into the spring. Suitable for all soil types. Height 35cm (14in), spread 60cm (24in).

6 *Erica* x *darleyensis* 'Mary Helen'
The golden-yellow summer foliage on this plant bears bronze tints in winter and displays its pink flowers in early spring.

CULTIVATION

Heathers are best planted in beds totally devoted to themselves, except for the addition of a few conifers or small evergreen shrubs to provide contrast in height and form. Heathers require open, preferably sunny positions, with well-drained soil. All the winter and spring-flowering species are lime-tolerant, whereas the majority of the summer and autumn-flowering species require acid soil. However, this can be overcome by planting them in tubs or troughs with ericaceous compost. Good results are achieved by planting in groups of three or five plants per cultivar, spaced 38-46cm (15-18in) apart. Trim foliage each year, immediately after flowering.

Suitable for all soil types. Height 25cm (10in), spread 45cm (18in).

7 *Calluna vulgaris* 'Dark Beauty' ♛
This outstanding plant has semi-double dark-cerise flowers, deepening to ruby on dark green compact foliage during late summer. Prefers acid soil or ericaceous compost. Height 25cm (10in), spread 35cm (14in).

8 *Calluna vulgaris* 'Peter Sparkes' ♛
Superb long spikes of double rose-pink flowers on dark-green foliage in early autumn make this an outstanding plant. Prefers acid soil or ericaceous compost. Height 40cm (16in), spread 55cm (22in).

9 *Calluna vulgaris* 'White Coral'
This spectacular compact plant displays pure double white flowers on bright-green foliage from mid to late summer. Prefers acid soil or ericaceous compost. Height 20cm (8in), spread 40cm (16in).

10 *Calluna vulgaris* 'Wickwar Flame' ♛
A sturdy plant with lavender flowers in late summer. The foliage is gold in summer, turning orange then red in winter. Prefers acid soil or ericaceous compost. Height 50cm (20in), spread 65cm (26in).

KINGFISHER NURSERY
Gedney Hill, Spalding, Lincolnshire PE12 0RU
T: 01406 330503 F: 01406 330078
E: sales@kingfishernursery.co.uk
W: www.kingfishernursery.co.uk
Contact: Mandy or Pete

Kingfisher Nursery has been established for over 30 years and has developed into one of the country's leading wholesale heather specialists, producing around 800,000 plants annually. Kingfisher heathers are supplied to leading garden centres throughout the country and can be recognised by the distinctive colour coding scheme, used to identify lime-tolerant varieties, and the little kingfisher at the corner of every label.

HEDGING PLANTS

AS RECOMMENDED BY BUCKINGHAM NURSERIES

Berberis darwinii

Euonymus fortunei 'Emerald 'n' Gold'

A hedge is a living barrier, providing privacy, beauty, shelter and a haven for wildlife. Depending on the position, different plants should be used, as these factors need to be taken into account before the perfect hedge can be chosen: height, evergreen or deciduous, soil, weather and future maintenance. As there are so many facets to be considered, it's a good idea to approach a specialist nursery, with a range of species.

1 *Amelanchier lamarckii* 'Snowy Mespilus' or 'Juneberry' ♆

An easy, deciduous hedge with leaves opening coppery-red; green in summer and red, orange and yellow in autumn. It produces dainty white flowers in spring followed by edible black berries. Suitable for hedges 1.5m (5ft). Needs sun or partial shade.

2 *Fagus sylvatica* ♆

Beech is a native plant with superb, shiny green leaves, which turn rich copper in autumn. It forms a dense screen all year and is suitable for hedges 1m (3ft 3in) and can grow 45cm (18in) a year.

3 *Berberis darwinii* ♆

Makes a colourful, fast-growing evergreen hedge with small holly-like green leaves tinged red when they are new. The hedge produces rich orange flowers from May to June, and blue barberries, excellent in jams and preserves. Grows 30cm (12in) a year, making a hedge between 1.2-2m (4-6ft 7in).

4 *Cotoneaster simonsii* ♆

A semi-evergreen hedge which often holds its glossy, dark-green leaves through to February. Leaves turn bright red before dropping. Small white flowers, tinged pink, appear in June, followed in autumn by bright-red berries. Between 1-1.5m (3ft 3in-5ft) tall, it can grow to 20-30cm (8-12in) a year.

5 *Escallonia* 'CF Ball'

An eye-catching evergreen hedge, with crimson-red flowers and glossy, deeply-toothed dark-green leaves. It is a sun-loving, fast-growing plant, suitable for hedges between 1-2m (3ft 3in-6ft 7in). It thrives on coastal sites, but is unsuitable for cold positions. Grows 30cm (12in) a year.

6 *Euonymus fortunei* 'Emerald 'n' Gold' ♗

A showy, evergreen dwarf hedge, displaying shiny leaves with a broad yellow margin, tinged pink in winter. Excellent for use in any aspect, it retains the bright variegation. Can be trimmed to between 20-60cm (8-24in). Growth of 5-7cm (2-3in) per year.

7 *Lonicera nitida* 'Twiggy'

Dense, non-flowering evergreen hedge with tiny golden leaves. Forms a solid hedge quickly, but needs sun to retain its colour. In shade use *L. nitida* 'Elegant' – with same habit and appearance but dark green leaves. Suitable for hedges 30-150cm (12-60in) tall, growing 20cm (8in) a year.

8 Mixed native hedging

A common sight in the countryside, and part of our heritage. A mixture that includes hawthorn (*Crataegus*), blackthorn (*Prunus spinosa*), dog rose (*Rosa canina*), field maple (*Acer campestre*), hazel (*Corylus*) and spindle (*Euonymus europaeus*). These plants give a variety of colours, flowers, perfumes, fruits and leaf forms. For hedges 1m (3.3ft) upwards.

CULTIVATION

Good ground preparation is essential for hedge planting, ideally before winter. Dig a trench at least 30cm (12in) wide. Remove perennial weeds, then fill with improved soil. Bare root plants are mainly used, and only available when dormant. Roots should be moist when planted. Spread them out to their original position and plant to the same depth as before. After planting, treat with a beneficial mycorrhizal fungi, and apply a mulch. Evergreens need protection from drying winds during their first winter.

---

9 *Rosa* 'Hansa'

Throughout the summer, 'Hansa' carries fragrant, fully double, crimson-purple flowers. In autumn it has large red hips, excellent for rosehip syrup or jelly, or food for birds if left on the tree. It is suitable for hedges 1.2-2.1m (4-7ft) in the sun.

10 *Taxus baccata* ♗

Yew is commonly used for hedging as it is naturally dense and bushy, with dark-green evergreen foliage and red berries on the female plants in winter. It grows between 15-25cm (6-10in) a year. Suitable for hedges 30cm-4.5m (12in-15ft).

BUCKINGHAM NURSERIES
Tingewick Road, Buckingham MK18 4AE
T: 01280 822133
E: web-enquiries@buckingham-nurseries.co.uk
W: www.buckingham-nurseries.co.uk

Buckingham Nurseries is run by Richard and Pauline Brown and their sons. The 11-acre site houses a Garden Centre with shop and restaurant, a wide range of container-grown trees and shrubs. During the 'dormant' season, bare-rooted hedging plants, young ornamental and forest trees are available. The nursery has supplied thousands of miles of hedging. Open Mar to end Oct, Mon to Sat 8.30am to 6pm; Sun 10.30am to 4.30pm; Nov to end Feb, Mon to Thurs 8.30am to 5.30pm; Fri to Sat, 8.30am to 6pm; Sun, 10.30am to 4.30pm.

HOLLIES

AS RECOMMENDED BY PHILIP LANC OF WELSH HOLLY

I. x meservae 'Blue Angel'

I. aquifolium 'Argentea Marginata'

Holly – also known as the genus *Ilex* – is found throughout the world from Japan to Africa to Europe. It is an important plant for the garden for its range of colour and leaf variation. It is a plant for all seasons, not just Christmas. In the spring its delicate flowers are followed by fresh, vivid growth, often with a deepening of colour in winter. It is little wonder the ancients revered it as a sacred plant. Here are our top 10 hollies.

1 *I. aquifolium* 'Alaska'
'Alaska' is the classic green-leafed holly with masses of red berries, even on young plants. The clusters of berries contrast with the dark green leaves. It is ideal for clipping and forms a dense bush.

2 *I. aquifolium* 'Argentea Marginata' ♈
This is an all year round plant, with a wide, creamy margin. You could easily overlook the reddish-pink young growth, but you'd be missing a treat. It is one of the signs that shows that spring has arrived. It is followed by whitish berries, which eventually turn red. It can grow to a height of 14m (46ft).

3 *I.* 'Harpune'
This female plant's harpoon-shaped leaves look nothing like traditional holly. It was

found as a sport of 'Alaska' in 1978. Although it does berry, its main interest is its unusual, long thin leaves. Older plants tend to have most fruit. It grows well in containers.

4 *I. aquifolium* 'Green Pillar'
As the name suggests, 'Green Pillar' grows as a pillar. It is an ideal low-maintenance plant, perfect to use in a pair to 'stand guard' at the front door. It needs top clipping once a year to restrict its height. It can grow to 7-8m (21-24ft). Once established it berries prolifically.

5 *I. x altaclerensis* 'Wilsonii'
The large flattish leaves never fail to impress. It was awarded an RHS First Class Certificate in 1899. It is a stunning reddish-orange colour in spring, and after that produces masses of glossy scarlet berries.

It has strong purple stems and is prickle-free. Height 8m (25ft).

6 *I. aquifolium* 'Elegantissima'

'Elegantissima' has to be one of the loveliest male pollinators. Its name oozes class and the plant itself is first-class. In the spring, large amounts of blossom are followed by delicate, pinky new growth. Clipping this holly produces a very dense bush, making it ideal for nesting birds.

7 *I.* x *meservae* 'Blue Angel'

'Blue Angel' has a leaf which changes colour during the year from green to almost blue. It is a dense plant, with a large amount of growth from the base. Its leaves look prickly but are actually quite soft.

8 *I.* x *altaclerensis* 'Ripley Gold'

'Ripley Gold' is a sport of 'Golden King'. The orange-yellow spring growth is a treat for those who look carefully. The leaves, with yellow central blotches, have a slight twist for added interest. It is female and can berry well.

9 *I.* 'J.C. Van Tol' ♛

There are three Van Tols, green-leafed 'J.C. Van Tol', a silver-edged 'Silver Van Tol', and a 'Golden Van Tol', with a gold-edged leaf. All are self-fertile and have prickle-free leaves. 'J.C. Van Tol' is quick-growing, hardy and can grow to 4.5m (14ft).

10 *I.* x *altaclerensis* 'Golden King' ♛

'Golden King' is a female despite its name. Its leaves have dark green centres and a wavy margin of creamy yellow. The young stems are purplish and quick-growing. The berries can vary from reddish-brown to red. It is ideal for Christmas wreaths. Height 6m (20ft).

> **CULTIVATION**
>
> Holly grows best in full or semi-shade. It doesn't like wet feet, so avoid waterlogged ground. If grown in pots, it can be planted at any time of year, while hollies transplanted from the ground should only be moved over winter. Holly responds well to being fed, enjoying foliar feeds and mulches. It doesn't always deserve its reputation for being slow growing; a good plant, well fed, can grow 3-6m (9-18ft) per year. Clipping is best done while the plant is growing, for example in August, but don't let that stop you from pruning it for Christmas foliage.

WELSH HOLLY
Tenby Road, St. Clears, Carmarthen SA33 4JP
T: 01994 231 789
E: info@welsh-holly.co.uk
W: www.welsh-holly.co.uk

Welsh Holly, a specialist holly nursery, was started by Philip and Fiona Lanc in 1998. From small beginnings and after many hard lessons, the nursery now sells ornamentals to the gardener and native provenance holly for environmental planting schemes. While the average garden centre may sell around five hollies, we grow over 100 cultivars and add to the list every year. Enquiries from around the UK and Europe result in hollies being couriered long distances.

HYDRANGEAS

AS RECOMMENDED BY CHRIS LODER OF HAVEN NURSERY

H. macrophylla
'Madame Emile Mouillière'

Hydrangeas - genus *Hydrangea* - are colourful plants that flower for weeks during summer. Their colours include pure blues, whites, pinks, reds and purples. Moreover, hydrangeas are easy, tough plants, which are spectacular and long-lived. They do well in shade, can be grown in towns or woodland and are good by the sea. They're also ideal for containers. Plus you can choose from three types of hydrangea flower:

1 Mophead types, which have big round balls consisting of lots of flowers
2 Lacecap types, which are generally flat, with flowers with showy petals in a ring around the outside
3 Panicles, which are cone-shaped, large and showy, on long stems

H. macrophylla 'Lanarth White'

H. macrophylla 'Générale Vicomtesse de Vibraye'

CULTIVATION

Hydrangeas are generally easy and reliable plants, needing little attention. They will grow in sun or in partial shade, and are ideal for north-facing beds and for open woodland. They do well in a wide range of soils except shallow, chalky and dry soils; plenty of humus (compost, manure, and so on) dug in and used as a mulch helps. The soil affects the colour of the flowers more than any other flower we grow. Many varieties produce blue shades on acid soils, but on neutral and alkaline soils they are pinker; to get them blue, water with aluminium sulphate.

H. macrophylla 'Nigra'

1 *H. macrophylla* 'Générale Vicomtesse de Vibraye' ♔

Not the easiest name, but an ever-popular and reliable mophead. It is a lovely pale to mid-blue colour in acid soil and a pleasant pale pink elsewhere. It can grow to 2m (6ft 7in) in moist, shady conditions.

2 *H. macrophylla* 'Lanarth White' ♔

This a strong grower, with brilliant white lacecap flowers over many weeks in high summer. White always stands out in a shady site and especially in evening light. On acid soil, the little fertile flowers in the centre are a lovely blue. Grows to 1.5m (5ft).

3 *H. macrophylla* 'Madame Emile Mouillière' ♔

This is a medium-growing white mophead, effective in shade and looking good at dusk. The individual flowers open with a blue eye on acid soils and the whole head assumes interesting green and pink shades as they age in autumn, so it's good for drying.

4 *H. macrophylla* 'Nigra' ♔

This large shrub – 2m (6ft 7in) tall – has pale pink or light blue mophead flowers, but it is the new black stems that are so distinctive, reminding one of black bamboo and suggesting a planting with gold bamboo. Found in China by EH Wilson.

5 *H. macrophylla* 'Schöne Bautznerin' (syn. 'Red Baron')

This sturdy mophead has rich, pink-red flattened mopheads and so is good on alkaline soil. It makes a very good plant for a tub or large pot. It turns bluer given an acid soil. In open ground, it can reach 1.5m (5ft) in height. Other good red mopheads include 'Leuchtfeuer' and 'Masja'.

6 *H. macrophylla* 'Tokyo Delight' ♈

This valuable lacecap form is a strong grower and the flowers go through a beautiful range of colours, opening white and ageing to pink and red. Some years, the autumn colours of the leaves can be spectacular rich red. *H. serrata* 'Grayswood' is similar, as is *H.* 'Preziosa'.

7 *H. paniculata* 'Kyushu' ♈

All forms of *H. paniculata* produce spectacular panicles of creamy-white flowers which age to pink and reddish tones. They can be pruned hard or allowed to grow into large shrubs, to 3m (10ft) tall. This clone has open panicles with fewer petals, which makes them less solid and more lacy.

H. serrata 'Tiara'

H. macrophylla 'Tokyo Delight'

H. paniculata 'Kyushu'

8 *H. quercifolia* ♈

The oak-leaved hydrangea is admired for its distinctive, architectural foliage and is particularly effective for its rich autumn colours. The flowers are in panicles of creamy-white, often held horizontally, and there are several forms including the dwarf 'Pee Wee', double 'Snowflake' and more upright forms. Can reach 2m (6ft 7in) tall, but it's usually less.

9 *H. serrata* 'Tiara' ♈

Serrata only grows up to about 1m (3ft 3in) tall, so is well suited for smaller gardens, front of borders and large pots and tubs. The leaves are smaller and more pointed than *macrophylla* types, and this well-named, very free-flowering variety has delicate pale-blue lacecap flowers, often out by midsummer.

10 *H. anomala* subsp. *petiolaris* ♈

The climbing hydrangea is a very versatile self-clinging climber that's good even on shady north walls, and looks very fine growing up a tree. It is vigorous, growing to 15m (50ft) but is easily cut back. The leaves are heart-shaped and the long-lasting flowers are white lacecaps. The stems grip like ivy.

HYDRANGEAS IN CONTAINERS

We started collecting hydrangeas about five years ago. We realised that they're the ideal summer shrub: long flowering, easy and suitable for any garden, from the smallest patio with tubs, through to the largest woodland gardens. They do well in pots and tubs, especially the compact (*serrata*) varieties. Use a mixture of compost and soil (acid, sandy if you want them blue), and it's well worth adding some water-retaining granules, as sold for hanging baskets. Remember to water and feed them regularly.

H. quercifolia

HYDRANGEA HAVEN (PART OF LODER PLANTS)
Market Garden, Cyder Farm, Lower Beeding, Horsham, West Sussex RH13 6PP
T: 01403 891412 F: 01403 891336
E: plants@rhododendrons.com
W: www.loder-plants.com
Open Monday to Saturday, 10am to 4pm, but call first

Loder Plants is a small, specialist nursery, also growing rhododendrons, azaleas and camellias. Larger specimens and standard-size stock are available. Chris Loder started the nursery in 1989, and it's now run by a team of five part-time enthusiasts, all passionate about plants and gardens. In the heart of the Sussex High Weald, the nursery is a sun trap on a south-facing slope. There is an encyclopaedic, website-illustrated catalogue.

IVIES

AS RECOMMENDED BY ANGELA TANDY OF FIBREX NURSERIES

H. helix 'Manda's Crested'

H. helix 'Ceridwen'

H. helix 'Midas Touch'

H. pastuchovii 'Ann Ala'

Although an ancient plant, ivy – genus *Hedera* – has only been used in the garden since the middle of the 19th century, when the Victorian plant hunters discovered variations in leaf forms and started to grow and name their finds. Classed as a climbing evergreen shrub, ivy is native to Europe, North Africa and Asia. There is a huge range of leaf size, shape and colour, making it possible to find an ivy to suit almost any place in any size of garden. When choosing my top 10, I have tried to pick ivies that will do different jobs in the garden.

1 *H. helix* 'Anita'
This small ivy is one of my favourites, with medium-green, deeply-cut arrowhead-shaped leaves and a compact habit. It is good for ground cover in small areas, and will climb or hang over low walls. It is excellent in a hanging basket or window box and for topiary, and is happy in either sun or shade.

2 *H. helix* 'Ceridwen' ♔
Traditional, medium-sized ivy-shaped leaves with a yellow edge and green and grey-green centre. This ivy is vigorous.

It climbs and will cover a wall or fence. Good as ground cover, it looks pretty in a hanging basket, pot or window box in sun or semi-shade.

3 *H. helix* 'Heise'
Introduced from Denmark in 1965, this ivy has medium-sized, traditional ivy-shaped leaves, with creamy white edges and green and grey-green centres. It is a fairly vigorous and useful climber. Good as ground cover and for hanging baskets, pots or window boxes, it will keep its colour in sun or shade.

4 H. helix 'Ivalace' ♛

Introduced from America in 1955, this ivy has small, square-shaped dark green leaves with a slight crinkle to the edges. A fairly slow grower, it is a well-behaved ivy for ground cover and, as it clips well, very good for topiary. Sun or shade.

5 H. helix 'Light Fingers'

This ivy has slender, yellow arrowhead-shaped leaves. It needs full sun to keep its bright yellow colour, but given semi-shade it fades to an attractive lime green. Not normally grown as a climber, it can be used as ground cover and is good in hanging baskets, pots or window boxes.

6 H. helix 'Manda's Crested' ♛

This medium-sized, medium-green wavy-edged plant is probably one of the best all-round ivies there is. It climbs and covers well, is good as ground cover and produces garland-like trails when used in a basket or window box. It turns copper in the winter and is happy in sun or shade.

7 H. helix 'Midas Touch' ♛

This ivy has medium-sized dark-green heart-shaped leaves, splashed and blotched golden yellow. Whenever we exhibit this ivy everyone loves it. It does not like competition from other plants and is a very slow grower, but well worth the wait. It has a prostrate habit and needs sun.

8 H. helix 'Spetchley' ♛

Probably the smallest-growing ivy there is, with tiny, dark-green, rounded arrowhead-shaped leaves on a densely growing plant. It looks wonderful planted to cover large rocks slowly. Best used as ground cover but it will climb a little. The leaves turn bronze in winter. Happy in sun or shade.

9 H. hibernica 'Rona'

This ivy has medium-to-large-sized leaves, traditionally shaped, marbled, and splashed cream, lime and dark green. It is slow at first, but once established is a bit of a thug. A good climber, it looks great grown as a specimen up a post or tree stump. Needs sun.

10 H. pastuchovii 'Ann Ala'

Collected in the wild by Roy Lancaster, this is a stunning ivy, with dark-green spearhead-shaped leaves, some 15cm (6in) long, which turn purple/black in winter. Best grown as a climber, it needs support on a wall or fence. It does not cling well, but looks good on a stout post.

FIBREX NURSERIES
Honeybourne Road, Pebworth,
Stratford-upon-Avon, Warks CV37 8XP
T: 01789 720788 F: 01789 721162
E: sales@fibrex.co.uk
W: www.fibrex.co.uk

✿   NCCPG National Collection holder of *Pelargoniums* and *Hedera*
Fibrex Nurseries was established in 1960 as a pelargonium nursery by Hazel and Dick Key. Now run by three of their children, it houses the National Collections of Pelargoniums and *Hedera*. Open Monday to Friday, 9am to 5pm (Sat and Sun, 10.30am to 4pm), March to July; Monday to Friday, 9am to 4pm, August to February. Call for details of holiday closures.

JAPANESE MAPLES

AS RECOMMENDED BY JUNKER'S NURSERY LIMITED

A. palmatum 'Autumn Showers'

A. palmatum 'Edna Bergman'

Japanese maples belong to the genus *Acer* and are a versatile and diverse group. Some will grow into wonderful long-lived specimens for the woodland, open garden or border, while others are perfect for pots on the patio. All develop fiery autumn tints, but some have brightly coloured spring growth or pretty summer foliage as well. Leaf shape varies from solid and fan-shaped to deeply dissected, while others have finger-like narrow lobes. In winter, their naked structure can be a feature in itself.

1 *A. japonicum* 'Green Cascade'
Its tremendously weeping habit results in a low, almost carpeting plant, unless a young shoot is trained up to form a leader, thus achieving a tumbling curtain of deeply incised, rich-green leaves. Autumn leaves pass through a kaleidoscopic display of all the bonfire colours. Height 3m (10ft).

2 *A. palmatum* 'Autumn Showers'
The deeply-lobed leaves are green in spring and summer, but the plant comes alive in autumn with some of the most spectacular colours of all Acers. It forms a graceful tree of 4m (13ft) in height and almost as wide.

3 *A. palmatum* 'Chitos-yama' 🏆
This old cultivar has softer, subtle tones. The deeply divided leaves unfurl pale crimson and open to a rich, deep purple. This fades to bronze-green in summer before erupting into crimson autumn colour. Arching in habit, it forms a broad shrub 3m (10ft) tall and wide.

4 *A. palmatum* 'Edna Bergman'
Similar to the well-known *A. palmatum* 'Osakazuki', this has a more upright habit, but similarly large, comparatively simple leaves, emerging rusty red before becoming rich green. 'Edna Bergman' turns to vibrant red almost as you watch. Height 6m (20ft).

5 A. *palmatum* 'Komon-nishiki'

The variegated cultivars give interest all summer. In spring, the fundamentally green new leaves are suffused with rose-pink, becoming variegated as they expand. Tiny, creamy-white markings speckle the leaves. The bright orange and crimson autumn colours are outstanding. It can mature to 3m (10ft) and is suited to pot culture.

6 A. *palmatum* 'Mapi-nomachihime'

With a rounded, dense habit, growing to only 2m (7ft) high, this lends itself to shaping into a miniature tree. Although essentially green in summer, the young growth opens chartreuse, edged with vibrant pinky-orange. Later in summer, it is highlighted against green mature foliage. Orange-red autumn colours complete the display.

7 A. *palmatum* 'Orangeola'

'Orangeola' shares the typical, deeply dissected ferny foliage of the Dissectum Group, but its habit and colouring are unique. Spring new growth is bright orange-red, maturing in summer to rich, reddish green. In autumn the process is reversed, with the leaves turning dark red and then orange-red. 'Orangeola' is particularly pendulous. Height 6m (20ft).

> **CULTIVATION**
>
> Japanese maples dislike extremes: excessive winter wet or summer drought. Therefore, a constant moisture level is the key. Plant in early autumn or late spring when the roots are active.

8 A. *palmatum* 'Tsuma-gaki'

Attracts attention in spring as new growth unfurls. Young leaves are acid green, with bright red tips to each lobe, toning down to a soft green as summer progresses. Autumn colours are crimsons and reds. Finally forms a shrubby plant; up to 3m (10ft) tall and wide.

9 A. *palmatum* 'Villa Taranto'

Deeply divided leaves with narrow lobes give a finger-like appearance. The leaves emerge crimson before turning green with reddish overtones. Autumn colours are yellows and golds. Can eventually grow to 3m (10ft) tall.

10 A. *shirasawanum* 'Autumn Moon'

Vibrant young growth includes shades of pinkish orange, before maturing to gold or yellow-green where shaded. Autumn colours are rich oranges and reds. Leaves are typically shaped, being almost circular in outline, with 11 short, pointed lobes. Height 10m (33ft).

JUNKER'S NURSERY LIMITED
Lower Mead, West Hatch, Taunton, Somerset TA3 5RN
T: 01823 480774
E: karan@junker.co.uk
W: www.junker.co.uk

We bought our current site in 1986, developing it from a green field, and gradually collected new and exciting plants. We do not buy-in plants to resell; we propagate everything ourselves from our own stock plants. We are a small, family-run unit, specialising in more interesting plants, most of which are woody; in addition to the maples, we have extensive collections of *Epimedium*, magnolia, *Daphne*, *Cornus*, *Hamamelis*, *Liquidambar* and *Viburnum* to name but a few. Visits are by appointment only.

LAVENDERS

AS RECOMMENDED BY SIMON CHARLESWORTH OF DOWNDERRY NURSERY

L. augustifolia 'Rosea'

L. augustifolia 'Beechwood Blue'

L. canariensis

L. x intermedia 'Edelweiss'

I have chosen these lavenders – genus *Lavandula* – for their broad appeal and versatility, and because I have found them to be among the easiest to grow and best loved. The *Angustifolia* and x *intermedia* cultivars are perfect for hedging and make great specimen plants.

The three prerequisites for successful lavender growing are loads of sun, well-drained poor soil and a jolly good prune at the right time! Pruning requires a strong constitution, so be bold to reap great rewards the following year. As soon as flowers fade, prune lavenders hard to small side shoots to encourage strong re-growth, thus ensuring plants can cope with adverse winter conditions.

1 *L. angustifolia* 'Ashdown Forest'

A marvellous, very bushy pale purple highly scented lavender, ideal for a low hedge, looking great in the green and exceptional in flower. 'Ashdown Forest' flowers through June and July. Clip to shape immediately after flowering. A robust lavender that can withstand all but the wettest soil conditions, it can grow to a height of 50cm (20in).

L. angustifolia 'Ashdown Forest'

2 *L. angustifolia* 'Beechwood Blue' 🏆

A lavender with colour to die for! The rich purple-blue flowers with their sweet scent rise above grey-green foliage during June and July and can reach a height of 60cm (24in). One of the earliest introductions, from around the 1920s, but little known. The colour is richer and less vulgar than 'Hidcote'.

3 *L. angustifolia* 'Betty's Blue'

A stunning, vibrant purple lavender with very uniform flowering and stiff erect stems through June and July that won't splay. The flowers have a soft, sweet scent. The stout stems make 'Betty's Blue' a great lavender for drying. The plant reaches about 60cm (24in).

4 *L. canariensis*

A breathtakingly beautiful lavender from Tenerife. The intense violet-blue flowers rising on long stalks above vibrant fresh green foliage are an astonishing sight

L. angustifolia 'Betty's Blue'

in summer. Can add a delicate touch to the border or pot. Well worth growing from seed, which germinates wherever it falls and the plant grows to 60cm (24in) in one season. Treat it like an annual.

5 *L. angustifolia* 'Rosea'

The brilliant green foliage in spring makes this sweetly fragranced pale-pink lavender distinctive. Growth is very dense, allowing hard pruning to easily maintain a height of 60cm (24in). 'Rosea' flowers in June and July and is a superb lavender to provide contrast with

L angustifolia .'Nana Alba'

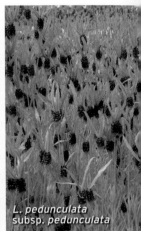

L. pedunculata
subsp. *pedunculata*

L. angustifolia
'Melissa Lilac'

purple lavenders or to cool down a border
in midsummer.

6 *L.* x *intermedia* 'Edelweiss'

A splendid fan-shaped bush forming a
perfect dome of strongly fragrant white
flowers rising above green-grey foliage,
'Edelweiss' makes a stunning specimen
feature, achieving a height of 75cm (30in).
This cultivar also perfectly partners purple
late-flowering lavenders like 'Grosso'.

7 *L. angustifolia* 'Nana Alba' ♔

A wonderful little strongly scented
white-flowered lavender with green-grey
foliage. It's the perfect lavender for edging
a border, growing to a height of 40cm
(16in). As with other *angustifolia*
lavenders, 'Nana Alba' flowers through
June and July and looks brilliant with the
pink and dark purple lavenders to add
contrast and interest.

8 *L. angustifolia* 'Melissa Lilac'

A real marshmallow of a lavender, with
beautiful furry buds and powder-purple,
mildly scented flowers. So mouthwatering
you feel you could eat it – so sumptuous
you feel you could sleep on it! The flowers
are beautifully displayed above the broad
grey-green foliage during June and July,
and can grow to a height of 60cm (24in).

9 *L.* x *intermedia* 'Grosso'

An amazingly blue-purple flowering

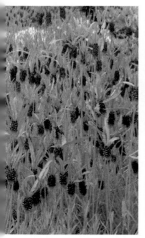

L. x intermedia 'Grosso'

lavender, which flowers profusely during July and August. This is the most widely grown lavender for oil in the world. This is because 'Grosso' is a very aromatic lavender. It also has large conical flowers and grey-green foliage, growing to 75cm (30in).

10 *L. pedunculata* subsp. *pedunculata* ♉

Often called 'butterfly lavender', this Spanish lavender is a graceful, upright plant. The long flower stalks (peduncles) are topped with purple flowers and long magenta 'ears' that look magical when fluttering in an early summer breeze. The flowers appear from late May to mid-June, above narrow pale green foliage reaching a height of 75cm (30in). You can encourage repeat flowering in the high summer by halving the height after the first flowering. This lavender requires very well-drained soil throughout the winter months.

DOWNDERRY NURSERY
Pillar Box Lane, Hadlow,
Tonbridge, Kent TN11 9SW
T: 01732 810081 F: 01732 811398
E: orders@downderry-nursery.co.uk
W: www.downderry-nursery.co.uk
Open May to Oct, Tue to Sun (and Bank
Holiday Mondays), 10am to 5pm

❀   NCCPG National Collection holder of *Lavendula* and *Rosmarinus*
Simon Charlesworth started **Downderry Nursery** in 1991. His collection of lavender was given National Plant Collection status in 1996. The nursery moved to a walled garden in Hadlow in 1997 and has risen to become the country's premier lavender nursery, offering unrivalled choice and expertise. Downderry has achieved several Gold Medals at both the RHS Chelsea and Hampton Court Palace Flower Shows, including Best Exhibit and Most Creative Exhibit in the Floral Marquee in 2005.

LILACS

AS RECOMMENDED BY GORDON LINK OF THE GOBBETT NURSERY

S. vulgaris 'Krasivitsa Moskvy'

Lilacs or *Syringa* are a group of hardy, deciduous trees and shrubs grown for their tiny, fragrant flowers, which scent the air of streets and gardens in late spring and early summer. The flowers, borne in profusion in graceful panicles, are used extensively for cutting. They come in a range of colours, from lilac itself to claret, red, pink, white and even pale yellow. There are tree lilacs, which are ideal for the back of the border, smaller-growing varieties for small gardens and dwarf varieties suitable for containers.

1 *S. vulgaris* 'Krasivitsa Moskvy' (syn. Beauty of Moscow)

Beautiful double white flowers follow lavender-rose-tinted buds. It is absolutely stunning when half the florets are open and the rest are still showing rose-pink buds. This is often regarded as the best lilac ever produced. Very fragrant.

2 *S. vulgaris* 'Katherine Havermeyer' ♔

I chose 'Katherine Havermeyer' because of its enormous panicles of double lilac-pink flowers and the exquisite scent that it produces. It is extremely fragrant and has proved to be a consistently reliable flowerer.

S. x *josiflexa* 'Bellicent'

S. *vulgaris* 'Katherine Havermeyer'

S. x *hyacinthiflora* 'Esther Staley'

S. vulgaris 'Lee Jewett Walker'

CULTIVATION

Of the 20 or so species of lilac, the most widely grown are the varieties of *S. vulgaris* (common lilac), of which there are hundreds, if not thousands. Lilacs are an easy-to-grow shrub. All they need is a soil that is reasonably well drained and a spot that gets at least four hours of sun a day. On acidic soil they do appreciate a handful of lime at planting time. Pruning should be done just after flowering, when about one third of the shoots should be cut back hard every year.

3 *S. vulgaris* 'Lee Jewett Walker'
Very beautiful single pale pink fragrant flowers – absolutely stunning. This lilac is a personal favourite of mine.

4 *S. vulgaris* 'Sensation'
I just had to pick this one, as no other variety is anything like it. It has single purple flowers with white edges to the petals, and is highly scented.

5 *S.* Josée
Single pale pink flowers cover this dwarf lilac that only grows to about 1.2-1.5m

S. vulgaris 'Sensation'

(4-5ft). It grows well and if deadheaded after flowering, will often bloom again.

6 S. x *hyacinthiflora* 'Esther Staley' 🏆

This beautiful hybrid flowers just before the *vulgaris* varieties. It is a vigorous plant with gorgeous red buds, which open into single, bright pink flowers. It is a very heavy bloomer with a lovely, very sweet fragrance.

7 S. *vulgaris* 'Primrose'

A bushy, upright plant, with heart-shaped green leaves. Yellow buds open to single white flowers with a hint of yellow. The only lilac with yellow in the flower. At 3.5m (11ft), it doesn't grow as big as most *vulgaris* varieties.

8 S. *vulgaris* 'Président Grévy'

An upright shrub, spreading with age. Gorgeous double lilac-blue flowers in immense open pyramidal panicles in mid to late spring. Grows to 4m (13ft). Very fragrant, easy to grow and a reliable flowerer.

9 S. x *josiflexa* 'Bellicent' 🏆

A beautiful hybrid between S. *josikaea* and S. *villosa* that produces huge panicles of clear rose-pink flowers. An elegant shrub of about 2.5m (8ft). Flowers just after the *vulgaris* varieties. Very hardy and a reliable flowerer, this was the first lilac I ever planted, and started me collecting lilacs.

10 S. 'Red Pixie'

Red buds open to light pink flowers on this newly introduced dwarf lilac. A really nice variety, with a deeper bud colour than most dwarf cultivars. 'Red Pixie' grows 1.2-1.5m (4-5ft) high and about 1.2m (4ft) wide. It is intensely fragrant.

S. vulgaris 'Primrose'

THE GOBBETT NURSERY
Farlow, nr Kidderminster, Worcestershire DY14 8TD
T/F: 01746 718647
E: christine.link@lineone.net
W: www.thegobbettnursery.co.uk
Open Monday to Saturday, 10.30am to 5pm

The Gobbett Nursery has specialised in lilacs for around 10 years. Gordon and Chris Link have a collection of about 120 varieties, but not all of them are available at any one time. They also grow a wide range of other shrubs and climbers at their nursery in the hills of south Shropshire. An up-to-date list can be found on their website.

MAGNOLIAS

AS RECOMMENDED BY BURNCOOSE NURSERIES

M. stellata

What other group of trees and shrubs produces such an abundance of flower before the leaves appear? Magnolias – genus *Magnolia* – are truly spectacular plants, many of which are very easy to grow, even in the smaller garden. As such, they are deservedly growing in popularity. The Burncoose Nurseries' recommended list is based on our experience, gained over many years, of growing over 150 different individual varieties of magnolia. It's also based on the practical knowledge gained from our sister gardens at Caerhays Castle, who are holders of the NCCPG National Collection of Magnolia.

M. 'Caerhays Surprise'

1 M. 'Caerhays Surprise'

An exceptional magnolia for the smaller garden. Unlike many grafted magnolias, it flowers within only two to three years. The buds are a bright violet-red, opening and fading to pinkish lavender. The flowers normally appear in late April to early May and the tree grows eventually to about 3-6m (10-20ft).

2 M. stellata ♔

A small shrub magnolia that everyone can grow in a container or the smallest garden. It has a dense, compact habit and is slow-growing, but white flowers profusely at an early age. The flowers appear in early March. The plant is wind-tolerant and copes with shade or sun. Grows to 2m (6ft) tall.

3 M. 'Summer Solstice'

A stunning new magnolia – one for the specialist magnolia grower rather than the general enthusiast. It flowers in late May

M. 'Summer Solstice'

to June, with lightbulb-shaped flowers which open individually rather than all at once. The sensational, highly-scented flowers open as a delicate pink and fade eventually to creamy white.

4 M. x soulangeana 'Lennei' ♔

'Lennei' grows quickly into a multi-stemmed shrub or small tree, whose branches touch the ground at maturity. The tulip-shaped, strongly-scented flowers are magenta-purple outside, white inside and appear in profusion in late April to May. Grows in clay soils or even poor shallow soils in chalky areas. Height reaches 6m (20ft).

5 M. grandiflora 'Exmouth' ⚱

For foliage texture alone, this ornamental, evergreen magnolia is a real winner. Its fleshy, creamy flowers are also very fragrant. 'Exmouth' is commonly grown against a wall or on the front of a house, where its strong scent and polished leaves, with their reddish-felted undersides, can be fully appreciated. Grows to 10m (33ft) tall.

6 M. x loebneri 'Leonard Messel' ⚱

The flowers are dark pink in bud, opening to a gentle, attractive pale lilac-pink. It grows into a magnificent small tree which can be quite breathtaking in full flower. This plant is very easy to grow, grows quickly and will tolerate most soil types, apart from chalk. Reaches a height of 8m (26ft).

7 M. wilsonii ⚱

This species forms a large, spreading multi-stemmed shrub and comes into flower in late May to June. The flowers are circular and pendulous, with clear white petals and vivid

M. 'Star Wars'

M. x loebneri 'Leonard Messel'

M. 'Elizabeth'

M. wilsonii

M. cylindrica

red or magenta stamens. Grow in partial shade or on a bank so you can admire the flowers from below. Grows to 7m (23ft).

8 M. 'Elizabeth' ♛

'Elizabeth' is the first good, widely available pale yellow magnolia. It has fragrant, uniformly yellow flowers and rose-coloured stamens. Its new leaves, which often emerge before the flowers are fully over, are a gentle copper colour at first, turning dark green later. Height reaches 5m (16ft).

9 M. cylindrica

This is a large shrub or small tree which is easy to grow and requires little space. Its flowers are white with a hint of red or pink at the base. They appear March to April and are followed by cylindrical fruits from which the plant takes its name. Grows to 5m (16ft).

10 M. 'Star Wars' ♛

This flowers not once, but twice a year. In early spring, before the leaf emerges, large, bright pink flowers are produced abundantly from an early age. Again in August or September, this small tree produces slightly smaller and darker purple-pink flowers amid its leaves. Grows to 5m (16ft).

TREE PEONIES

AS RECOMMENDED BY DAVE ROOT OF KELWAYS PLANT CENTRE

P. 'Black Pirate'

P. rockii

Tree peonies – part of the genus *Paeonia* – are the most outrageously flamboyant spring-flowering shrubs that can be grown outside in all parts of the UK. They flower during April and May with individual blooms up to 30cm (12in) in diameter, in every shade from the deepest crimsons and purples through all shades of pink, orange and yellow, to white. They form stout shrubs with architectural foliage which emerges red before turning green, then back to fiery red again for an autumn finale. They make wonderful specimen plants for even the smallest garden and are among my favourite plants.

1 P. 'High Noon'

One of the best garden cultivars with medium-sized, strongly scented blooms up to 12cm (5in) across in rich lemon-yellow with deep raspberry flares in the centre of each petal. It forms an attractive, dense bush up to 1.2m (4ft) height and spread.

2 P. *suffruticosa* 'Yachiyo-tsubaki' (syn. Eternal Camellias)

Worth growing for its foliage alone: the leaves retain their silvery-purple colouration alongside bright red stems until leaf fall. The flowers are freely produced even on young plants and are an almost iridescent coral pink.

3 P. 'Oriental Gold'

An 'intersectional' hybrid, showing the best qualities of herbaceous and tree peonies. Early June flowering, it forms a medium-sized shrub up to 80cm (31in) in height, with a mound of rich, broad leaves upon which apricot-yellow blooms rest.

4 P. *suffruticosa* 'Shimane-hakugan'

A true horticultural diva. Not the most free-flowering peony, even a little temperamental, needing encouragement to produce a multi-stemmed bush. However, it's worth it for the sight of the flowers, which are of singular beauty; purest milky-white, with a bright red cherry- like carpel in the centre of the petals.

5 P. *suffruticosa* 'Renkaku' (syn. Flight of Cranes)

One of the earliest to flower, with immense white blooms with two rows of petals, each one with a slightly fimbriated edge, that tremble in the slightest breeze. A really free-flowering and easily-grown tree peony.

6 P. 'Mikuhino Akebono'

One of the most unusual and beautiful cultivars. It has large, white blooms with each petal deeply shredded (although sometimes, confusingly, it produces normal flowers). Grows vigorously to form a large shrub 1.5m (5ft) high.

7 P. rockii

The most famous peony and one of the most desirable woody plants, *P. rockii* is a large

shrub 2m (6ft 6in) tall with small palmate leaves. The flowers are medium-sized, white with a blotch of deepest maroon-purple, and an intoxicating scent. Variable, so always see the plant in bloom before you buy.

8 P. 'Black Pirate'

The darkest red of all flowers, this is a much-improved hybrid derived from *P. delavayi*. Medium-sized blooms are held like small trumpets, opening wider as the day progresses then closing at night. Give it a really rich soil.

9 P. suffruticosa 'Cardinal Vaughan'

One of the earliest-flowering tree peonies. Semi-double blooms of deep episcopal-purple, a colour which appears rarely in such a rich form. The colour slowly turns more maroon as the flower ages. This most captivating tree peony is always reliable.

10 P. suffruticosa 'Shimanishiki'

Chimera variegation in flowers happens only occasionally, and this unique peony is always a talking point. Individual blooms might be scarlet, white or a mixture of the two. 'Shimane Nishiki' forms a well-rounded shrub with purplish foliage. Not readily offered, so snap it up if you see it.

CULTIVATION

Tree peonies will survive almost anywhere but are happiest with some shade and rich, well-drained soil. They relish chalk but do not grow well in very acidic conditions. Plant in the autumn for best results. They are usually grafted, so plant with the graft level around 10cm (4in) below the soil level for a strong plant. Feed with a general fertilizer in spring, then again in autumn with a high potash feed such as bonemeal. Prune very hard if necessary to encourage multiple stems. Cut off any stems that suddenly wilt from *Botrytis* in the spring.

KELWAYS PLANT CENTRE
Langport, Somerset TA10 9EZ
T: 01458 250521 F: 01458 253351
E: sales@kelways.co.uk
W: www.kelways.co.uk

✿ NCCPG National Collection holder of *Paeonia lactiflora* (pre-1940s cultivars)
Founded in 1851 by James Kelway, this is one of the oldest nursery businesses in the world. Peonies have been a dominant crop for over 130 years. Based in the Somerset levels, the nursery excels in the production of many other plants too, including irises. The plant centre holds many unusual plants including a wide range of traditional roses. Kelways is famous for its floral displays at the Chelsea Flower Show and sends its peonies throughout the world. Open 9am to 5pm Monday to Saturday, 10am to 4pm Sunday and Bank Holidays.

PALMS

AS RECOMMENDED BY THE PALM CENTRE

Chamaerops humilis

Palms have come to symbolise the tropics and the Mediterranean, and inspire memories of hot summer holidays in the sun. More and more people are discovering how palms' architectural forms of palms can make an exotic difference to even the smallest garden. From an arid garden which needs the bare minimum of watering, to the exotic jungle look, palms provide the essential ingredient.

1 *Trachycarpus fortunei* ♔
The Chusan palm, which has been popular since Victorian times, is most gardeners' first palm. It is a solitary-trunked species with a crown of dark green, fan-shaped leaves, 1m (3ft 3in) or more in diameter. Happy in full sun or half shade, it is very cold-tolerant, and ultimately grows to 6-10m (20-33ft) or more. H3-4

2 *Trachycarpus wagnerianus*
The miniature Chusan palm or waggy is a distinctive species with small, stiff leaflets, and is considerably more wind-tolerant than the Chusan palm. It is ideal for the smaller, or windier garden. Perfect for the lawn or flower bed, it's just as hardy as its bigger cousin. Reaches a height of 6-8m (20-26ft). H3

3 *Chamaerops humilis* ♔
The Mediterranean fan palm is an attractive, small palm. It's relatively low-growing and extremely drought-tolerant. *C. humilis* needs virtually no care once established. There are several forms with different leaf sizes or colours. Reaches a height of approximately 2m (6ft 7in). H3

4 *Chamaerops humilis* var. *argentea*
A gem from the High Atlas Mountains of Morocco, the blue Mediterranean fan palm can tolerate extreme temperatures.

It develops silver-blue leaves as a defence against the intense light of its habitat. Easy to care for and grown in most garden soils, requiring no watering once established. Grows slowly to 1.8m (6ft). H3

5 *Phoenix canariensis* 🏆

Popular as a houseplant for decades, the Canary Island date palm is recently being discovered as an outdoor subject, too. It ultimately grows to a large tree, 6m (20ft) tall or more, so allow plenty of space if planting out. Full sun and deep, rich soil suit it best. Inexpensive to buy. H1

6 *Butia capitata*

The jelly or butia palm is an attractive, stout-trunked palm with grey-green feather-shaped leaves which are strongly recurved, giving it a distinctive appearance. Very hardy to both cold and drought, it's an excellent choice for the exotic garden where it will grow slowly, to about 6m (20ft). H1

7 *Brahea armata*

The stunning Mexican blue fan palm has big, ice-blue, fan-shaped leaves. It requires a warm and dry spot, ideally in a south-facing position. It's extremely hardy and tolerates several degrees of frost when mature. It's a real *prima donna*, however, and will not like any competition! It grows to 3m (10ft) or more, but slowly. H1

8 *Jubaea chilensis*

This monster grows a trunk which can be 92cm (36in) or more in diameter, supporting a crown of dark green, feather-shaped leaves. If nothing else, the Chilean wine palm will certainly be a talking point with the neighbours! Deep, rich soil will get it off to a good start, but position with care. Grows to 10m (33ft) tall. H3

9 *Chamaedorea radicalis*

The hardy chamaedorea palm is happy in deep shade and will grow slowly into an attractive multi-trunked specimen. When mature it produces clusters of bright red fruits. Moist and rich soil suit it best, and it will tolerate temperatures as cold as -8°C. Grows to 2-3m (6ft 7in-10ft). H3

10 *Trithrinax campestris*

The striking South American caranday palm has silvery-blue fan leaves that are as stiff as metal. It can also can withstand severe frosts and drought once established. Not cheap but a focal point in the exotic garden. Grows to 3-4m (10-13ft). H3

RHODODENDRONS AND AZALEAS

AS RECOMMENDED BY DAVID MILLAIS OF MILLAIS NURSERIES

R. 'Fantastica'

R. augustinii

Rhododendrons – genus *Rhododendron* – range from dwarf plants through evergreen and deciduous azaleas, to towering species such as *R. sinogrande*, with its 75cm (30in) leaves. The season starts with winter-flowering varieties in January and finishes with summer-flowering plants during July and August. While most varieties will grow in sun or shade, dappled shade will suit best. Hardy hybrid rhododendrons make ideal screening plants. With their downward-pointing large leaves and dense habit, they are one of the most effective sound barriers and give a wonderful display of flowers in the spring.

1 *R. augustinii*

One of the smaller-leaved rhododendrons, its flowers can range from lavender to deep violet-blue. The clone *R. augustinii* 'Electra' is the bluest of all, but not the hardiest, and needs extra protection from cold winters when young. Grows to 1.5m (5ft) in 10 years.

2 *R.* 'Fantastica' ♛

Deep red in bud, this opens deep pink with red edging, which fades to pale pink during late May. The flowers are set off by the dark green foliage. Ideal for containers or small gardens, it will form a dome-shaped plant about 1m (3ft 3in) high after 10 years. H4

3 *R.* 'High Summer'

This was raised by my father, Ted Millais. It flowers in June when most other varieties have either finished or are white in colour. It is a good creamy-yellow, set off by pale green, new foliage. Grows to 1.8m (6ft) in 10 years.

4 *R.* 'Kermesinum Rosé'

This evergreen azalea features rose-pink flowers with a white picotee edge. Although the flowers are small, there are so many of them that they completely hide the leaves during May. It grows to around 50-60cm (20-24in) in 10 years.

5 R. 'Lem's Monarch' ♔

Some plants are so spectacular that everyone who sees them has to have one. This outstanding plant was raised by breeder Halfdan Lem. The flower buds are red, opening to huge pink trusses with red edging, fading to pale pink. Height reaches 1.5-1.8m (5-6ft) in 10 years. Just stunning! H4

6 R. *maccabeanum* ♔

One of the largest-growing rhododendrons, the shiny leaves can be up to 35cm (14in) long with whitish, woolly indumentum on the underside. It has trusses of yellow flowers in March and April and is a choice architectural plant for the woodland garden. H3-4

7 R. 'Narcissiflorum' ♔

Deciduous azaleas give the most vibrant colours. The dainty double flowers are pale yellow, but darker in the centre and on the outside. A real favourite, due to its sweet-scented flowers and its good autumn-foliage colour. Reaches 1.5-1.8m (5-6ft). H4

8 R. *pachysanthum* ♔

This is a first-class foliage plant with pinky-white flowers in May. The leaves have a silvery indumentum which matures to a rusty brown on the lower surface. It forms a dense, compact plant, around 1m (3ft 3in) in 10 years. Millais Nurseries' clone, 'Crosswater', is particularly fine. H4

9 R. 'Wee Bee' ♔

This must be the best deep-pink dwarf rhododendron. It's almost red in bud, opening deep pink during April, fading paler with a slight creamy centre. It forms a neat mound, about 30cm (12in) high, after 10 years. 'Ginny Gee' (pale pink) and 'Patty Bee' (yellow) are also recommended. H4

10 R. *yakushimanum* 'Koichiro Wada' ♔

If you only grow one rhododendron, make it this. Deep pink in bud, the flowers open pale pink, fading to white during mid-May. The shrub reaches a height of only 60cm. H4

CULTIVATION

Rhododendrons are shallow-rooting, and should not be planted deeper than the top of the pot or root ball. Plant in autumn to aid establishment before flowering and growth, but water well for the first two seasons or more.

MILLAIS NURSERIES
Crosswater Farm, Crosswater Lane, Churt, Farnham, Surrey GU10 2JN
T: 01252 792698 F: 01252 792526
E: sales@rhododendrons.co.uk
W: www.rhododendrons.co.uk
Hours: Monday to Friday, 10am to 1pm, 2pm to 5pm; Saturdays, late Feb to June and mid Sept to Oct; Sundays, late April to early June

Millais Nurseries is one of the country's leading rhododendron specialists, growing one of the largest ranges available. It won the RHS Rothschild Cup for the best display of rhododendrons at Chelsea for 2005 and 2006. The business, started by Ted and Romy Millais, is now run by their son David. Many new species and hybrids raised by Ted can be seen flowering in the woodland gardens at Crosswater Farm, open daily in the spring.

RHODODENDRONS AND AZALEAS

SCENTED TYPES AS RECOMMENDED BY KENNETH COX OF GLENDOICK GARDENS AND GARDEN CENTRE

R. luteum

R. decorum

This huge group of spring-flowering plants is very popular all over the UK, except in areas with alkaline soil. Many of them have scented flowers, especially in varieties with paler flowers: white, pink and yellow. The hardiest scented varieties are the deciduous azaleas, and the species and hybrids of subsection *fortunea*. These are hardy enough for anywhere in the UK. If you garden in a relatively mild climate – western Britain and most of Ireland – you can grow the many scented *maddenia* and *edgeworthia* species and hybrids outdoors.

FORTUNEA SPECIES

Every garden with space or shelter should have one of these medium to large shrubs or small trees, from 2-3m (6ft 7in-10ft) to 6m (20ft), in height.

1 *R. decorum* ♀

This rhododendron has white to pale pink scented flowers in May and June. It is a beautiful and vigorous, easy species, and adaptable to dry sites and neutral soil. H4.

2 Loderi Group ♀

One of the finest hybrids ever raised. The huge, pale pink, cream or white flowers have a magnificent, sweet scent. It grows large, forming a tree, and is best in light shade in southern areas. H4

DECIDUOUS AZALEAS

These are very tough and tolerant of exposure and are useful for their relatively late flowers (June-July). They reach 1-2m (3ft 3in-6ft 7in) or more after 10-20 years. All H4

1 *R. arborescens*

The sweet azalea is the best of the white, scented species for Scotland and cool climates. It has attractive, tubular, white or pale pink flowers, sometimes with a yellow flare with contrasting purplish red styles.

2 *R. luteum* ♀

A spreading and vigorous, deciduous azalea with fine autumn leaf colour. The flowers are funnel-shaped, yellow and sweetly fragrant, held in a trusses of 7-17. It is easily grown and is good for naturalising in British gardens.

3 R. 'Fragrant Star'

This is a Franken rhododendron, created in a test tube, a tetraploid version of the natural hybrid 'Snowbird'. 'Fragrant star' has thicker leaves and a more upright and rigid habit. Slow growing, it has small, very sweetly scented white flowers, maybe the strongest scent of all rhododendrons.

MADDENIA AND EDGEWORTHIA SPECIES

These are superb garden plants for mild gardens or for cool greenhouses and conservatories elsewhere. Most are epiphytic (growing on logs, other plants and on cliffs), so they need a coarse growing medium and sharp drainage; they do well in raised beds, old tree stumps or mossy logs in wet areas. In pots allow them to become a little pot-bound. They can be hard pruned after flowering to improve habit.

1 R. edgeworthii 🏆

One of our favourite rhododendrons with large white, pink-flushed flowers in May and attractive, dark rugose foliage with indumentum. It is a very popular scented species that is reasonably hardy in a raised bed. 1.2m (4ft) tall. H3

2 R. lindleyi

An outstanding plant with large white, lily-like flowers in May. It is hardy at Glendoick except during severe winters. Requires good drainage. It grows to a height of 2m (6ft 7in). H2-3

3 R. maddenii subsp. crassum

The strongly scented white flowers in June are often striped and flushed pink and yellow. It is well worth trying in good microclimates, and it is best in some shade. It grows to 2m (6ft 7in) tall. H2-3

4 R. 'Lady Alice Fitzwilliam'

With scented white flowers in April and May, it is similar to the well-known 'Fragrantissimum', but is more compact. Hardy outdoors on a sheltered wall at Glendoick, it should be fine in similar climates and good in a greenhouse or conservatory. It grows to 1.5m (5ft). H2-3

5 R. 'Tinkerbird'

This breakthrough plant is a compact, scented dwarf that grows outdoors at Glendoick and should be hardy enough to grow outdoors in all but the coldest inland gardens, with a little shelter. It bears masses of scented, creamy flowers in early May and will make a fine pot plant – much more compact than most hybrids of this type. To 75cm (30in). H3-4

GLENDOICK GARDENS LTD AND GLENDOICK GARDEN CENTRE
Glencarse, Perth PH2 7NS
T: 01738 860205 F: 01738 860630
E: orders@glendoick.com

The Cox family is Scotland's rhododendron and plant-hunting dynasty. Euan Cox accompanied Reginald Farrer to Burma in 1919 and founded the gardens at Glendoick in the 1920s. Euan and his son, Peter Cox VMH, started the mail order nursery. The Coxes have discovered and introduced many plants from the wild and bred a very successful range of rhododendron and azalea hybrids. Garden Centre opens 9am to 5.30pm Monday to Sunday (summer), 9am to 5pm Monday to Saturday, 10am to 5pm Sunday (winter). Nursery and gardens by appointment.

ROSES – DISEASE-RESISTANT

AS RECOMMENDED BY MATTOCKS ROSES

R. Temptress

The rose – genus *Rosa* – is the quintessential part of the 'chocolate box' garden and is still much-loved by most gardeners. Feed your roses in the spring and again after the first flush of flowers, to keep them performing at their best. They always enjoy a good helping of organic matter too, which keeps a good level of soil organisms to help absorb minerals and nutrients better. Pruning regimes will depend on the type of rose you have, so always refer to a good book for specific guidance.

1 *R.* Temptress
Fantastic foliage that starts red and finishes a dark glossy green. It is a repeat-flowering climber that produces deep red flowers and has exceptional disease-resistance.

2 *R.* Royal William ♔
One of the finest dark red hybrid tea roses available. A previous Rose of the Year winner, this variety has strong, healthy stems to support the fragrant flowers, which is unusual with roses of this colour.

3 *R.* Lancashire ♔
Winner of many awards, this ground cover variety produces masses of cherry red blooms in large clusters and repeats over a very long period.

R. Lancashire

4 R. Champagne Moments
This variety was a very recent Rose of the Year and deservedly so, with the awards it has picked up. It produces clusters of large scented apricot to cream flowers over a long period above very glossy foliage.

5 R. Gertrude Jekyll ♈
This shrub rose produces deep pink, exceptionally fragrant blooms that can be smelt from quite a distance. It is an excellent variety for the middle to back of a border in the garden.

6 R. Summer Beauty ♈
This floribunda rose produces medium-sized apricot blooms on reasonably compact stems, covered by deep glossy green foliage.

7 R. 'Arthur Bell' ♈
This must be one of the finest yellow floribundas available. Arthur Bell produces

R. Red Finesse

R. Summer Beauty

bright golden flowers with a good fragrance and quite dark green foliage.

8 R. 'Compassion' 🏆

This climbing rose produces large orange-salmon fragrant flowers. It is also a repeat-flowering variety.

9 R. Red Finesse

This floribunda variety is one of our highest awarded roses, picking up 12 international awards in just a few years. It produces clusters of crimson red blooms throughout the whole summer.

10 R. Sunrise

This is a very colourful and 'happy' looking climber variety. This rose produces orange blooms with slightly deeper copper red shadings. It appears slightly ruffled and looks great against walls and over arches. It is a repeat flowering variety and has attractive foliage.

MATTOCKS ROSES
c/o Notcutts Nurseries, Woodbridge, Suffolk IP12 4AF
E: webenquiry@notcutts.co.uk
W: www.mattocks.co.uk

Established in 1875, **Mattocks** have earned a reputation over the years for introducing novel disease-resistant rose varieties. **Mattocks** provide roses in a good range of colours, selected for their health, fragrance and outstanding garden performance. It has close links with Kordes Roses, one of the world's leading and most prolific rose breeders, ensuring a steady stream of innovative new varieties.

ROSES – EASY TO GROW AND SCENTED

LOW-MAINTENANCE AND PERFUMED VARIETIES AS RECOMMENDED BY PHILIP AND ROBERT HARKNESS OF HARKNESS ROSES

R. Fellowship

R. Easy Going

LOW-MAINTENANCE ROSES

Low-maintenance roses or *Rosa* should be right at the top of the wish-list for any serious rose breeder. The goal is simple: it's all about giving value-for-money in the garden, helping inexperienced gardeners to get great results without great effort. Healthy roses keep on growing, and a rose that keeps on growing keeps on flowering. Disease tolerance is uppermost at Harkness, where roses prove themselves for up to six years in a no-fungicide environment. The most successful do not suffer from disease at all; or if they do, it is not serious enough to stop them growing and flowering. Here are the top five.

1 *R.* Easy Going

Easy Going can be planted and grown with confidence, even if never treated against blackspot. It flowers from June to November, has a light perfume and grows to 90cm (35in). For continuity of bloom, ease of cultivation and robust resistance to disease, it is matched only by Fellowship, its orange twin.

2 *R.* Fellowship ♛

A wonderful, warm colour, Fellowship is considered by many to be the best orange bedding rose available. It gives a great show, growing easily and blooming repeatedly, even if more or less neglected. It remains in robust health with no protection from diseases like blackspot. It can reach heights of up to 90cm (35in). H4

3 R. Penny Lane ♈

The first climber to be Rose of the Year, in 1998. The honey-champagne flowers blush to pearl late in the season. It is pleasingly perfumed, with an easy-growing habit, disease-tolerant foliage and abundant flowers. A genuine repeat-blooming climber, ideal for training on pillars, pergolas, etc. Does well in moderate shade. It can grow to 3m (10ft). H4

4 R. Pride of England

This hybrid tea gives a terrific show, and is long-lasting when cut. What makes it stand out is the speed at which it re-blooms.

Re-bloom cycle is often a function of disease tolerance, which goes hand-in-hand with low maintenance, providing continuous growth and bloom. It reaches 1.15m (3ft 9m).

5 R. 'Susan Daniel'

This marvellous rose is one to gladden the heart. The effect of sunlight on the subtle shadings at different stages of the opening bloom can be described as 'translucent', a miracle of pearly amber, transparent gold and gossamer blush. Easy to look after and growing up to 1m (3ft 3in), it gives superb results without trouble.

R. Penny Lane

R. 'Susan Daniel'

R. Pride of England

CULTIVATION

Roses grow easily given reasonable soil, a sunny position and an adequate supply of water. A helpful booklet is enclosed with each order supplied by Harkness Roses. The same information is on www.roses.co.uk following the link to 'Rose Care'.

PERFUMED ROSES

The notion that modern roses aren't perfumed comes from the flower shop, not the garden. These days, special roses raised just for floristry are almost never perfumed, as perfumed roses have less shelf life. A floristry rose has to travel from a developing nation to a flower auction in Europe, then to a flower shop or market, and finally to the consumer. It's a long journey, and the softer petals of perfumed roses survive less well. So florists sell roses that don't smell. For the garden, there are plenty of new varieties with fantastic perfume. This is the top five.

R. 'Caroline Victoria'

R. Chandos Beauty

R. L'Aimant

1 R. 'Caroline Victoria'

At first encounter, this light, creamy rose evokes serenity and grace. Its perfume is exceptional, a foundation of citrus with raspberry overtones. It is a delightfully fresh and rewarding scent – heady, with no hint of heaviness. Growing to 90cm (35in), the plant forms a sturdy bush, suitable for group planting.

2 R. Chandos Beauty

This hybrid tea brings style, elegance and a terrific perfume to the summer garden. It is easy to grow, and tolerates disease well. Growth is vigorous – up to 90cm (35in) – and branching, with repeat-blooming over an extensive flowering season of June to November. The perfume is strong,

R. Salvation

releasing fruity blackcurrant notes and a hint of cinnamon.

3 *R.* L'Aimant

L'Aimant is a heady mix of strong perfume, healthy foliage and beauty of bloom, capturing the romance of old-fashioned roses without the drawbacks. Its soft colour combines well in mixed plantings and its rich, fruity perfume makes L'Aimant one of the most popular roses for cutting. It can grow up to 90cm (35in). H4

4 *R.* Margaret Merril

The delightful, citrus-based perfume of Margaret Merril is legendary. It is so well-known as a rose of stunning beauty for cutting that its value in the garden can be overlooked, but it is reliable and free-flowering, though less disease-tolerant than the best new varieties. It can reach up to 90cm (35in) in height. H4

5 *R.* Salvation

This rose is a rising star, and it's easy to see why. Its prettily-formed urn-shaped flowers are glowing amber infused with apricot, and release a rich, spice-based perfume. Repeat blooming, Salvation is an all-rounder, ideal for planting out, as well as a delight to cut for indoors. It grows to 80cm (32in).

A HANDY TIP

Advice seen in the catalogue of Heirloom Roses, Oregon: '...start by digging a really BIG hole...' This simple advice shows understanding of a rule that often underlies basic procedures in gardening: the greater the effort, the better the reward. The 'really BIG hole' allows space for nutrients to be added below the roots, and space for plenty of friable soil mixed with nutrients to fill in.

HARKNESS ROSES
The Rose Gardens, Cambridge Road, Hitchin, Herts SG4 0JT
T: 0845 331 3143 F: 01462 422170
E: harkness@roses.co.uk
W: www.roses.co.uk

Founded in Yorkshire in 1879 by John and Robert Harkness, today the nursery is in the hands of the fourth generation, Philip and Robert Harkness. The nursery breeds roses of all types: bedding, garden shrub, patio and border, and repeat-blooming climbers. The goal is to breed for improvements in perfume, bloom quality and profusion, and disease-resistance. The rose store is open Monday to Sunday, 10am to 4pm (phone for details of December to January opening).

ROSES – ENGLISH

AS RECOMMENDED BY DAVID AUSTIN ROSES

R. William Shakespeare 2000

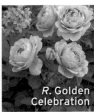

R. Golden Celebration

R. Darcey Bussell

David Austin, the award-winning rose breeder, has achieved worldwide recognition for his English roses or *Rosa*. Their flowers and growth habits are reminiscent of the old roses and yet have a unique charm and particular beauty. They are some of the most fragrant of all roses and are available in many different and rich shades, including apricots and yellows. English roses also repeat flower well, providing flushes of bloom from late May until the first frosts and forming attractive, rounded shrub roses which are tough, reliable and healthy.

1 *R.* Crocus Rose
A robust, free-flowering rose, bearing large, rosette-shaped flowers that are cupped at first; the petals are later reflexing. The colour is soft apricot, paling to cream with age. It has a delightful tea fragrance. This variety form a dense shrub of exceptional vigour. Height and spread 1.2 x 1m (4 x 3ft).

2 *R.* Darcey Bussell
The flowers are not excessively large, but are produced freely and the colour is a deep, rich crimson, with hints of mauve before the petals drop. It has a pleasing, fruity fragrance. Excellent for containers. Height and spread 1 x 0.6m (3 x 2ft).

3 *R.* Golden Celebration ♔
It is rich golden yellow and forms a large, but nicely rounded shrub. It is very healthy, with glossy, pale green foliage. The flowers initially have a strong tea scent, developing

hints of wine and strawberry. Grow as a specimen or in borders. Height and spread 1.2 x 1.2m (4 x 4ft).

4 *R.* Grace
One of the most beautiful shrub roses, producing many perfectly-formed blooms. The colour is a mixture of shades of apricot, deepening towards the centre. Grace is very healthy, repeat flowers well and is a very reliable garden plant. There is a delicious, warm fragrance. Height and spread 1.2 x 1.2m (4 x 4ft).

5 *R.* Jubilee Celebration
Large, domed flowers of rich pink with tints of gold on the underside of the petals. The flowers are produced exceptionally freely. The growth is vigorous, building up into a fine, rounded shrub. There is a deliciously fruity rose scent. Height and spread 1.2 x 1.2m (4 x 4ft).

6 R. Lady Emma Hamilton

The tight buds are a wonderful dark red with dashes of orange. The flowers are rich shades of tangerine-orange and yellow. It forms an upright but bushy shrub that flowers freely and has a strong fruity fragrance. Height and spread 1.2 x 1m (4 x 3ft).

7 R. Molineux ♛

The flowers are a rich yellow, tinged with orange at first. They have a tea fragrance with a musky background. Molineux has even, upright growth. Excellent for bedding, although may be grown in a large container. Height and spread 1 x 0.6m (3 x 2ft.)

8 R. Princess Alexandra of Kent

The glowing pink blooms are full-petalled and deeply cupped, enclosed by a ring of outer petals of softer pink. They have a delicious fresh tea fragrance. Height and spread 1.1 x 0.8m (3.5 x 2.5ft).

9 R. Wildeve

This is a robust, healthy rose, producing long arching branches that flower very freely. The buds are blush pink, opening to flowers with a pink and apricot colour. Wildeve is vigorous, with a soft but pleasant, fresh fragrance. It flowers well in less than ideal conditions. Height and spread 1.1 x 1.1m (3.5 x 3.5ft).

10 R. William Shakespeare 2000

One of our most popular roses, a superb variety with exquisite blooms of the richest velvety-crimson, gradually developing rich purple tones. This rose has the strong, old rose fragrance that we expect, but do not always find, in deep red roses. Height and spread 1.1 x 0.8m (3.5 x 2.5ft).

PLANTING SHRUB ROSES

Bare root roses should be planted between November and April. Containerised roses can be planted all year round, but will require careful attention to watering if planted during the summer months. Select a site with at least a few hours of sun each day where the roots of the rose will not be in competition with the roots of other plants. Shrub roses look superb planted in groups of three or more of one variety, about 45cm (18in) apart. They will then grow together to form one dense shrub.

DAVID AUSTIN ROSE NURSERY LTD
Bowling Green Lane, Albrighton, Wolverhampton WV7 3HB
T: 01902 376300
W: www.davidaustinroses.com
E: retail@davidaustinroses.com

✿ NCCPG National Collection holder of *Rosa* (English roses, bred by David Austin) **David Austin Roses** is a specialist rose nursery founded by David Austin in 1969. It maintains one of the largest collections of containerised roses to be found anywhere in the country, including English roses, old roses, climbers, ramblers, species, standards and modern roses. From mid-November to March, around 800 varieties of bare root roses are available. David Austin's rose gardens are open during nursery hours with free entry.

ROSES – MODERN

AS RECOMMENDED BY ANGELA PAWSEY OF CANTS OF COLCHESTER

R. Liliana

R. Fascination ('Poulmax')

Roses or *Rosa* rightly remain the nation's favourite flower and, contrary to what you might think, are quite happy in drought conditions. They come in all colours, shapes and forms, and can be used in shrubberies, borders, beds and edging, and on arches and walls. How can we select just 10 when, in the UK alone, there are nearly 3,500 varieties? Here, we have decided to focus on modern free-flowering, disease-resistant varieties.

1 *R.* 'Just Joey' ♛
A free-flowering, coppery-orange, fragrant hybrid tea, elected the world's favourite rose in 1994. Bred by Cants, named after Roger Pawsey's first wife Joanna, it is the first hybrid tea into bloom. It grows to 50cm (20in).

2 *R.* 'English Miss' ♛
Bred by Cants and achieved the equivalent of the Rose of the Year award. A free-flowering light pink fragrant floribunda rose, which, when blooms are fully open, has the appearance of a camellia. It is of branching habit with an unusual purplish foliage verging on dark green. It reaches 50cm (20in).

3 *R.* Britannia
One of many excellent varieties bred by Fryer's of Knutsford, it grows to a height of around 50cm (20in). This free-flowering

hybrid tea stands out with its unusual blend of apricot and gold-coloured buds that develop into nectarine orange blooms. The plants are of even branching habit, which shows the blooms off to stunning effect.

4 *R.* Liliana
Liliana is a particular favourite, being a lovely subtle, soft apricot colour with beautiful quartered blooms. Repeat-flowering with a lovely fragrance. Upright growth, with good disease-resistant mid-green foliage. Height 1.2-1.5m (4-5ft).

5 *R.* Summer Wine ♛
This climber from is from German breeders Kordes, who were responsible for the first truly repeat-flowering climbers. It has dense, deep green glossy foliage, masses of fragrant bright coral pink, open blooms. It has the

added attraction of being suitable for a north-facing aspect, and grows to 4m (13ft).

6 R. Fascination ('Poulmax') 🏆

This award-winning Poulsen floribunda is amazing for the enormous amount of blooms to a cluster. Classified as shrimp pink and fragrant, this exceptional free-flowering variety was awarded Rose of the Year for 1999. Plants are bushy, with dark green glossy foliage, growing to 60cm-1.5m (2-3ft).

7 R. Gertrude Jekyll

The David Austin English shrub roses are very popular and Gertrude Jekyll is a firm favourite that has strong, upright healthy growth, and stunning large, deep cerise-pink old-fashioned rosette blooms. Grows to around 1.2m (4ft) as a shrub, but can also be trained as a short climber.

8 R. Trumpeter 🏆

This floribunda remains a favourite, with masses of eye-catching orange-scarlet double blooms throughout the summer and autumn. If you only need one rose of limited height and like lots of colour this is the one for you. It reaches a height of around 60cm (2ft).

9 R. Ingrid Bergman

This velvety red rose is considered to be the *crème de la crème*, having received the accolade as the world's favourite rose of 2000, is Ingrid Bergman. Beautiful, deep-red, velvety blooms on a strong upright plant, with healthy, glossy dark-green foliage. It grows to 65cm-1m (2ft-3ft 3in).

10 R. Fellowship

I prefer floribunda roses to hybrid tea, and this is one of many varieties bred by Harkness Roses. This deep orange floribunda is colourful and free-blooming with a delicate fragrance, flowering late into autumn. It reaches 60cm-1.5m (2-3ft).

CULTIVATION

If a little time is taken to prepare the soil well, then planting and looking after roses is comparatively simple. Choose a site with good drainage, and incorporate well-decomposed material, open holes and plant the rose with the union just below the soil level. Remember to prune all bush roses hard in March. Deadhead roses when necessary to prolong flowering. Plant bare-rooted plants at approximately the end October to the end of March. Containerised plants come into their own from approximately April to July.

CANTS OF COLCHESTER
Nayland Road, Mile End, Colchester, Essex CO4 5EB
T: (01206) 844008 F: (01206) 855371
E: enquiries@cantsroses.co.uk
W: www.cantsroses.co.uk

Established in 1765, **Cants of Colchester** is the oldest family-run rose growers in the UK. A summer highlight is to walk round their rose fields, open to view late June to the end of September (phone for details). Cants grow a large selection of all types of roses but specialise in modern, long-flowering disease-resistant varieties. The firm is owned and run by Martin, Roger and Angela Pawsey (their mother was a Cant) with a small but enthusiastic staff.

SHRUBS – FLOWERING

AS RECOMMENDED BY NOTCUTTS NURSERY

Hydrangea macrophylla Endless Summer

Cornus alba 'Sibirica Variegata'

Hibiscus syriacus 'Woodbridge'

This hard-working group of plants can add structure to your garden, around which you can have fun filling in with herbaceous perennials, bulbs and annuals. Generally, a little tidying up and re-shaping after flowering will suffice, together with a dose of general fertiliser in spring. However, as this is such a diverse group of plants, refer to the plant label or a good reference book for specific advice. This selection reflects those plants that have earned the title 'good do-er' among our plantsmen, requiring little in the way of specialist knowledge to be successful in the garden.

1 *Choisya ternata* Sundance 🏆
An evergreen, rounded shrub, with a height and spread of 2.5m (8ft). The glossy foliage is bright golden-coloured all year round, with leaves consisting of three leaflets. This shrub has a neat habit and produces fragrant white flowers in spring.

2 *Coprosma repens* Pacific Night
An evergreen shrub, proving to be one of the hardiest Coprosmas (down to -5°C), with rich, deep purple glossy foliage. Growing to 1.5 x 1.5m (5 x 5ft) it has a neat, upright habit, which makes it perfect for patio pots.

3 *Cornus alba* 'Sibirica Variegata'
This compact variety of the red-barked dogwood has attractive cream and pale-green variegated foliage. It turns bright red in autumn, then falls to reveal attractive scarlet stems for winter interest. Height and spread 1.5 x 1.2m (5 x 4ft).

4 *Hibiscus syriacus* 'Woodbridge' ♔
This deciduous, upright shrub has large,
rich pink flowers throughout the summer,
right through until mid-autumn. It is hardy
throughout the UK, although it is best in a
sheltered, sunny spot. Height and spread
3 x 3m (10 x 10ft).

5 *Hydrangea macrophylla* **Endless Summer**
This deciduous shrub, also known as bailmer,
has the unique ability to flower on old and
new wood, so even if caught by a late frost or
pruned incorrectly it will still produce large
mop-head flowers in shades of blue or pink
throughout the summer. Height and spread
1.5 x 1.8m (5 x 6ft).

6 *Physocarpus opulifolius* 'Diabolo' ♔
A deciduous shrub with a height and spread
of 1.8 x 1.2m (6 x 4ft) which has outstanding,
rich purple foliage and contrasting white
flowers in early summer. It requires sun and
fertile, but not too dry, soil. Prefers acid soil.

7 *Physocarpus opulifolius* 'Seward'
(**syn. Summer Wine**)
This more compact *Physocarpus* is
available for gardens where space is limited.
Height and spread 1.5 x 1.8m (5 x 6ft).
It is fully hardy.

8 *Prunus incisa* 'Kojo-no-mai'
This shrub has a long season of interest.
In early spring, pale pink flowers smother
the naked branches. Fresh green foliage
turns a rich shade of orange-red in autumn,
then the twisted stems are revealed,
providing winter interest. It grows to
1.2 x 0.9m (4 x 3ft) so is ideal for a
patio pot.

9 *Rhus typhina* **Tiger Eyes**
This deciduous shrub, also known as
Bailtiger, is grown for its brightly-coloured
golden-green foliage, which takes on
brilliant shades of orange and red in
autumn. Requiring sun and well-drained
soil, it is a compact *Rhus*, 2 x 2m (7 x 7ft)
which, so far, appears not to sucker as other
types do.

10 *Robinia pseudoacacia* 'Lace Lady'
This *Robinia* has unusually twisted
stems and foliage. In autumn, the rich
green foliage turns butter yellow, and in
winter highly ornamental zig-zagged
stems are revealed. It eventually makes
a large shrub or small tree 2.5 x 2.5m
(8 x 8ft) and is excellent in containers
where its twisted stems give it a bonsai-
like appearance.

SHRUBS – FOLIAGE

AS RECOMMENDED BY IMOGEN AND RICHARD SAWYER OF LANE END NURSERY

Leucothoe 'Scarletta'

t is always tempting to buy that shrub, covered in glorious flowers, so carefully placed near the tills at the nursery or garden centre. Once the flowers are gone, however, you will be left with the foliage to provide interest for the rest of the year and if it is dull, it is dull for an awfully long time. I always select shrubs for foliage interest, making sure that I have a mixture of leaf sizes, colours, shapes and textures. All my top 10 foliage shrubs are easy to grow, relatively pest and disease-free and widely available.

1 *Sambucus nigra* 'Eva' (syn. 'Black Lace')
This large, fast-growing, deciduous elderberry is one of the darkest purple foliage plants available. It is tolerant of any soil, sun or shade. Large heads of scented flowers appear in late spring, followed by deep purple edible berries in autumn. Attractive to bees, butterflies and humans, 'Eva' can grow up to a height of 6m (20ft).

2 *Luma apiculata* 'Glanleam Gold' 🏆
A beautiful, aromatic evergreen shrub with varied foliage interest all year round. The leaves have creamy yellow margins which

stay bright even in midwinter. The new shoots have a deep red tinge and often the colour reappears in autumn. The small white flowers are scented and are followed by edible black and red berries. The plant can grow up to 6m (20ft) in height.

3 *Sorbaria sorbifolia* 'Sem'
This little deciduous shrub is a treasure. In spring the new leaves are bright pinky-red, with feathery gold foliage which turns green. In summer, creamy white flowers appear followed by autumn colour. It thrives in moist soils, flowers best in full sun and seems happy in a large pot.

4 *Leucothoe* Scarletta

This dainty little evergreen shrub develops coppery new shoots in spring. Little white flowers appear, pretty and delicate against the foliage. In autumn and winter outer leaves turn deep maroon-red. They must have moist acid soil and shade. The plant grows to a height 1m (4ft) with a spread of 3m (10ft).

5 *Acer palmatum* 'Shindeshōjō'

If you only have room for one maple in your garden, make it this one. This graceful shrub gives one of the best displays of autumn colour. In spring the new shoots are a deep pinky-red. It is best grown in acid soil, with some shade and out of a cold wind.

6 *Ilex* x *alterclerensis* 'Golden King' ♛

The beauty of holly foliage seems only to be appreciated in the weeks before Christmas when everyone wants them for decoration. For the best bright golden variegation the female 'Golden King' is hard to beat. Tolerant of most soils, they can grow to 6m (20ft).

7 *Cornus controversa* 'Variegata' ♛

People are often surprised to learn that this spectacular shrub is actually a dogwood. Part of the attraction is the layered effect.

Clusters of cream white flowers open in May to June followed by black berries and deep yellow foliage in autumn. It's best in sun or part shade, any soil, and reaches heights of 6m (20ft).

8 *Hebe* 'Red Edge' ♛

This useful garden shrub has attractive blue-green leaves with a maroon-red margin. In summer, small spikes of lilac to white flowers complement the foliage, especially if sited in full sun. In winter the maroon colour deepens and brightens up the winter garden.

9 *Pittosporum tenuifolium* ♛ 'Irene Paterson'

'Irene Paterson' is a beautiful variegated form. The new leaves emerge a rich cream colour then turn marbled cream with a pink tinge in winter. The stems are black and so this plant is widely used in floristry. Plant in well-drained soil in sun.

10 *Cotinus* 'Grace'

This fast-growing, deciduous shrub has large oval leaves of exquisite purple. They have a translucent quality best appreciated in sun. In autumn the leaves change from purple to outrageous scarlet. Any reasonable garden soil will do but avoid waterlogging. 'Grace' can grow to a height of 5m (16ft).

LANE END NURSERY
Old Cherry Lane, Lymm, Cheshire WA13 OTA
T: 01925 752618 E: rsawyer@onetel.net
W: www.laneendnursery.co.uk

Imogen and Richard Sawyer have owned **Lane End Nursery** since 1994. Over the years they have gradually expanded the business into a much-loved local nursery. The site has a huge range of perennials, trees, shrubs, herbs, bedding and bulbs with many unusual varieties. They run a range of garden courses, demonstrations and events each year - please see website for details. The nursery is open 9.30am to 5.30am Monday to Sunday (closed Wednesday).

TREES AND SHRUBS

AS RECOMMENDED BY ROBERT VERNON OF BLUEBELL ARBORETUM & NURSERY

Quercus rhysophylla

These trees and shrubs are ideal for people who prefer a 'woody' garden. Once established, they create a lovely, slightly wild effect that can add interest to nearly any area. We have chosen these plants as they are easy to grow, hardy in our climate and are some of our favourite plants in both the nursery and our own arboretum. They also represent an excellent selection of some of the more beautiful trees and shrubs that are now becoming available in the UK. Here are our top 10.

Cercis canadensis 'Forest Pansy'

Tilia henryana

PLANTING TREES AND SHRUBS

In windy sites a small stake can be useful to help anchor the plant until it has become established. Once planted, a thick layer of bark mulch, 8-10cm (3-4in) around the base of each tree, can help keep the weeds down and reduce the amount of moisture lost from the soil by evaporation. These trees should grow well without any plant feed. In the case of *Cercis canadensis* 'Forest Pansy', feeding it will actually damage the root system.

1 *Quercus rhysophylla*

This very rare evergreen oak, native to Mexico, is a small-to-medium-sized tree – 10m (30ft) – that prefers lime-free soil and a warm site. The bold, shiny green leaves, shaped like laurel but lighter in texture, are topped in spring by handsome new growths of young rich-purple foliage.

2 *Tilia henryana*

A rare, choice and slow-growing small-to-medium-sized tree, reaching up to 10m (30ft). The huge, ovate leaves of Henry's Lime are edged with bristle-like teeth and are a beautiful silvery pink as they unfold in spring. Creamy-white, fragrant flowers are borne in profusion on mature plants in September.

3 *Acer tegmentosum*

One of the loveliest of all snake-bark maples, *A. tegmentosum* has magnificent jade-and-silver striated bark, with mahogany-coloured buds in winter. This plant is almost as spectacular in summer as it is in the depths of winter, with lush green leaves and an excellent display of bark, and reaches up to 3m (10ft) in 10 years.

Sequoiadendron giganteum 'Glaucum'

4 *Cercis canadensis* 'Forest Pansy' ♔

The sun shining through the rich-purple, heart-shaped foliage of this redbud tree is one of the wonders of the garden. Some leaves reflect light while others appear translucent. Rose-pink flowers appear in late April and the foliage colour lasts from mid-May until November. *C. canadensis* can reach a height of 10m (30ft).

5 *Betula utilis* var. *jacquemontii* 'Doorenbos'

Variant *jacquemontii* is white-trunked form of the Himalayan birch. 'Doorenbos' is a superb, fast-growing, hardy, slender and medium-sized tree, growing to 10m (30ft) with fine, peeling white bark. Excellent as a single plant and striking when planted in groups.

6 *Malus* 'Evereste' ♔

A fantastic crab apple tree. In spring it is covered with beautiful pale pink and white flowers, followed in autumn by masses of yellow and red fruit and excellent yellow autumn tints. It is a small tree, growing

Liquidambar styraciflua 'Festival'

to 7m (23ft), with less invasive roots than flowering cherries, making it a good choice for smaller gardens.

7 *Cornus kousa* var. *chinensis* 'China Girl'

Introduced from China in 1910, *C. kousa* is a first-class large shrub or small tree. This improved form of *C. kousa* var. *chinensis* has an impressive display of white flower bracts in June, pretty autumn tints and strawberry-like fruits. They are hardy but originate from countries with hot summers. *C. kousa* can reach heights of 7m (23ft).

Cornus kousa var. *chinensis* 'China Girl'

8 *Sequoiadendron giganteum* 'Glaucum'

A rare and vigorous giant redwood, with striking steel-blue foliage and chestnut-red bark. With a life span of 3,000 years and requiring little room (other than air space) it is one of the finest trees for commemorative planting. A fast-growing, 30m (100ft) windproof conifer, it thrives in the UK.

9 *Liquidambar styraciflua* 'Festival'

This sweetgum cultivar has the finest, rich burgundy autumn colours of any *Liquidambar*. The autumn display often lasts from September into November. Although *Liquidambar* is happy in moist, retentive soils, once established, with the addition of manure, it seems equally happy in well-drained soils. It can grow to up to 30m (100ft).

10 *Styrax japonicus* ♔

A small, very choice tree 15m (50ft) tall with excellent yellow autumn tints. The undersides of the fan-shaped branches are covered in trailing, bell-shaped, white flowers in June hence the name snowbell tree – plant where these flowers can be best admired from below. It needs lime-free soil in sun or light shade and shelter from wind.

BLUEBELL ARBORETUM & NURSERY
Annwell Lane, Smisby, nr Ashby de la Zouch, Derbyshire LE65 2TA
T: 01530 413 700
E: sales@bluebellnursery.com
W: www.bluebellnursery.com

BlueBell Arboretum & Nursery specialises in rare and unusual trees and shrubs. The nursery is surrounded by a beautiful three-acre arboretum, planted with both native trees and rarities from all over the world. It sells a huge range of plants, both on site and via its online mail order service. Open Monday to Saturday 9am to 5pm, Sunday 10.30am to 4.30pm (March to October); Monday to Saturday 9am to 4pm, closed Sunday (November to February).

TREES AND SHRUBS FOR SMALL GARDENS

AS RECOMMENDED BY CHEW VALLEY TREES

Crataegus persimilis 'Prunifolia Splendens'

Malus 'Evereste'

Photinia x fraseri 'Red Robin'

Trees and shrubs provide the essential framework to the visual structure of every garden. The difference between a small tree and a large shrub seems to boil down to whether it has a clear stem. Hawthorn (*Crataegus*) is usually regarded as a hedging plant but will grow as a single-stem tree with a defined head if left unchecked, whereas hazel (*Corylus*) will always sucker from the base, and though will usually grow tall must still be considered a shrub.

TREES

1 *Crataegus persimilis* 'Prunifolia Splendens'

There are numerous hawthorns available but this frosted thorn has to be the overall winner. A display of white flowers in early summer is followed by shiny red berries. It has fabulous autumn colouring and thrives provided the soil is well-drained. It grows to a height of 8m (26ft).

2 *Cotoneaster frigidus* 'Cornubia' ♔

The multi-talented 'Cornubia' is a semi-evergreen, producing frothy, white flowers in June followed later by bright red berries. Its leaves are long and narrow on arching branches, providing a useful screen. It can grow to 6m (20ft).

3 *Malus* 'Evereste' ♔

This handsome ornamental crab apple brings a billowing cloud of first blush pink, then white flowers in spring, and miniature yellow-orange ornamental apples subsequently appear during the autumn. This cultivar is an ideal choice where space is limited, given its rather conical habit.

4 *Sorbus* 'Joseph Rock'

This yellow-berried rowan is a popular ornamental rowan for the small garden with its display of white spring flowers and yellow berries in the autumn, with late autumn leaf colours of crimson and purple. The leaves are somewhat fern-like in appearance, casting a light shade on the ground below. It grows to 15m (50ft).

5 *Salix integra* 'Hakuro-Nishiki'

For gardeners requiring a very small specimen, perhaps for a container, this 'form of willow is dainty and appealing.

The foliage is shrimp pink becoming variegated mottled cream and light green.

SHRUBS

1 *Amelanchier lamarckii* ♆
The silvery leaves of the snowy mespilus unfold in April, and a mass of tiny white flowers then bursts at the end of each shoot as the unfolding leaves take on a pale copper-bronze, turning orange and red in autumn. It grows to 6m (20ft).

2 *Photinia* x *fraseri* 'Red Robin' ♆
An evergreen plant found mostly as a shrub. Glossy red leaves at the end of each shoot turn this otherwise laurel-like shrub into an attractive selection. It can be grown as a hedge and prefers a sunny position. It grows to 6m (20ft).

3 *Elaeagnus* x *ebbingei* 'Limelight'
This evergreen cultivar, with variegated foliage providing colour, is a reliable old favourite with its textured oval leaves splashed with gold on green. It can grow to a height of 5m (16ft).

4 *Escallonia* 'Iveyi' ♆
'Iveyi' could be planted either as a specimen

CULTIVATION

Depending on your choice of species, plants are available container-grown for year-round planting, or alternatively bare-root plants can be obtained from specialist nurseries. Bare-root plants are lifted straight from the soil during the autumn and winter months when they are not growing (or 'dormant'). Another term for bare-root is 'field grown'. When planting your tree or shrub the removal and subsequent control of grass and weeds around the base is essential in their establishment. The staking of trees and larger shrubs will anchor the roots ensuring they can penetrate the surrounding soil.

or as a hedge and has the characteristic leaves of highly-polished dark green. This cultivar has an upright shape featuring scented, white flowers in a long-lasting display from mid-summer to autumn. It can grow to 6m (20ft).

5 *Ceanothus thyrsiflorus* var. *repens* ♆
There are many species of ceanothus all with their signature bright blue flowers in early April, but this creeping blueblossom has a low and spreading habit. It is an evergreen, flowering in spring and, prefers a sheltered, sunny spot. It grows to 1.5m (5ft).

CHEW VALLEY TREES
Winford Road, Chew Magna, Bristol BS40 8HJ
T: 01275 333752 F: 01275 333746
E: info@chewvalleytrees.co.uk
W: www.chewvalleytrees.co.uk

Chew Valley Trees are specialist growers of hardy, native and ornamental trees, shrubs, hedging and fruit trees. Professional and amateur gardeners alike benefit from their helpful service and advice. The nursery, established in 1986 by directors Julia and David Scarth, stocks both container-grown and bare-root plants. The 18-acre nursery located five miles south of Bristol on the B3130 welcomes customers weekdays and Saturdays throughout the year (although closed on Saturdays in July and August).

APPLES

AS RECOMMENDED BY CROWN NURSERY

'Elstar'

Each year, over 55 million tonnes of apples are commercially grown worldwide. These varieties tend to be reliable croppers, with colourful skins, good disease resistance and lengthy storage qualities. Although old varieties often offer superior flavour, many have died out because they do not meet commercial requirements. Recently, with increased awareness of this loss, efforts have been made to make old varieties more available, and our 10 favourites are described here. If you need an excuse to plant an apple tree, remember the old proverb, 'An apple a day keeps the doctor away'. Research now suggests that apples may reduce the risk of many cancers, and can help fight cholesterol, heart disease and some neurodegenerative diseases.

'Baker's Delicious'

'Red Pippin'

'Egremont Russet'

1 'Baker's Delicious'

A medium-sized tree with a good crop of smooth-skinned dessert apples. These are flushed bright orange-red over gold and are rich and juicy with a deep-cream flesh. The acidity is quite strong, but there is an aromatic flavour and lots of natural sugar. Pick in early September and store only until the end of that month.

2 'Elstar'

An intensely flavoured dessert apple with very honeyed, sweet, crisp and juicy flesh. The fruits are coloured by flush and stripes, with some russet. It is a reliable, prolific cropper that should be picked in early October. Store until late October to December. It is widely grown on the continent, but less well known in the UK.

3 'Fiesta' (syn. 'Red Pippin')

An excellent garden tree similar to 'Cox's Orange Pippin'. Indeed, it is a cross of this and 'Idared', but it is easier to grow, requiring very little pruning or spraying, making it an excellent choice for organic growers. The tree is virtually self-fertile giving heavy, regular crops of medium-sized dessert apples that are similar in flavour to 'Cox's Orange Pippin' – sweet and tangy. A fairly new introduction from Kent.

4 'Norfolk Royal'

A good, regular cropper with medium to large dessert apples. They are very pale yellow to pale whitish yellow in parts, with a quarter or almost the whole surface flushed with brilliant red. The flesh is creamy white, tinged with pink near the skin, but not hard. The flavour is crisp and juicy with a slightly sweet aroma.

'Tydeman's Late Orange'

'Lord Derby'

'Doctor Harvey'

5 'Egremont Russet'

An easy-to-grow dessert apple, requiring the minimum of pruning or spraying. The yellow-green, rough skin of the apples is covered with brown 'russet', and the flesh is creamy, aromatic, sweet and juicy. Apples keep well into the winter, while the tree is also a great pollinator of other apple trees.

6 'Tydeman's Late Orange'

The medium-sized fruits of this dessert apple have pale yellowish skin that becomes dull greenish yellow to dull brownish purple. The flesh is creamy yellow, firm, fine-textured and juicy. It also keeps well, being rich and aromatic in December, and sweeter and only lightly aromatic in March.

7 'Lord Derby'

A mid- to late-season cooking apple that shows resistance to scab and tolerates wet soils. The skin of the fruit is bright green, later becoming yellow, often with whitish dots, smooth and dry. The flesh is greenish white, with a slightly coarse texture. It is a hardy, prolific and regular cropper, requiring thinning to obtain a larger fruit.

8 'Doctor Harvey'

A moderately vigorous cooking apple with an upright-spreading habit. The fruits are yellow-orange with a greyed-orange flush. The flesh is creamy white with a firm, fine texture and a good flavour that is sub-acid. They break up completely on cooking. The apples can keep until mid-December.

9 'George Cave'

A fairly hardy, upright-spreading dessert apple of moderate vigour. It bears good crops, although the fruits drop quickly. The apples are pale yellow-green, becoming yellow, and are half covered with a red flush. The creamy white flesh is soft, fine-textured and juicy, sometimes flushed green under the skin, with a slightly sweet aroma. Pick and eat during early to mid-August.

10 'Tydeman's Early Worcester'

A moderately vigorous dessert apple with long, arching and spreading lateral branches. The apples are greenish yellow, becoming pale yellow, with half or almost the entire surface covered with a crimson-red flush. The flesh is white and finely textured, with a distinct strawberry flavour when ripe. Best picked late August to early September.

'George Cave'

'Tydeman's Early Worcester'

BERRIES

AS RECOMMENDED BY PHIL CORBETT OF COOL TEMPERATE

Cornus canadensis

Berberis vulgaris

Between the tall hawthorns and the ground-hugging alpine strawberry, these berry plants have a wide range of shapes and sizes. Something from this selection will suit most growing spaces. Most of these plants have few pests and diseases, and are undemanding. As well as giving fruit, some will make low hedges or spiny barriers, some can tolerate adverse or coastal conditions and some will fix their own nitrogen fertiliser. They give a great deal and ask for very little, and all have their own particular beauty.

1 *Amelanchier laevis*

Amelanchier or juneberry are small deciduous trees or shrubs, often suckering, with starry white flowers in spring, whose young foliage may be tinted bronzy-pink. *A. laevis* is perhaps the tallest species. Usually seen in cultivation as the hybrid 'Ballerina' it reaches 6m (20ft), has larger than average fruit and can crop heavily.

2 *Aronia melanocarpa*

The black chokeberry is a deciduous shrub about 2m (7ft) tall, like a cross between a hawthorn and an apple, with simple foliage and clusters of white flowers or black berries.

Fruit ripens fully a few weeks after it has turned black, with a hint of morello cherry.

3 *Berberis vulgaris*

Berberis or barberry is a large genus of prickly-leaved shrubs, excellent for deterrent hedging. Yellow-orange flowers are succeeded by fruits of various colours. Some species have dry, seedy fruits, but *B. vulgaris*, the native barberry or *B. darwinii* are juicy with a lemony sharpness, useful for preserves.

4 *Cornus canadensis* ♔

Although the fruits of dogwoods can be bitter, this particular species is an exception.

A carpeting plant for dappled shade in acid woodlands, including under conifers. Fruits have a pleasant flavour, can be eaten raw or cooked, and are rich in pectin. Also try *C. kousa* var. *chinensis* and *C. mas*. H4

5 *Crataegus pinnatifida* var. *major* 'Big Golden Star'

Our native hawthorns are small-fruited and seedy, but several species give larger, more useful fruit, flowers and autumn colour. 'Big Golden Star', a crop in China, grows up to 6m (20ft) tall and has red fruit 2.5cm (1in) in diameter, which can be eaten raw or cooked.

6 *Elaeagnus angustifolia*

Elaeagnus are nitrogen-fixing, with scented flowers and edible fruit, are fast-growing and usually tough. The deciduous types like *E. angustifolia* are spring-flowering with an autumn crop. This shrub can grow like a small tree with grey leaves, occasional spines and yellowish flowers ripening to sweet but mealy fruit. Height 7m (23ft).

7 *Fragaria vesca* 'Semperflorens'

The wild Alpine strawberry spreads by runners and fruits around midsummer. The Alpine strawberry generally has no runners and flowers nearly year-round when the weather is suitable. A few do have runners, removing the need for re-sowing every year, and their flavour is exquisite. Try also the cultivars 'Running Alpine' from this nursery.

8 *Fuchsia magellanica*

The hardiest fuchsia, with over 150 cultivars. In milder areas it can be grown as a hedge. It has a plum like fruit with peppery overtones, but these are seldom formed in most cultivars. Use flowers for wine-making and fruits for jelly or raw eating. Good cultivars are 'Globosa', 1m (3ft), and 'Gracilis', 2m (7ft).

9 *Hippophae rhamnoides* ♔

The sea buckthorn is the native deciduous shrub of dunes, where it fixes nitrogen and stabilises the sand with suckering shoots. The berries are rich in vitamins and cultivated for preserves and drinks. It grows to a height of 3m (9ft 10in). Tolerates coastal conditions. H4

10 *Ugni molinae*

The Chilean guava is an evergreen shrub that grows to about 1.5 x 1m (5ft x 3ft), sometimes grown as an ornamental. Pink flowers are followed by red fruits ripening in November to December. Hardy to about -10°C. The fruit has a wild-strawberry taste, was loved by Queen Victoria and was grown especially for her in Cornwall. H3

COOL TEMPERATE
45 Stamford Street, Awsworth,
Nottinghamshire NG16 2QL (office contact address)
T/F: 0115 916 2673
E: phil.corbett@cooltemperate.co.uk
W: www.cooltemperate.co.uk

Phil Corbett set up **Cool Temperate** in 1996. Since then, climate change and the oil crisis have come to the fore, and plants that can find their own food and water, and serve a variety of functions, are the ones he believes we shall be increasingly turning to. **Cool Temperate** specialises in practical plants – fruit, hedging and nitrogen fixers (sometimes all three in one) and fruit trees grown on their own roots. If planning to visit, please phone for more details.

PEARS

AS RECOMMENDED BY SIMA AND HAMID HABIBI OF KEEPERS NURSERY

'Beth'

Pears were first domesticated in the ancient Near and Middle East from wild *Pyrus communis*. They were probably first introduced to Britain by the Romans. Early European pears were mainly hard and gritty, suitable only for culinary use. Modern European dessert pears as we know them, with their softer, juicier flesh, are of more recent origin. Today, there are 469 varieties of pear in the National Fruit Collection and many more have probably existed in the past. With their beautiful white blossom and delicious fruit, pear trees are an essential component of any fruit garden.

'Merton Pride'

'William's Bon Chrétien'

'Onward'

'Beurré Hardy'

ROOTSTOCKS

Pears are grafted onto rootstocks, which determine the size and vigour of the tree. The common rootstocks are Quince A (semi-dwarfing) and Quince C (dwarfing), with seedling pear (vigorous). With the correct choice of rootstock, pear trees can be used for a wide range of situations, from large country gardens to rooftop patios. They're suitable for training as fans, espaliers or cordons. All forms need regular annual pruning, both to develop a good shape and to rejuvenate fruit-bearing wood. To ensure regular crops, two or more compatible varieties must be grown together for cross-pollination.

1 'Beth' ♛
One of the earliest ripening pears. A small- to medium-sized fruit with a pale green skin, turning to yellow when ripe. It has a soft, very juicy flesh, with a pleasant sweet flavour. It produces a small compact tree suitable for small gardens and restricted forms. Season: August to September.

2 'William's Bon Chrétien' ♛
Originating from a chance seedling in the garden of a schoolmaster in Aldermaston, this is now the most widely grown pear in the world. It has smooth, pale green skin turning pale yellow when ripe. The flesh is white and juicy with a strong, musky flavour. Susceptible to scab. Season: September.

3 'Merton Pride'
This is a very good garden variety. The fruit is large and has a heavily russetted skin. The creamy white flesh is very juicy and sweet, with an excellent flavour. It is a triploid, meaning it forms a vigorous tree that can't pollinate other pear trees. Season: September.

'Conference'

'Doyenné du Comice'

4 'Onward' ♔

This is an excellent garden variety. The smooth skin is yellowish green with a red flush and stripes. The creamy flesh is juicy, with an excellent flavour. It is rich and sweet with some balancing acidity. It's a good, reliable cropper and will grow well in most parts of the country. Season: September to October.

5 'Beurré Hardy' ♔

A popular variety on the Continent, where it's grown commercially. It is a large fruit with bronze, russetted skin and creamy white, tender juicy flesh. It's sweet with an outstanding aromatic flavour and a hint of rosewater. Crops well but is slow to come into bearing. Season: October.

6 'Louise Bonne of Jersey'

This is an excellent, heavy-cropping garden variety, suitable for growing in most parts of the country. The fruit is very attractive,

with smooth yellowish-green skin and a prominent dark red flush. Its white juicy flesh is sweet, but also, quite unusually for a pear, it has some good acidity. Season: October.

7 'Conference' ♔

The most widely grown pear in the UK, with recognisable long, thin fruit. It's sweet with good, but not outstanding, flavour. 'Conference' is one of the most reliable pears for British conditions and also one of the few self-fertile pears to produce a crop on its own. Season: October to November.

8 'Doyenné du Comice' ♔

One of the finest dessert pears. It has largish fruit, with green skin covered in variable amounts of fine russet and often faint red stripes. The pale yellow flesh is juicy and sweet with a delicious flavour. It needs a warm, sheltered location for best results. Season: October to November.

9 'Durondeau'

This produces the most attractive fruit, with a yellow skin covered with a fine golden russet and often a faint red flush. The combination of golden fruit and red leaves can give a spectacular autumn display. The fruit is juicy and sweet, with a pleasant flavour. Season: October to November.

10 'Catillac' ♈

This is an old-fashioned cooking pear, with spectacularly large and quite attractive fruit, which has a green skin with patches of red flush. The white flesh is hard and gritty, requiring cooking for quite a while; ideal for making pickled pear. The blossom is large and attractive. Season: December to March.

'Durondeau'

CULTIVATION

Pears are less suited to the British climate than apples, because they flower earlier and require warmer, sunnier summer weather to ripen well. However, with some care in the choice of varieties and location, pears can be grown in most regions. Pear trees are best planted bare root in late autumn and winter. They will grow on a wide range of soils other than very alkaline, but do best on a well-drained, moisture-retentive soil with a pH of 6.0-7.0.

'Catillac'

KEEPERS NURSERY
Gallants Court, East Farleigh, Maidstone ME15 0LE
T: 01622 726465 F: 0870 705 2145
E: info@keepers-nursery.co.uk
W: www.fruittree.co.uk

Keepers Nursery is a specialist nursery offering probably the largest range of fruit varieties in the world. Established in the early 1980s, it has been run as a family business by Sima and Hamid Habibi since 1996. Nearly all the trees are produced at the nursery and supplied bare root in late autumn and winter, mainly by internet and mail order. Although the nursery is generally not open to visitors, open days are held in autumn (call for dates).

SUMMER FRUITS

AS RECOMMENDED BY BLACKMOOR NURSERIES

Damson 'Merryweather'

Blackcurrant 'Ben Lomond'

Fruit trees and soft-fruit bushes are a very sound investment and add a new dimension to your garden. Properly cared for, they respond by producing attractive blossom, in turn followed by a crop of luscious fresh fruit. The 10 plants listed below are in no particular order and represent some of our most popular fruit varieties. For more advice on growing and caring for fruit, visit our 'Fruit Growers Handbook' at www.blackmoor.co.uk/handbook.php.

1 Apricot 'Flavourcot'

This highly recommended new apricot variety has many advantages over 'Early Moorpark', another popular apricot. 'Flavourcot' comes into cropping earlier in the tree's life and produces heavier, better-flavoured fruits. The tree is also self-fertile.

2 Blackberry 'Ashton Cross'

A vigorous wall or fence plant with large, juicy fruit. Plants will spread 5-7m (16-23ft). Fruit ripens from mid July right through till late September. Thornless varieties include 'Adrienne' and 'Thornfree'.

3 Blackcurrant 'Ben Lomond' 🏆

Blackcurrants are a very good source of vitamin C and are easy to grow, cropping in July and August. This variety bears heavy crops of large, sweet berries on a compact bush, and is resistant to mildew. Plant 1m (3ft 3in) apart, firmly and deeply.

4 Blueberry 'Blue Crop'

Blueberries are among the healthiest fruit you can eat, say medical experts. They must have moist, distinctly acid soil. 'Blue Crop' has a vigorous, upright habit with bell-shaped flowers in spring, followed by heavy crops of good-flavoured fruit. Plant at least 1.5m (5ft) apart.

5 Cherry 'Stella'

'Stella' is the number one sweet cherry for the garden, and the blossom can pollinate itself. The flavour is good and the flesh is juicy. Fruits are dark red or near black. Pick during late July, but protect from birds.

6 Damson 'Merryweather'

Damsons have a spicy, tart flavour and are used for cooking, jam and wine making. 'Merryweather' is a very hardy tree, which succeeds where a plum would fail. The blossom is self-fertile. The large, blue-black fruit with yellow flesh is juicy and acidic and ready during late August.

7 Peach 'Avalon Pride'

This outstanding new variety represents the biggest advancement in peach breeding for many years – 'Avalon Pride' appears to be completely resistant to peach leaf curl – a common disease of peaches in the UK. The blossom is self-fertile with pretty pink flowers and bears delicious juicy large fruits from early August. Peaches are best grown against a south-facing wall.

8 Plum 'Victoria'

Plums are the most popular of the stone fruit and they are also the easiest to grow. Many varieties are self-fertile. 'Victoria' is the number one plum, still the most popular with both amateur and commercial growers. The flesh is yellowish-green, and this plum is self-fertile, hardy, delicious and a reliable heavy cropper.

9 Raspberry 'Autumn Bliss'

Raspberries are good for pies, jam or eating fresh, and this one is recommended. The fruit starts ripening in August and goes on into September. Plant 45cm (18in) apart and cut the canes to ground level after fruiting. Note that raspberries require a free-draining soil and do not like getting wet feet.

10 Strawberry 'Cambridge Favourite'

Strawberries are the most popular soft fruit for growing at home and 'Cambridge Favourite' has been the number one choice for years. It crops well, is thoroughly reliable and has a long, productive life with good disease-resistance. Plant 35-40cm (14-16in) apart in rows, with 1.5m (5ft) between the rows.

Strawberries

AGAPANTHUS

AS RECOMMENDED BY PINE COTTAGE PLANTS

A. 'Exmoor'

Agapanthus have been popular in gardens since they were first introduced to Europe from South Africa in the 17th century, and can be seen at their best in warm coastal gardens. The flowers are produced between July and the end of September. Fifty or more stems may appear on established plants. Here's our selection of the top 10 agapanthus that we believe to be reasonably hardy in all but the colder districts of the UK.

1 A. 'Arctic Star'
This semi-deciduous cultivar with large white flowers grows to 65cm (26in) and has distinct greyish-green leaves. It flowers in early July and usually into August, and is one of the best whites around – both for outdoor planting and in containers.

2 A. 'Liam's Lilac'
A distinctive new selection of agapanthus, with few flowered umbels. The individual flowers are flared and nodding. The colour is lilac, which becomes a deeper violet towards the base of the tube, and purple pedicels. It is another late-season agapanthus, which can grow up to 1m (3ft 3in) in height.

3 A. 'Luly'
A soft-blue cultivar raised by Lewis Palmer, from whom it takes its name. An old favourite, this is a strong-growing plant with upright stems up to 90-100cm (35-39in) tall. The flowerheads are a good size, appearing later in August. Awarded a First Class Certificate (FCC) by the RHS in 1977.

4 A. 'Midnight Star'
This darker-blue cultivar is always in great demand with gardeners. The flowers are held up on strong stems of 80cm (32in) or so. It quickly makes large clumps, producing numerous flowers and can be relied upon to give an eye-catchingly good display. A bestselling cultivar.

5 A. 'Exmoor'

The wonderful dark stems supporting deep blue flowers mark this out from all the rest. Flowering in August. A hardy deciduous, it can grow to a height of 110cm (43in).

6 A. 'Tarka'

Lovely lilac flowers in full heads, with distinct reflex tepals. The pedicels are speckled with dark violet. The height can go up to 1m (3ft 3in) and the leaves are semi-evergreen. Flowers during August.

7 A. 'Taw Valley'

A dark blue hardy deciduous cultivar, 70cm (28in) tall, flowering mid-season. From the same stable as 'Nikki', which was awarded an FCC by the RHS in 2003, flowering only slightly later in August.

8 A. inapertus 'Crystal Drop'

This tall-growing *inapertus* hybrid has a pearly-pink flush on mainly white flowers. A lovely plant which grows 90-110cm (35-43in) tall. Some *inapertus* produce flowers of the darkest inky-blue, as in 'Black Magic', while the drooping habit of the tubular flowers adds an extra dimension to the late summer border.

9 A. inapertus 'Lydenburg'

One of the most attractive of all the *inapertus* types, producing long-lasting, deep blue pendulous flowers, each flared towards the apex. A feature in South Africa's national Botanical Garden at Kirstenbosch.

10 A. inapertus subsp. pendulus 'Graskop'

A wonderful dark blue form also from Kirstenbosch, where it was first introduced many years ago and where it always makes an impression on visitors. Shorter than most *inapertus*, being only 60-80cm (24-32in), it's nevertheless quite impressive when fully established into a large clump. Very desirable.

GROWING AGAPANTHUS IN CONTAINERS

Excellent results can be achieved with containers. Use a traditional clay pot and bring it into the cold greenhouse before the frosts. Evergreen types are best suited to pot culture. Container-grown plants may be plunged (not planted) in a border for the summer, but lifted again in autumn. For winter storage, aim to keep just frost-free and moist.

PINE COTTAGE PLANTS
Fourways, Eggesford, Devon EX18 7QZ
T: 01769 580076 E: pcplants@supanet.com
W: www.pcplants.co.uk

✿ NCCPG National Collection holder of *Agapanthus*
Pine Cottage Plants is a small nursery established in 1996. It grows a limited range of unusual plants, with special emphasis on agapanthus. It produces an illustrated mail-order catalogue. The nursery is open all year, Monday to Saturday, 10am to 4pm. Please call prior to visiting as they attend many shows in the summer. The garden is open at certain times for viewing the National Collection and is also open under the National Garden Scheme (NGS).

ASTERS

AS RECOMMENDED BY OLD COURT NURSERIES AND THE PICTON GARDEN

Asters in The Picton Garden

The numerous species and cultivated varieties of autumn-flowering asters – genus *Aster* – are well known as Michaelmas daisies. Bringing drifts of subtle colours into our gardens in September and October, these easily-grown herbaceous perennials have been popular for over 100 years. Most varieties derive from species native to North America and smaller numbers are of European and Asiatic origin. (The recently published *Flora of North America* has adopted a re-classification, placing most of the familiar species into the genera of *Symphyotrichum* and *Eurybia*). Asters are an important cut-flower crop with worldwide production.

1 *A. amellus* 'Gründer'

One of the most robust varieties in the group, bearing sturdy flowering stems up to 80cm (32in) tall. The well-shaped, lilac-blue flowers are around 7.5cm (3in) in diameter and appear in September and October. The stems need support to look their best. 'Gründer' is an excellent cut flower.

2 *A. amellus* 'Rosa Erfüllung'

Healthy growth in generous mounds up to 50cm (20in) tall, and masses of rich, purple-pink flowers in September and October make this variety the best in this colour range. The name is sometimes translated as 'Pink Zenith'. 'Jacqueline Genebrier' is a good alternative, with flowers of a slightly deeper hue.

3 *A. laevis* 'Calliope'

A late-flowering, imposing plant with large, deep green leaves and virtually black stems. Robust shoots grow to 2m (6ft 7in) tall by the time the lilac-blue flowers appear in mid-October. Fairly resistant to mildew. Best grown in a sunny site and left undivided.

A. laevis 'Calliope'

A. 'Little Carlow'

4 *A. lateriflorus*

This is one of the easiest asters to grow and creates a colourful display. The leaves are bronze-purple in spring. Plants grow up to 1m (3ft 3in) tall in sun or partial shade. In October there is an explosion of flowers, with central discs starting yellow and becoming purple-red.

5 *A.* 'Little Carlow' ♔

The Michaelmas daisy to beat all others for clouds of lavender-blue. Vigorous, compact, woody clumps give rise to masses of stems with broadly lance-shaped green leaves to 1.2m (3ft 11in) tall, with 2.5cm (1in) diameter, beautiful bright lavender-blue flowers. Grow in a sunny site in good soil and support the stems before heavy rain.

6 *A. novae-angliae* 'Anabelle de Chazal'

One of the newer, most popular varieties

A. novae-angeliae 'Helen Picton'

CULTIVATION

The most colourful and varied range of *Michaelmas* daisies are the cultivars of *Aster novi-belgii*. Grow them in a sunny site, with fertile soil, and don't allow them to become too dry in the spring and summer. Spray through the growing season to prevent mildew. Varieties taller than 45cm (18in) will need support. *Aster novae-angliae* requires similar conditions, but plants are resistant to mildew. *Aster amellus* and *Aster* x *frikartii* are also resistant to mildew. They need to be grown in fertile soil with good winter drainage. Must be planted in spring only.

A. novi-belgii 'Jenny'

of 'New England' aster, this one is mildew-resistant. It creates an eye-catching display of 5cm (2in) wide, rosy-pink flowers in October, about 1m (3ft 3in) tall. Divide clumps every three to four years, in early spring. First-year plants may need quite a lot of support. Best planted in fertile soil and sunlight.

7 A. novae-angliae 'Helen Picton'

A comparative newcomer to the ever-growing list of trouble-free asters. The flowers are 5cm (2in) diameter and deep blue-purple in colour. Stems grow up to 1.2m (4ft) tall with rich green leaves. 'Helen Picton' is vulnerable to damage

A. novi-belgii 'Marie Ballard'

from heavy rain and support is essential. Grow in rich soil in sun.

8 A. novi-belgii 'Jenny'

Everyone's favourite dwarf Michaelmas daisy. Neat clumps give rise to sturdy, upright stems 40cm (16in) tall, and broad heads of large flowers 5cm (2in) across, with bright purple-red rays and yellow discs. Superb for the front of borders or containers, and a good cut flower. Spray against mildew. Divide plants every spring.

9 A. novi-belgii 'Marie Ballard'

Here is perfection in the formality of the double flowers and the clean, lavender-blue of the rays. The flowering stems grow to 1m (3ft 3in) tall, and closely-packed sprays produce long-lasting blooms in September and October. The heavy stems need support and need to be sprayed against mildew.

10 A. novi-belgii 'Mount Everest'

'Mount Everest' was raised before 1930 and its graceful spires have yet to be bettered. It reaches a height of 1.6m (5ft 5in) when the plants are growing in fertile soil and kept well watered. A suitable cut flower for harvest festivals. Divide annually. Spray against mildew and keep well supported.

OLD COURT NURSERIES and THE PICTON GARDEN
Colwall, nr Malvern, Worcestershire WR13 6QE
T: 01684 540416 E: paulpicton@btinternet.com
W: www.autumnasters.co.uk

✿ NCCPG National Collection holder of *Asters* (autumn-flowering)
Old Court Nurseries has specialised in breeding and growing Michaelmas daisies since 1906, and other late-season perennials, trees and shrubs for autumn interest are available. Plants are sold by mail order and to customers visiting the nursery. **The Picton Garden** is part of the same enterprise, designed to grow the NCCPG National Collection of autumn-flowering asters. For opening times for the nursery and garden, call or visit the website.

BEAUTIFUL BULBS

AS RECOMMENDED BY CHRIS IRELAND-JONES AND ALAN STREET OF AVON BULBS

Allium 'Globemaster'

Lilium regale

Our entry to this book is a distillation of all the gorgeous bulbs that are available. They have been chosen for ease of growing and the satisfaction that they should bring, as well as representing a wide range of seasons. Bulbs are explosive early-flowering plants with impact and rich colours to offer. They add sparkle to your displays at any time of year, though dominating in the spring.

1 *Gladiolus communis* subsp. *byzantinus* ♔
With its magenta flowers and sword-shaped leaves, this plant has been known and loved in the British garden for 300 years. Each flower spike carries up to 20 flowers arranged to one side. The sturdy stems are 70cm (28in) tall, and the plant makes a good cut flower.

2 *Leucojum aestivum* 'Gravetye Giant' ♔
The summer snowflake comes into flower after the snowdrops have finished, with similar nodding, emerald-tipped flowers hanging from upright bare stems, amid

graceful dark green leaves. It can reach a height of 50cm-1m (20-40in). It likes damp situations, although it prefers good drainage, and can tolerate drought.

3 *Lilium regale* ♔
A wonderful garden bulb with its large trumpet-shaped white flowers, flushed pink, with yellow anthers and pollen. It grows to 1.5m (5ft) high, giving a fine focal point to any border. It is happiest with its head in sun and its root in shade.

4 *Narcissus poeticus* var. *recurvus* ♔
A late-flowering narcissus from Alpine

meadows, suited to naturalising. It is sweetly scented with a spicy tinge, so plant in pots where you can appreciate its perfume. It likes its roots in shade, in grass or with other plants around it and looks especially fine in dappled light. It can reach heights of 24cm (9in).

5 *Scilla peruviana*
Broad, fleshy, nearly evergreen leaves grow through winter and in April dramatic dark blue buds appear, followed in June by a pyramid of steely-blue, star-shaped flowers with bright yellow anthers, perhaps 15cm (6in) high. Suitable for containers but do not like being moved.

6 *Tulipa* 'Shirley'
A tulip to watch through the season. The buds open creamy-yellow, becoming white with purplish speckling over the petals. As they mature, the speckling spreads until the flower is darkly stained purple at flowering time in late April or early May when they will be about 60cm (24in) tall.

7 *Allium* 'Globemaster' ♕
A 20cm (8in) violet-purple sphere on a 90cm (35in) stem is not something that will be overlooked in the garden. The already satisfactory flowering season is extended as, after the first flourish, new florets appear for a subsidiary display. Best planted in groups, 45cm (18in) apart, in a sunny situation.

8 *Erythronium* californicum 'White Beauty' ♕
In spring the mottled leaves form a loose clump from which rise several stems carrying the creamy flowers about 24cm (9in) tall in April. Once established they clump up well in moisture-retentive, fertile soil in dappled shade, where roots of shrubs and trees take away excess moisture in summer.

9 *Eucomis comosa*
The pineapple flower is from South Africa, so it likes wet summers and dry winters. If planted deeply enough it persists from year to year. The fleshy star-shaped flowers are white, green or pink with darker edges and ovaries, growing up a spike between 60cm-1.2m (24-47in).

10 *Galanthus* 'S. Arnott' ♕
A honey-scented tall, 25cm (10in)-tall vigorous snowdrop with a deep green heart-shaped mark on the inner petals. The flowers last, even when the weather is sunny. Plant in light shade, under trees and shrubs, where they will increase steadily. Buy 'in the green' in spring and plant deeply.

AVON BULBS
Burnt House Farm, Mid Lambrook,
near South Petherton, Somerset TA13 5HE
T: 01460 242177
E: chris@avonbulbs.co.uk W: www.avonbulbs.com

Avon Bulbs are a family firm based in south Somerset from where they provide these and many more great bulbs by mail order. Having gained 20 Gold Medals at the Chelsea Flower Show it can also be said that they also know how to grow and display what they sell. Avon Bulbs specialise in *Galanthus* and *Eucomis* (spring), *Alliums*, *Iris unguicularis* and historical daffodils (autumn) and amaryllis (late summer). Opening times vary seasonally - telephone for details.

BULBS FOR NATURALISING

AS RECOMMENDED BY JOHN SHIPTON AND ALISON FOOT OF SHIPTON BULBS

Hyacinthoides non-scripta and *Silene dioica*

Wildflower gardening is becoming very popular, with more people aware of the value of their gardens as a refuge for wildlife. Shipton Bulbs grows bulbs native to Britain, and a range of native perennials and ferns for woodland, wetland and meadows. To increase diversity, they also grow a range of other bulbs to naturalise in the garden, including many historical daffodils, tulips and crocuses to provide colour and interest for most of the year.

1 *Hyacinthoides non-scripta*

Everybody knows and loves this familiar flower. Often known as a bluebell, Shipton Bulbs has been growing stock in west Wales for over 25 years and can vouch for its authenticity. Easy to grow in shady spots or more open areas, it flowers in May, reaching its glorious peak in the middle of the month.

2 *Narcissus pseudonarcissus* ♆

Known as the Lent lily, this is the main daffodil species of Britain, and the one that impressed Wordsworth so much. A short plant of 20-30cm (8-12in) in height, with pale petals and deep yellow corona, it's found in damp woods and grassland, where it naturalises readily. It flowers in March.

3 *Galanthus nivalis* ♆

Native to Wales and the South West, the snowdrop has naturalised in most parts of Britain. It's found in damp woods and can be grown in most soils and grass. It's one of the earliest of flowers, appearing from January to March.

4 *Fritillaria meleagris*

The fascinating native fritillary, with red-purple to cream flowers, chequered dark and light, occurs naturally in damp meadows in southern England. It is now rare in the wild. Planted in soil that does not dry out, and in full sun, it flowers in April.

5 *Anemone nemorosa* ♆

Called the windflower, this is one of our loveliest woodland flowers, with its delicate white blossoms and ferny foliage. It prefers damp soil and light shade, so it's suited to hedgerows and areas under deciduous shrubs and trees, where it will spread very happily.

Hyacinthoides non-scripta

6 *Primula vulgaris* 🏆

The primrose is a favourite spring pale yellow flower, and one of the earliest. Some can begin flowering in January, continuing through to April and May. It grows well in woodland, on hedge banks or in grass that's only mown in late summer.

7 *Silene dioica*

Known as snake's flower' in Welsh, the campion has a long flowering season from spring through to summer, and looks absolutely stunning with bluebells. It flowers freely, with male and female flowers on different plants, in shades of rich pink,

CULTIVATION

All Shipton Bulbs' bulbs and plants are suitable for naturalising, given conditions close to their natural habitat; woodlanders are happy in the shade from shrubs and garden trees, while wetland plants thrive in a boggy area around a garden pond. Bulbs grow best planted in late summer and autumn. Plant in large drifts, in grass or under trees. Most of the perennials and ferns can be planted at the same time, but spring is best for autumn flowerers. The key to successful planting is good preparation, making sure that the ground is weed-free and the grass cut short.

Narcissus 'White Lady'

Fritillaria meleagris (white form)

in woods, hedge banks and meadows. It spreads in most soils.

8 *Dryopteris affinis* ♛
Ferns are ideal for damp woodlands and shaded borders, and are becoming fashionable again. They're fascinating in their own right. This one is commonly called the golden scale fern and it is a fine feature in our woods and hedge banks, with its golden scales covering the fronds.

9 *Narcissus poeticus* var. *recurvus* ♛
The fragrant old-fashioned pheasant's eye narcissus is an old variety of the species found in meadows in central Europe. With its pure white petals and shallow greenish-yellow cup with a crimson rim, it flowers late in the season, well into May.

10 *Narcissus* 'White Lady'
This charming, delicately scented variety was introduced before 1898. Raised by the Reverend GH Engleheart, this mid-season daffodil was a stalwart of the florists' industry for many years. The flowers are a beautiful shape with satiny white petals, and a lemon cup.

SHIPTON BULBS
Y Felin, Henllan Amgoed, Whitland,
Carmarthenshire SA34 0SL
T: 01994 240125 F: 01994 241180
E: bluebell@zoo.co.uk W: www.bluebellbulbs.co.uk

With hedgerows, woodland and hay meadows disappearing under the onslaught of construction and modern farming methods, the sight of our native flowers is fast becoming a memory to many people. This inspired John Shipton and Alison Foot in the early 1980s to start growing native bulbs on their Welsh smallholding. Over the years they've added many beautiful wildflowers to their list, as well as some of the most striking native ferns and many old daffodils.

BULBS – UNUSUAL

AS RECOMMENDED BY JACQUES AMAND OF JACQUES AMAND

Arisaema candidissimum

When considering bulbs, the best-known ones, such as tulips, crocuses and daffodils, usually spring to mind. Bulbs, or bulbous plants, include what are, botanically, corms, tubers and rhizomes, all adaptations by nature to form a store of nutrients and moisture so they can survive in their natural habitat. Nearly 75% of the bulbs planted in gardens each year are those that flower in spring, with daffodils, tulips, hyacinths and crocuses predominating. With diversity now in fashion, the time may have come to try some of the more unusual bulbs currently offered by the UK's specialist nurseries.

1 *Arisaema candidissimum* ♛

One of the most attractive and dependable of the many hardy species and, unlike most other *Arisaema*, has a beautiful rose-like fragrance. The blooms are pink and white. Plant in spring in an only lightly-shaded, well-drained spot. It emerges in May and is normally in full bloom in June. It grows to 10-15cm (4-6in) tall, with a spread of 30-45cm (12-18in), and is frost hardy. H4

2 *Arisaema sikokianum*

Native to Japan, where it grows in woodlands, this is perhaps the most striking of all Arisaemas, its marshmallow-like central spadix arousing curiosity in all who see it. Flowering in May to June, it prefers leafy, well-drained soil with shade. It's also frost hardy and grows to 30-50cm (12-20in), with a spread of 30-45cm (12-18in). H3

3 *Eremurus* 'Joanna'

Raised in Holland and named after John Amand's daughter, this spectacular, frost-hardy cultivar, with hundreds of individual white flowers on a giant spike in June, is ideal for the back of a sunny, sheltered border. The octopus-like roots are planted in autumn with their central crown just below the surface. Reaches a height of 2.4m (8ft).

4 *Lilium nepalense*

A strangely beautiful species lily from the Himalayas, with yellowish-green and maroon-red flowers in July, always much admired in our Chelsea displays. Once established it grows to about 1m (3ft 3in), with one to three blooms on a stem, and should be planted in spring in a shady, woodland position with humus-rich, free-draining soil. Frost hardy. H2

Lilium nepalense

CULTIVATION

Even though their homelands can be diverse, most bulbs have one common requirement – the need for good drainage. Mix in a generous amount of coarse sand or grit with the existing soil, especially if this is naturally heavy. Depth of planting is also important; 'the larger the bulb, the deeper it should be planted' and 'cover the bulb with up to twice its own height' are good rules of thumb. As always, there are exceptions to such rules so, if in doubt, check with your supplier, a good reference book or on the internet.

Allium 'Globemaster'

Fritillaria imperialis 'Striped Beauty'

5 *Lilium majoense*

One of the best of the recently introduced species from China, deserving to be more widely grown. It has several large, creamy-white flowers, heavily speckled with dark purple. The bulbs are planted in spring in similar conditions to those advised for *Lilium nepalense* and, when established, will flower in July. Frost hardy, it reaches a height of 1.2-1.5m (4-5ft). H2

6 *Iris* 'Katharine Hodgkin'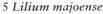

A little gem of the bulb world, perfect for the rockery or a special corner in the garden, growing to just 13cm (5in). It comes into bloom between January and March, an exquisite blend of creamy-yellow overlaid with azure and sea-green veins merging into a golden yellow crest on the falls. Plant bulbs in September to October. Suitable for sun or shade, it's a hardy plant that requires dry soil. Also poisonous. H4

7 *Allium* 'Globemaster'

Growing to 75cm (30in), this is an outstanding cultivar, deservedly at the forefront of the explosion in popularity of Alliums during the 1990s and into the new millennium. Bulbs planted 12.5cm (5in) deep in autumn flower during May and June with huge, ball-shaped heads, each made up of innumerable individual flowers in a most-attractive shade of aster violet. Fully hardy, 'Globemaster' is suited to full sun and dry soil. H4

8 *Fritillaria imperialis* 'Striped Beauty'

'Striped Beauty' flowers in April with a circular cluster of pendulous, yellow

Eremurus 'Joanna'

to orange bells, heavily veined with carmine-orange, all atop a stout stem crowned with a tuft of leaves. Plant in the autumn, about 15cm (6in) deep, ideally in a sunny position with rich, free-draining soil. Reaches a height of 60-90cm (24-36in).

9 *Trillium grandiflorum* ♆

Trilliums are definitely among the most attractive of North American woodland plants, and this species, the wake robin is one of the finest and easiest. Three-petalled, white flowers are held on slender stalks in April to May. Planted with plenty of leafmould, and given time to establish, this lovely woodlander will prove long-lived and trouble-free – it's fine in sun or shade, and dry soil. It grows to 30cm (12in) tall. H4

10 *Narcissus cyclamineus* ♆

With its deep yellow, tubular trumpet and petals sweeping straight back, this species daffodil is one of those 'once seen, never forgotten' gems of the bulb world. Usually in full flower in early March, it's perfect for naturalising in partly-shaded spots with damp, acid soil beneath deciduous trees. Grows to a height of 15cm (6in). H4

JACQUES AMAND
The Nurseries, Clamp Hill, Stanmore, Middlesex HA7 3JS
T: 020 8420 7110
E: info@jacquesamand.co.uk
W: www.jacquesamand.co.uk

Jacques Amand, a family firm founded in 1927, moved to its North London site in 1986, and over the years has gained an enviable reputation for its wide range of bulbs. The nursery's catalogues, nursery and displays at shows throughout the country are an Aladdin's cave for those seeking rare and unusual bulbs. Specialities include *Arisaema*, *Trillium*, *Fritillaria* and *Lilium*. Separate catalogues are issued for autumn and spring and will happily be sent, free of charge, on request.

CHRYSANTHEMUMS

AS RECOMMENDED BY HAROLD WALKER AT HAROLD WALKER NURSERIES

C. 'Beacon'

C. 'Fairweather'

Chrysanthemums – genus *Chrysanthemum* – are very useful in the garden as they provide late summer and autumn colour during their season of flower. Some late varieties even carry on well into autumn, although it's a good idea to stake or support them so that they don't topple over. There is a huge range of flower shapes, grouped into 10 different categories, from simple daisy-like flowers to pompons and elaborate spider forms. Below I have listed my 10 favourites, all of which have 'incurved' or 'intermediate', spherical flowerheads. Many are ideal for exhibition, should you wish to enter them in your local flower show.

1 C. 'John Hughes'
This chrysanthemum is a pure white incurve of perfect short upright habit, growing to a height of 1.2m (4ft).

2 C. 'Yellow Fairweather'
A cultivar with a clear yellow incurved flowerhead that appears late in the season and grows to 1.2m (4ft).

3 C. 'Max Riley' ♔
Good incurves are hard to come by and this deep yellow form is always in demand. A good globular form with hard petals that flowers in early autumn and grows to a height of 1.1m (3ft 7in).

4 C. 'Alan Foxall'
This golden bronze incurve of classic form that flowers late in the season grows to 1.3m (4ft 3in).

5 C. 'Beacon' ♔
This late-season chrysanthemum is aptly named for its very bright, red and gold flowerheads. These are in the 'intermediate' category, very similar to 'incurved' types. It is a decorative plant carrying a heavy crop, growing to 1.2m (4ft).

6 C. 'Gingernut'
The very neat, light bronze 'gingernut' flowerheads of this chrysanthemum

appear in early autumn and are intermediate in shape. Some of the flowerheads at the top form a perfect incurved shape. The plant can grow to a height of 1.2m (4ft).

7 C. 'Fairweather'

A very neat medium incurve that flowers late in the season. The flower colour is light purple, showing more silver on the reverse side. It is a short, stocky grower, reaching a height of 1.1m (3ft 7in).

8 C. 'Ermine'

The perfectly incurved white flowerheads of this early season chrysanthemum are always greatly admired. They are large flowers carried on good stems 1.2m (4ft) high with small leaves.

9 C. 'White Fairweather'

The medium-sized, incurved flowerheads of this chrysanthemum are borne in late autumn on 1.2m (4ft) tall stems.

10 C. 'Emma Lou'

The large yellow incurved flowerheads of 'Emma Lou' are something of a rarity these days. The incurved shape goes back to the stem and finishes well on top. Tends to

C. 'Max Riley'

C. 'Emma Lou'

flower in October. This plant can grow to a height of 1.2m (4ft).

CYCLAMEN

AS RECOMMENDED BY PETER MOORE OF THE TILE BARN NURSERY

C. coum

C. hederifolium

I saw my first cyclamen – genus *Cyclamen* – as a boy while walking in Austria and this started my interest in the genus. Over the course of many years I built up my collection of plants. Eventually I joined the Cyclamen Society and in 1983 became its secretary. I was lucky to be chosen to go on field trips to Turkey, Israel and Greece and the Greek islands of Crete, Kithera and Rhodes. As well as being a total joy to see the plants growing in the wild, the trips were also a valuable insight into the natural habitats of cyclamen. We stock a number of other plants, which make good planting companions for cyclamen and I have included two of these in my top 10.

1 C. cilicium ♈

C. cilicium has either white or pink flowers, which usually bloom after *C. coum*. Its oval-shaped leaves are covered with a delicate pattern of white markings, the perfect background to the equally delicate flowers. They must have a well-drained site in dappled shade. It grows to 10cm (4in) in height. H2-4

2 C. coum ♈

This cyclamen thrives in dappled shade. As long as the soil is not waterlogged, it will be very rewarding. It flowers late winter to early spring, when there is little else to brighten dull days. There are white, pink or magenta flower forms. It can reach 10cm (4in). H4

3 C. cyprium

Indigenous to Cyprus where it grows in the mountains, this has strong-scented white flowers with purple marks at the base in late autumn to early winter, extending the flowering period. The leaves are olive green with light green blotches. In the garden a shady position is essential. It grows to a height of 10cm (4in). H3

4 C. *graecum*

If I have a favourite cyclamen, this is probably it. It grows wild in Turkey and Greece, with white or pink flowers in autumn when the leaves appear, with very varied patterns and shades. It needs full sun and a good baking in summer, growing to 10cm (4in). H3

5 C. *hederifolium*

C. *hederifolium* flowers in autumn when the garden is becoming dull, with white or pink flower forms. Grow it in dappled shade in well-drained soil. It is a very strong-growing plant with attractive foliage and can swamp C. *coum*, so keep them separate or planted in groups. It can reach a height of 10cm (4in).

6 C. *mirabile* ♔

This native of Turkey can withstand the cold of the UK, but must have a well-drained site in dappled shade. It has white or pink flowers, and in many plants the upper white markings of the young leaves are carmine-pink. It makes an excellent cold greenhouse plant. It reaches a height of 10cm (4in). H2-3

7 C. *persicum*

C. *persicum* flowers in the spring and the foliage and flowers are larger than other species of cyclamen. The colour of the flowers ranges from deep magenta, to pink and through to pure white. The leaf patterns are very varied and beautiful. There is a silver-leafed form which is particularly striking. It grows to a height of 30cm (12in). H1

8 C. *peloponnesiacum* ♔

This species is a spring-flowering woodland plant with delicate flowers, pink to dark pink with a carmine nose. The pattern on the leaves is frequently covered with bright silver splashes. The addition of leaf mould or other organic material is especially beneficial to this species. It grows to 30cm (12in). H2-3

9 *Erythronium revolutum*

For visitors to the nursery we have for sale a range of bulbs apart from cyclamen. This hardy woodland plant has beautiful mottled leaves, and rose-pink reflexed flowers in the spring. It makes an excellent plant for the cold greenhouse and grows to 20-30cm (8-12in).

10 *Narcissus cyclamineus*

This narcissus has bright golden flowers with reflexed perianth segments. In the garden both this narcissus and the *Erythronium* above require similar conditions to cyclamen and look very well growing amongst them. This narcissus reaches a height of 15cm (6in).

TILE BARN NURSERY
Standen Street, Iden Green, Benenden, Kent TN17 4LB
T/F: 01580 240221
E: sales@tilebarn-cyclamen.co.uk
W: www.tilebarn-cyclamen.co.uk

The nursery became a full time occupation for Peter Moore 20 years ago during which time he has seen interest in cyclamen steadily growing during this period. He says he hopes they have helped to dispel some of the misconceptions that cause many gardeners to dismiss cyclamen as difficult. Please send an SAE for a catalogue. The nursery is open Wednesday to Saturday - call for times. Mail order plants are sent out all the year round.

DAFFODILS

AS RECOMMENDED BY RON SCAMP AT QUALITY DAFFODILS

N. 'Rapture'

N. 'Avalanche'

N. 'Cape Cornwall'

N. poeticus var. recurvus

The culture of the genus *Narcissus*, or daffodil as it is popularly known, has been well documented. By the mid 1800s great steps were taken to produce new, more suitable varieties for the flower market. This has continued over the years and is still being developed today in many parts of the world. Narcissi can be found primarily in the temperate regions of Europe, though some species are found in the Mediterranean and western Asia. I have chosen the varieties for their colour, shape, scent, season and vigour in growth, and I think that all the daffodils mentioned here are admirably suited for the garden.

1 N. *poeticus* var. *recurvus* ♔
Commonly know as the pheasant's eye, this can be found in the wild, growing in the Pyrenees. It is superb in large, naturalised drifts. I like to have a vase indoors where the delicate scent can really be appreciated. It can grow to a height of 42cm (17in).

2 N. 'Rapture' ♔
One of the best of this group, best described as a larger smoother N. *cyclamineus* 13Y-Y with a gracefully reflexed perianth and a long slender corona. Wonderful when grouped at the front of the border, it flowers early and lasts a long time.

3 N. 'White Lady'
A wonderful old variety. As a boy I always got my quota quickly when picking for market, such was the quantity of bloom and length of stem. The flowers are white with a soft yellow, small cup and delicate perfume. It grows up to 45cm (18in) in height.

4 N. 'Blisland'
I could describe this as a modern-day pheasant's eye. This is one that I have bred and is a strong, robust plant with very special quality blooms that have won many prizes. It flowers just a little bit later in the season. It also has a very pleasant scent.

5 N. 'Avalanche' ♔
Although grown for 50 years or more, this has not been widely distributed until now. Possibly a little tender in some regions, but one of the hardiest of its kind. Plant it in a

sunny aspect at the back of the border as it will grow quite tall, to 35cm (14in).

6 N. 'Madam Speaker'

Many double daffodils have the fault of the stem bending over and spoiling the bloom – this is one that I have bred that resists this. There are many fine doubles that I have bred, but if I could have only one in the garden, this would be it.

7 N. 'Rainbow'

There are many daffodils with pink in the cups, but this one has proved itself on the show bench and in the garden, where its consistency, bloom, vigour and habit make it a must. Plant it in sun and it will reward you with its charm. It can grow to 45cm (18in).

8 N. 'Rosemoor Gold'

I have bred and introduced many jonquil hybrids, which are all highly scented. Most will give several flowers on the stem and mature bulbs will give several secondary stems. The bulbs appear to be disease-resistant, and 'Rosemoor Gold' was selected by the RHS as its Bicentenary Daffodil.

CULTIVATION

Daffodils are not demanding plants, but are best suited to an open aspect with plenty of light and moisture-retentive, well-drained soil, as they do not like to be dry during the growing season. It is best to plant the bulbs with at least 12-15cm (5-6in) of soil covering the bulb, the smaller varieties with a little less. They can be planted in grass and natural surroundings and left for many years undisturbed to develop into bold displays. Always leave the foliage to die back naturally, as the premature loss of the foliage can be a cause of loss of blooms next year.

---

9 N. 'Cape Cornwall'

This is one of the most consistently smooth and faultless flowers for the show benches and looks stunning in the garden. The flowers are large, brightly coloured and stand well on stiff upright stems.

10 N. 'Gillan'

For years, the split corona daffodils weren't that popular, but attitudes have changed. This is one we introduced a few years ago – the bulbs produce an astonishing number of blooms with glowing colours.

R. A. SCAMP - QUALITY DAFFODILS
14 Roscarrack Close, Falmouth, Cornwall TR11 4PJ
T/F: 01326 317959
E: info@qualitydaffodils.co.uk
W: www.qualitydaffodils.co.uk

Ron's association with daffodils goes back over 55 years when, as a child, he lived in the Tamar Valley, a prominent flower and daffodil-producing region in Cornwall. Today his collection numbers almost 2,500 kinds of daffodils, which are sent all over the world. Through **Quality Daffodils**, Ron has displayed at many major shows, and achieved several RHS Gold medals. In 2006, Ron was awarded the prestigious American Daffodil Society Gold Medal for his work with daffodils. Please contact the nursery for more information about purchasing.

DAHLIAS

AS RECOMMENDED BY DAVID HALL OF HALLS OF HEDDON

D. 'Pooh'

How do you choose a top 10? The varieties of dahlia – genus *Dahlia* – I have selected are just some of those that stood out for me over the years. Some come from memories of my first association with dahlias when going to shows with my father or 'helping' on the nursery, others are good all-round varieties suitable for general planting in today's gardens. I have a particular fondness for the collerettes and dwarf bedder dahlias because of their free-flowering nature – they provide a great splash of late summer colour when many other plants are over. Cactus dahlias have silky, ball-shaped flowerheads.

D. 'Black Monarch'

D. 'David Howard'

D. 'Fashionmonger'

1 D. 'Doris Day'

The flowers of this small cactus dahlia are a rich red and held on slender stems. Growing to about 1.1m (3ft 7in), 'Doris Day' makes an ideal garden variety, being very free-flowering – it is the first dahlia I have seen recommended for pots because of its free-flowering nature. It is also good for cut flowers. H2-3

2 D. 'Black Monarch'

The dinner plate flowers of this giant decorative are either loved or hated. Deep purple with almost black shadings, this variety grows to about 1.5m (5ft). The flowers are at their biggest when only three or four stems are allowed to grow and disbudded so the main flower develops. H2-3

3 D. 'David Howard' ♛

This miniature decorative variety, introduced in 1960 by David Howard from Norfolk, has been one of my favourites for a long time. With its bronze foliage and burnt orange flowers, it is ideal in borders for a summer-long display, contrasting well with other plants and giving a tropical feel to the planting. H2-3

4 D. 'Fashionmonger'

This particular variety, also known as collerette, is just eye-catching with its the combination of raspberry-red and cream flowers, which are extremely attractive to butterflies. Growing to about 1.2m (4ft), it blends well in a typical cottage garden where it begins its continuous show of flowers from early August to the frosts. H2-3

5 D. 'Pooh'

We came across this dahlia by chance in a 'lucky dip' consignment we received from America. Free-flowering and upright-growing to 1.2m (4ft), this variety, also known as collerette, stood out the first year we planted it and was one of the most requested varieties of those we had on trial that year. H2-3

CULTIVATION

Land for dahlias should be well dug and manured in the autumn and a complete fertiliser applied at the rate of 75-100g (3-4oz) per square metre, about two weeks before planting. If you have a heated greenhouse you can take delivery of mini plants from April onwards. On receipt, plants should be potted on into 10-13cm (4-5in) pots, shading from direct sun for the first few days. Grow on in a frost-free environment, being careful not to overwater in the early stages. When plants are about 25cm (10in) high, remove the growing tip to encourage bushiness.

D. 'Staleen Condessa'

6 *D.* 'Tudor 1'

The name 'Tudor' refers to the creamy-white flowers with chocolate-coloured centres, reminiscent of Elizabethan ruffs. The flowers contrast well with the bronze foliage to make this an excellent dwarf bedder dahlia suitable for pot culture, growing to about 45cm (18in) in height, with an equivalent spread. H2-3

7 *D.* 'Bryn Terfel'

This giant decorative dahlia created an immediate impact on the show bench and in our nursery trial beds when we first grew it. A stunning variety that is big and bright, with a slightly twisted petal formation, the plant itself is very robust with strong stems growing to 1.5m (5ft) in height. H2-3

8 *D.* 'Staleen Condessa' ♟

We grew this medium semi-cactus dahlia in our fields along with 6,000 other plants and it is one of the best we have seen. The colour

D. 'Tudor 1'

D. 'Teesbrooke Redeye'

D. 'Doris Day'

and form of the flowers is excellent. Cuttings are very easy to root and the plant itself has a very strong upright habit, growing to a height of 1.5m (5ft). H3

9 D. 'Teesbrooke Redeye'

This variety does well on the show bench. Also known as a collerette, it is an excellent garden variety, notable for its slightly reddish serrated leaf and the chocolate eye in the centre of the freely-borne lilac pink single flowers. An excellent choice for the herbaceous border, mixing very well with other plants. H2-3

10 D. 'Charlie Dimmock'

We introduced this small waterlily dahlia, raised by Ken Stock of Bournemouth, in 2005. It is superb for mixed borders and, with its strong stems, excellent for cutting. It is also a good choice for exhibition, as the flower formation is good. H2-3

DELPHINIUMS

AS RECOMMENDED BY KEN AND AUDREY HARBUTT OF ROUGHAM HALL NURSERIES

D. 'Albert Shepherd'

No planting scheme of hardy perennials is complete without the inclusion of *Delphinium elatum*, the 'queen of the border'. This stately hardy perennial will give height, beauty and years of pleasure to any garden. Cultivars derived from this species range from pure white through to cream, pink, mauve, light and dark blue, and also very dark purple. Different-coloured eyes add to the beauty of the flowers. Delphiniums are also very popular cut flowers for indoor arrangements, either for a very bold display, such as on a pedestal or using the small florets for a table decoration. These are our top five cultivars.

1 *D.* 'Christine Harbutt'

Without doubt, one of the most free-flowering delphiniums in cultivation today. Pure white with attractive cream eyes, and lovely light green foliage. Height reaches up to 1.3m (4ft 4in). To encourage repeat flowering, remove any spent flower stems to ground level. The original plant of this cultivar at Rougham Hall Nurseries is 18 years old and still flourishing.

2 *D.* 'Cream Arrow'

This lovely delphinium has tall, majestic stems of cream florets with an attractive deeper cream eye. A vast improvement on all others in the 'cream' group. It can grow up to 1.6m (5ft 3in). It has a true perennial habit and is a cultivar that is becoming increasingly popular with both the specialist cut-flower grower and the amateur gardener.

D. 'David Mannion'

3 *D.* 'Albert Shepherd'

A very free-flowering cultivar of great merit. Lovely pale blue, lightly flushed pale pink with a very attractive fawn eye, that will flower repeatedly. Grows up to 1.3m (4ft 4in) tall, and is a trouble-free cultivar if the flowering stems are not overcrowded; thin them out to seven or eight.

> **CULTIVATION**
>
> For the best results, choose a well-drained, but moisture-retentive, soil in full sun. Plant from March to the end of September, spacing at least 60cm (24in) apart. Do not plant in winter. Mildew is caused through dryness at the roots and overcrowding of flower stems, so ensure roots are kept moist by scrupulous watering, mulching well and thinning flower stems to no more than eight. Feed with a well-balanced fertiliser; never a high-nitrogen feed. Keep a sharp lookout for slug damage, especially during the winter and spring months.

4 *D.* 'Alie Duyvensten'

Rich violet-purple with a conspicuous white eye. Beautiful-shaped florets, evenly spaced on strong, elegant stems, with attractive mid-green foliage. A tall, majestic cultivar attaining a height of up to 1.9m (6ft 3in). Robust and long-lived, this cultivar should be given consideration by the keen exhibitor.

5 *D.* 'David Mannion' ⚜

Ultramarine-blue with attractive brown-black eye; neatly-placed florets on strong, stiff stems, up to 1.3m (4ft 3in) tall. Given the RHS Award of Garden Merit recently, following extensive trials at Wisley. A long-lived, trouble-free perennial.

ROUGHAM HALL NURSERIES
A14 Rougham, Bury St Edmunds, Suffold IP30 9LZ
T: 0800 970 7516
E: sales@roughamhallnurseries.co.uk
W: www.roughamhallnurseries.co.uk

❀   NCCPG National Collection holder of *Delphinium* and gooseberries
Rougham Hall was established in 1960 by Ken and Audrey Harbutt, specialising in field-grown hardy perennials. Later, container-grown plants were added to meet growing demand. The nursery is a regular exhibitor at RHS flower shows. Recently, Kelvin, the eldest son, has taken over the management of the nursery, still specialising in hardy perennials, but adding a good range of fruit trees and bushes, trees and shrubs. Open seven days a week, 10am to 4pm.

DIANTHUS (PINKS)
AS RECOMMENDED BY MR AND MRS JAMES OF ALLWOODS

D. 'Doris'

Pinks are in the *Dianthus* family and have been known in cultivation as far back as 300BC. The genus was given the name *Dianthus* from the Greek '*dios*', which means 'divine', and '*anthos*', meaning 'flower' – and they really are 'a divine flower'; with their heady perfume, stunning colours and different types, dianthuses are a must for all gardeners. Traditionally grown in cottage gardens, they have adapted to our modern gardening styles and add a touch of class and scent to any garden.

1 D. 'Doris' ♈
Introduced in 1945, this is the most famous pink of them all, named after the wife of Montagu Allwood, one of the nursery's founders. This long-flowering pink, with a bushy habit, is ideal in any garden. It is clove-scented, grows to 30-35cm (12-14in) and is ideal for growing as a cut flower.

2 D. 'Summerfield Amy Francesca'
Developed in 2000, this is a compact, bushy variety that produces fully-double, slightly fringed flowers, with a rose-pink ground and velvety crimson centres. It is clove-scented and compact, reaching a height of 20-25cm (8-10in) with a long flowering season.

D. 'Summerfield Amy Francesca'

D. 'Fleur'

3 *D.* 'Show Beauty'

Developed pre-1939, this plant, as the name suggests, was used for show purposes. The flowers are large, showy and deep rose-pink with a bold maroon eye. They have a strong clove scent and are excellent for cutting. The plant has a long flowering season. It grows to 30-35cm (12-14in).

4 *D.* 'Mrs Sinkins' ♆

The pink everyone knows! Developed in 1868, this pure white frilly flower is unbeatable. Heavily clove-scented, it is still as popular now as it has always been. Growing to 25-30cm (10-12in), it makes a good bushy plant and flowers easily. It can be found on the Slough coat of arms.

5 *D.* 'Fleur'

A fantastic double variety developed in 1971, with blooms of pale pink, striped with coral red. 'Fleur' makes a good compact plant and repeat-flowers over a long period.

D. 'Mrs Sinkins'

Reaching a height of 20-25cm (8-10in), it is clove-scented, but the unusual blooms are its biggest feature!

6 D. 'Laced Mrs Sinkins'

The age of this plant is unknown. However, it is a vigorous grower – a sport from the famous white 'Mrs Sinkins' – with a wonderful strong clove scent and big, bushy flowers of deep pink with a darker pink central zone and lacing. It grows to a height of 25cm (10in).

7 D. 'Becky Robinson'

One of the laced varieties, developed in

CULTIVATION

Pinks are hardy perennials. They are fairly drought-tolerant – very useful in our ever-changing climate. They like a sunny spot and good drainage around the roots. If you're on heavy clay, add grit to the soil or grow your dianthuses in containers. Flowering times vary depending on the variety. Old varieties, like 'Mrs Sinkins', have a general flush in May and June, whereas modern varieties repeat-flower from April until the frosts. Feeding is essential for good growth and an abundance of flowers. A balanced feed is ideal, and should be started soon after dianthuses are planted into the ground or pots.

D. 'Laced Mrs Sinkins'

1984, with superb rose-pink ground colour, a crimson centre and lacing. This is a good, compact grower with long-flowering abilities and a wonderful clove scent, making it a great cut-flower plant. It grows to around 30cm (12in).

D. 'Pheasant's Eye'

8 D. 'Pheasant's Eye'

This is one of the oldest pinks around. Developed pre-1600, this highly-serrated flower with a white ground has a deep red-brown eye. It is heavily clove-scented and reaches a height of 25cm (10in).

9 D. 'Helena Hitchcock'

Developed in 1990, this is a very pretty flower, with a pure white ground colour, laced rosy-purple. It grows to a height of 25-30cm (10-12in) and is richly clove-scented.

D. 'Helena Hitchcock'

10 D. 'Rainbow Loveliness'

Developed by Allwoods in the 1920s and still incredibly popular, this annual pink has a heady perfume and fantastically divided petals, unrivalled by any other pink. It flowers throughout the summer in pastel shades of lavender, pink and white; it is seed-raised, so each year you never know what you're going to get.

D. 'Rainbow Loveliness'

ALLWOODS
London Road, Hassocks, West Sussex BN6 9NB
T: 01273 844229
E: info@allwoods.net W: www.allwoods.net
Open Monday to Saturday, 9am to 5pm (Sundays and Bank Holidays, 10am to 4pm), March to June only

The three Allwood brothers founded the nursery back in 1910, and made many introductions, such as 'Doris', probably the most famous pink in existence. In 1960 **Allwoods** was sold. The firm then had many owners and a chance conversation in 1992 enabled the current owners to buy it. It was being run-down for closure and was in a poor state, but they managed to buy it in time and rescue its unique collection of plants.

EUPHORBIAS

AS RECOMMENDED BY DON WITTON OF DON'S HARDY EUPHORBIAS

E. polychroma

E. amygdaloides var. robbiae

The genus *Euphorbia* is one of the largest in the world. It contains about 2,000 species which grow in almost every corner of the planet. It is a diverse family containing succulents, trees and shrubs, as well as the herbaceous perennials outside in the garden. This latter group come mainly from Europe and Asia and make delightful garden plants. The flowers consist of petal-like bracts in colours from lime to gold, orange-red and white. They start flowering in late winter and can bloom for months, peaking in May and giving zingy splashes of colour to the garden.

1 *E. characias* subsp. *characias* 'Humpty Dumpty'

A 90cm (35in) evergreen perennial, this variety prefers plenty of sun and a free-draining aspect. It will produce over 60 floral stems annually. Bright grey-green leaves are topped with cylindrical flower heads. It flowers from February to June.

2 *E. characias* subsp. *Wulfenii* 'Purple and Gold'

A delightful form of this popular garden plant. The evergreen foliage turns rich purple from October onwards, remaining impressive throughout the winter. Then golden flowers appear on the foliage from March, lasting until June. It can grow to 1.1m (3ft 7in) and thrives in a sunny, sheltered position in the garden.

3 *E. cornigera* 🏆

Mid-green leaves with a white midrib are produced on deep red annual stems topped with much-branched yellow flowers. It produces flowers later than most Euphorbias, peaking in July. It grows up to 1m (3ft 3in) and looks good in a summer herbaceous border.

4 E. griffithii 'Dixter' ♈

Deep bloodshot green leaves are produced on red annual stems topped with vermillion-red floral leaves with yellow nectarines from April to June. The plant grows to about 70-80cm (28-31in) and forms a large clump, but can be divided in late winter to keep it compact. This variety needs more moisture-retentive soil than the average *Euphorbia*.

5 E. x martini ♈

E. x *martini* tolerates a wide range of aspects but can be short-lived. Deep red stems are clothed with rich green evergreen leaves containing more than a hint of purple. Acid green flowers, each with a pretty red eye, are produced from March to July. It never grows more than 75cm (30in).

6 E. mellifera ♈

E. mellifera is a shrub which may grow to more than 1.5m (5ft) but can be pruned to keep it compact. It has large glossy, light green evergreen leaves, often with a maroon edge. The flowers are pale buff-yellow, appearing from April to June. Place in a sunny, sheltered spot.

7 E. myrsinites ♈

Prostrate stems support small, glaucous evergreen foliage. The lime-yellow bracts are produced from March to April. No more than 30cm (12in) high, it is usually wider than it is tall. It needs a sunny, free draining aspect and is best grown on a sloping rockery, the top of a wall or in a container.

8 E. polychroma ♈

A wonderful border perennial which makes a neat, compact clump up to 60cm (24in). A deciduous species, the attractive green leaves appear in February. By April and May they are covered in stunning acid yellow. It copes with light shade but in full sun makes an eye-catching luminous dome.

9 E. Redwing ♈

An excellent hybrid with an extremely long period of interest. Rich evergreen foliage turns purple-red at the stem tips in January to February. The plant is then smothered in yellow bracts from March to July. It has a compact habit, and can grow up to 70cm (28in). Grow in sun or part shade.

10 E. amygdaloides var. robbiae ♈

Shiny evergreen, leathery-textured leaves are attractive throughout the winter, and topped with lime bracts 75cm (30in) from March to June. This plant does well in full sun but is better known as evergreen ground cover in dry shade, where it thrives.

DON'S HARDY EUPHORBIAS
26 Casson Drive, Harthill, Sheffield S26 7WA
T: 01909 771366 E: donshardyeuphorbias@btopenworld.com
W: www.euphorbias.co.uk

✿ NCCPG National Collection holder of *Euphorbia* (hardy)
Don's Hardy Euphorbias is a small, appointment-run nursery specialising in Eupho nursery is based around Don's NCCPG National Collection with over 150 differen⁺ cultivars. He produces Euphorbias in a wide range of varieties, usually around ⸢ one year, including rarities. Limited mail order available between October an⸢

FERNS

AS RECOMMENDED BY THE FERN NURSERY

Dryopteris affinis

Asplenium trichomanes

In the garden, ferns provide many interesting foliage effects and strong architectural shapes, especially for difficult places where nothing else will grow, since their lack of flowers and fruits means their need for light, food, and even water is often slight. Their herbaceous habit means that they require little or no maintenance, especially when compared to other foliage features, such as topiary. For the collector, they provide a vast range of plants suited to every imaginable garden situation, with many cut-leaved, crested and other fancy forms in cultivation. Here are our top 10 ferns.

1 *Dryopteris filix-mas* ♕

Perhaps the best known of our native ferns, D. *filix-mas* or the male fern is one of the toughest of all plants, thriving on neglect, in sun or shade, wet or dry. It grows to a tall waist-height of 1.2m (4ft). The form ˈˈarnesiae' has outstandingly stately fronds.

stichum setiferum ♕

wn as soft shield fern this can grow vhere, in lime or acid soil. It ˈoking, but reliably evergreen, ong outline. Its new fronds spring, covered in a soft ˈs to silver as it unfurls.

3 *Athyrium filix-femina* ♕

The lady fern is a beautiful British native with delicate-looking, but actually very tough fronds that grow to waist height. It is reputed to prefer shade and moist soil in the wild, but is in fact tough, easy and accommodating in the garden. The forms 'Frizelliae' (a dwarf form), 'Axminster' and 'Victoriae' are recommended.

4 *Athyrium niponicum* var. *pictum* (syn. *A. niponicum* f. *metallicum*) ♕

A small fern ideal for a sheltered spot, as it is easily damaged by wind and sun. The most colourful of all ferns, with grey, silver, pink

reach 0.8m (2ft 6in) high. The plant prefers moisture and partial shade. A superb fern that will thrive in the border or container. H4

6 *Blechnum chilense* 🏆

This magnificent plant originating in South America grows quickly to form a spreading clump in full sun (and almost any other conditions) providing the roots are not allowed to dry out. The upright or arching, evergreen leathery fronds can reach 1.6m (5ft) in height, with new fronds red-gold. H3

7 *Osmunda regalis* 🏆

The royal fern is another plant that likes moist conditions, often growing along water edges and in full sun. The rich leafy green fronds can reach 1.6m (5ft) and form large clumps after a few seasons. The fronds die back over winter but give a good gold-yellow colour in autumn. H4

8 *Polystichum vestitum*

The prickly shield fern is a New Zealand native fern with finely dissected, dark-green glossy fronds that can grow to 1m (3ft) in length. Extremely hardy and growing in a wide range of moisture, soil and sun conditions. A great specimen plant for ground or container planting. H3

9 *Cyathea medullaris*

This exceptionally striking black tree fern from the Pacific Islands and New Zealand. Very vigorous, with massive lacy fronds that can grow to 3m (10ft). The sturdy stems are covered in hairy, jet-black scales. Give frost protection if kept outside. H2

10 *Matteucia orientalis*

The Oriental ostrich fern is the Asian version of the shuttlecock fern, needing much less moisture, and more tolerant than its European cousin. The broad, bright green feather-like fronds form a flat rosette from the central crown.

FOXGLOVES

AS RECOMMENDED BY THE BOTANIC NURSERY AND GARDEN

D. purpurea

D. grandiflora

Our native foxglove, *Digitalis purpurea*, is the best known in cultivation, yet there are 25 other species and distinct forms found throughout central and southern Europe. All make exciting, summer-flowering plants for sun or light shade. With the exception of the *D. purpurea* and *D. ferruginea* forms, which flower in their second year, all species are perennial. The foxglove, so much a part of our British countryside, is one of the few natives to be well received in gardens. Once there, few gardeners have the heart to remove them, thus ensuring more in future seasons, for foxgloves are great self-seeders.

1 D. 'Glory of Roundway'
A perennial foxglove with lovely, rich apricot-pink flowers produced on multiple spires. They make good cut flowers and the foliage is attractive too. Grows well in any soil in sun or part shade, reaching a height of about 1.2m (4ft).

2 D. dubia
The silvery grey, hairy leaves of this Spanish native remind us that this perennial foxglove loves a hot and sunny spot. The flowers are a very pretty pink. It can grow to a height of 35cm (14in).

3 Digitalis purpurea 'Pam's Choice'
This really is a splendid example of our native foxglove, isolated from the Giant Spotted Group (which have heavily spotted throats to their flowers). It has large white flowers with chocolate-maroon spots and splashes in the flower throat.

In its second year, it can grow up to 2.2m
(7ft 2in) high.

4 *D. parviflora*

The 'chocolate' foxglove is a sound perennial
that produces many spires of small orange-
brown, chocolate-coloured flowers, to
1m (3ft 3in) tall. The leaves form a large
elongated rosette at ground level, which
looks good even in winter. Grow in sun or
light shade.

5 *D. ferruginea* ♈

Many people admire this foxglove for its
tall, branching stems of densely-packed,
honey-brown flowers with hairy interiors.
When it flowers in its second year, it can
grow up to 2m (6ft 6in) high. Even in winter
the plant looks attractive, with its ground-
level rosettes of long, deeply-veined, dark
green leaves.

6 *D. thapsi*

A rare species in cultivation, and an
undiscovered gem, originating from Portugal
and Spain, with leaves covered in golden
hairs. The purple flowers rise in spires up to
45cm (18in) tall, and are paler in the throat
and spotted red within. Grow in sun or light
shade, in well-drained soil.

7 *D. cariensis* f. *trojana*

This is a rare but exciting plant, because it
is the only perennial foxglove with white
flowers. Individually they are small and
intricately marked, almost orchid-like,
with a large white lip. They are carried on
branched spires to about 35cm (14in) high.

8 *D. lutea*

The willowy, 1m- (3ft 3in) high wands of
soft yellow flowers of this perennial foxglove
are small but plentifully produced. It is a
very pretty species for naturalising in either
sun or shade.

9 *D. purpurea* 'Sutton's Apricot' ♈

This native foxglove is notable for its tall
spires of salmon-coloured flowers, to
1.5m (5ft) high. It only lives for two years,
flowering in its second summer before
setting seed.

10 *D. grandiflora* 'Carillon'

This compact variety of the large yellow-
flowered foxglove is an easy and versatile
perennial species. It bears soft yellow
flowers intermittently all summer long,
in spires no more than 35cm (14in) tall. Best
grown in sun or part shade, it naturalises
well in wild areas.

GERANIUMS
AS RECOMMENDED BY EAST LAMBROOK MANOR GARDENS

G. macrorrhizum 'Czakor'

G. sanguineum 'Album'

G. wlassovianum

Once geraniums – genus *Geranium* – were only considered fillers in the garden, but over the years they have come into the spotlight, with new varieties introduced every year. Margery Fish, creator of East Lambrook Manor Gardens, wrote: 'I have a very large collection of hardy geraniums in different parts of the garden, and find them a most adaptable and generous family. Many of them flower throughout the season, they fit in anywhere, and in many cases good foliage is another recommendation.'

1 G. *sanguineum* 'Album' ♈
One of the smaller geraniums, only growing to 30cm (12in) with a 30cm (12in) spread, but one of the bigger *sanguineum* varieties. It likes a sunny position but will tolerate some shade. Has white flowers from June onwards.

2 G. *sylvaticum* 'Album' ♈
This lovely geranium has white flowers from May onwards. It will tolerate a wide range of positions from sun to shade, which makes it very appealing to gardeners, and also does well on dry soil. Grows to 60cm (24in) in height with a spread of 45cm (18in).

3 G. x *oxonianum* 'Walter's Gift'
Delicately-veined pale pink flowers appear on this stunning geranium from May onwards. It has orange-brown leaf growth in spring with dark markings. It reaches 30cm (12in) in height with a 50cm (20in) spread. It tolerates

a range of positions from sun to shade and prefers a good garden soil. It seems ideal for most gardeners.

4 G. x *oxonianum* 'Lambrook Gillian'
This variety was found here at East Lambrook and is available from our nursery. It has very pale-pink, almost translucent silvery flowers and early foliage has brown markings. Reaches around 45-60cm (18-24in) in height with a 60cm (24in) spread. It grow in sun or shade on any good garden soil.

5 G. Rozanne
Rozanne has large, slightly cupped and upward-facing blue flowers with paler centres from May to November. An easy geranium, like 'Buxton's Variety', but with larger flowers and over a much longer season. Grows to around 40cm (16in) in height with a spread of 60cm (24in). Prefers a sunny position.

CULTIVATION

Geraniums are very adaptable and will generally grow very well without too much input. However, selecting the correct spot will enhance their growing potential dramatically. Because the genus is so vast it is recommended that you enquire as to the optimum growing conditions for each species or cultivar when purchasing. Give plants in your border a good mulch in the spring, just as the leaves are pushing through the surface of the ground, to conserve moisture and feed the plants throughout the summer. Regular deadheading or cutting back to ground level after flowering can induce a second flush of flowers.

6 G. *psilostemon* ♛

If not the tallest, then one of the tallest geraniums, reaching around 90-120cm (36-48in), with a spread of 60cm (24in). Large black-eyed magenta flowers adorn it from June onwards. The foliage is also stunning with large, dark-green leaves. Tolerates sun or partial shade on good garden soil.

7 G. 'Lambrook Helen'

A stunning new introduction from East Lambrook. A low-growing and long-flowering alpine, its unique bright pink colour with a dark eye makes it ideal for a pot or trough on the rockery. Grows approximately 10cm (4in) in height with a spread of 25cm (10in). Prefers a well-drained, sunny spot.

8 G. *wlassovianum*

Reaches around 45-60cm (18-24in) in height with a spread of 60cm (24in). A clump-forming hairy perennial, with leaves deepening to red in autumn. From midsummer to early autumn it bears long-lasting purple-blue flowers. Plant in sun or semi-shade. I love seeing it over a low wall where it can cascade downwards.

9 G. *phaeum* 'Lily Lovell'

This has particularly large bluish-purple flowers with reflexed petals from May onwards. Grows to around 45cm (18in) in height with a spread of 60cm (24in). Readily attracts wildlife, good in sun or shade and will also tolerate dry conditions.

10 G. *macrorrhizum* 'Czakor'

Strongly-scented aromatic foliage with small magenta-pink flowers from June onwards. It grows to 20-30cm (8-12in) in height with a spread of 40-50cm (16-20in). Will tolerate sun or shade on good garden soil. Some years it has stunning red autumn foliage.

EAST LAMBROOK MANOR GARDENS
South Petherton, Somerset TA13 5HH
T: 01460 240 328 F: 01460 242 344
E: enquiries@eastlambrook.co.uk
W: www.eastlambrook.co.uk

James Coles is the head nurseryman at the Margery Fish Plant Nursery at **East Lambrook Manor Gardens**. The gardens and nursery were made famous by the late Margery Fish from the 1940s to 1969. The gardens are now Grade I Listed and are recognised internationally. The nursery evolved from Mrs Fish's generosity, as she would often dig up plants for interested visitors. Open 10am to 5pm, Monday to Sunday.

GLADIOLI

AS RECOMMENDED BY GILL AND JOHN HAZELL OF GREAT
WESTERN GLADIOLUS

G. 'Flevo Junior'

Many gardeners are familiar with the half-hardy, summer-flowering *Grandiflorus* gladioli (genus *Gladiolus*), which vary in height from under 1m (3ft 3in) up to 2m (6ft 6in). They make outstanding cut flowers and come in all colours, so make sure you plant a few extra so you can cut some for indoors. There is also a large, lesser-known group of species and interspecific hybrids, which are generally much shorter, often scented and occasionally hardy. These flower from late winter to midsummer. A further group, the *Primulinus* hybrids, are known for their enchanting, hooded summer flowers on slender, whippy stems.

1 G. 'Côte d'Azur'
Bred in England, this is a unique, dark lavender, giant-flowered *Grandiflorus* hybrid. The early-summer flowers have a ruffled appearance, with paler throats. As many as nine flowers will be open at one time on the tightly packed spikes. Height 1.7m (6ft). H2

2 G. 'Of Singular Beauty'
A New World gladiolus with giant, all-white summer flowers of perfect form. The blooms are lightly ruffled. It is very easy to grow, giving impressive results, up to 1.5m (5ft). H2

3 G. 'Drama'
A large-flowered Canadian beauty in red and primrose, which grows up to 1.7m (6ft) tall. It is a *Grandiflorus* hybrid with slightly ruffled petals and yellowish, speckled throats. It tends to flower later in the summer, with up to 10 flowers in bloom at any one time on the tightly packed buds. H2

4 G. 'Sophie'
An elegant and beautiful, large-flowered white gladiolus that blooms from midsummer, is long-lasting, even in hot weather, and can reach up to 1.2m (4ft). H2

5 G. 'Purple Prince'
An unusual medium-flowered, inky violet with lightly ruffled flowers that contrast well with light green sepals. They appear from midsummer and grow up to 1.4m (5ft). H2

6 G. 'Flevo Junior'
A miniature-flowered, velvety red. The deep colour of the white-veined flowers against dark green foliage makes a bold statement in the garden. A dwarf type, up to 60cm (24in), it does not need staking. H2

7 G. 'Hastings'
A unique *Primulinus* hybrid, with coffee- and orange-coloured flowers with cream throats. These appear in midsummer on a petite plant. About six flowers open at any one time. It grows up to 1m (3ft 3in) tall. H2

8 G. 'Scarlet Lady'
A red-flowered *Primulinus* hybrid of great beauty. There are purple markings on the blooms, carried on tight spikes on top of a thin stem. Height up to 1m (3ft 3in) tall. H2

9 G. tristis
Pale yellow or cream flowers in spikes, up to 1.5m (5ft) tall, appear in spring. They are strongly scented and can be used for cutting. Allow the plant to die down in summer; it may survive a mild winter in a sheltered spot. H2

10 G. carinatus
The blue Afrikaaner is a richly scented, miniature species in shades of blue and yellow, which grows up to 40cm (16in) tall. Flowers appear from late winter to spring. It is best in a pot, in free-draining compost, where it can be grown in a sunny place under glass. H1

CULTIVATION

The species vary in their treatment and growers should consult the nursery for more information. Summer-flowering hybrids should be planted in spring in a sunny situation at a minimum of four times the depth of the corm. Fertilise every 10 days up until flowering, once flower spikes reach about half their height. Use a high-potash liquid feed, such as tomato fertiliser. Most gladioli are not hardy in the British Isles and need some kind of stake to support them. A booklet is available from our nursery, which deals with all aspects of cultivation and covers the esoteric world of exhibiting.

GREAT WESTERN GLADIOLUS
17 Valley View, Clutton, Bristol BS39 5SN
T: 01761 452036
E: clutton.glads@btinternet.com
W: www.greatwesterngladiolus.co.uk

Great Western Gladiolus was founded in 1996 by Frank Hartnell. The current owners are well-known horticulturalists Gill and John Hazell. It is the only gladiolus nursery in Britain and produces two catalogues: one in October – for summer-flowering hybrids of all shapes and sizes for cut flowers, borders, tubs and exhibition – and one in July – for the connoisseur interested in species and other rare bulbous plants. Open by appointment only.

GRASSES & PERENNIALS

AS RECOMMENDED BY KNOLL GARDENS

Eupatorium maculatum

Grasses are among the most successful plant groups in the world. They are tough, adaptable and versatile. They are beautiful ornamental plants that bring fluidity and grace to our gardened landscapes in a way that eludes most other plants. In the UK, our gardens can be bright and colourful in spring, but lack substance as the season ages. The grasses recommended here, and the perennials to grow with them, address this shortcoming and will allow you to enjoy your garden for much more of the year.

GRASSES

1 *Anemanthele lessoniana* ♛
Highly adaptable and happy in full sun, this is the star grass for dry shade, where few others survive. It can grow to 60-90cm (24-35in), and its gracefully drooping foliage turns through a procession of colours including greens, tans, reds and cinnamon. During the summer months flower stems cover the plant in a pink haze. H4

2 *Calamagrostis brachytricha* ♛
This grass has mounds of soft foliage and feathery plumes of greyish-pink flowers.

Close up the flowers have a purplish hue, but like many grasses, their colours change as they age. It prefers a sunny, open position and provides a distinct outline in the garden in both summer and winter. It can grow up to 90cm-2m (3-6.5ft).

3 *Miscanthus sinensis* 'Flamingo' ♛
'Flamingo' is among the first rank of *Miscanthus*, chosen for its pendulous, soft-pink flowers, produced in abundance during summer. It has a great presence, growing up to 1.8-2.1m (6-7ft). Although the flower colour fades with age, the plant seems to gain in stature. H4

4 *Panicum virgatum* 'Shenandoah'

The prairie switch grasses are underused. 'Shenandoah' is a great selection, chosen specifically for its foliage, which turns dark burgundy-red from high summer onwards. Its tiny red flowers are produced in such profusion they look like fluffy clouds. It grows up to 90cm-1.2m (3-4ft).

5 *Pennisetum alopecuroides* 'Hameln'

Though all the fountain grasses, or pennisetums demand full sun and a soil that doesn't waterlog in winter, the profusion of this plant's flowers is amazing – each year, masses of pale, fluffy flowers seem to explode from a mound of foliage. 'Hameln' can grow to 80cm-1.1m (3-3.5ft). H3

6 *Rhynchospora latifolia*

I first saw this growing in the US through lawn grass. Its distinctive, leafy white bracts create a bewitching scene. I have grown it in a pot, a border and even in the pond. It is slow-growing – up to 60-90cm (24-35in) – but flowers over a long period. H2-3

PERENNIALS

7 *Echinacea purpurea* 'Leuchtstern'

With so many popular cultivars of coneflower to choose from, I find myself drawn to this seed-raised strain. Its simple beauty and enthusiastic growth, up to 80cm-1m (31-39in), is equal of any other. There is variation in flower size, shape and colour depending on its strain.

8 *Eupatorium maculatum* 'Atropurpureum' ♔

My favourite of the Joe-Pye weeds, with its imposing dark stems supporting domed heads of rosy-purple flowers. The individual flowers are tiny, but together produce imposing heads that can be seen from a distance. 'Atropurpureum' can grow up to 2-2.4m (6.5-8ft). H4

9 *Phlomis russeliana* ♔

With its large, felty leaves and striking flowers, the Jerusalem sage is perfectly designed to go with grasses. The plant can grow to 80cm-1m (31-39in). When dark brown they combine well with lighter, beige-coloured grasses such as Panicums during the autumn and winter. H4

10 *Sanguisorba tenuifolia* 'Purpurea'

The *Sanguisorbas* makes a well-behaved garden plant. This one can grow up to 1.8-2.1m (6-7ft) and is useful for gaining height among *Miscanthus* and Panicums. Tidy mounds of delicately-cut leaves send up spikes of pendulous, dark red cylindrical flowers.

KNOLL GARDENS
Hampreston, Wimborne, Dorset BH21 7ND
T: 01202 873931 F: 01202 870842
E: enquiries@knollgardens.co.uk W: www.knollgardens.co.uk

❀ NCCPG National Collection holder of *Ceanothus* (deciduous cultivars), *Pennisetum* and *Phygelius*
Knoll Gardens offers one of the country's most exciting and varied selections of grasses and perennials. It has a well-established reputation for both modern design and the introduction of new plants. Now, Knoll is pioneering the concept of 'livable landscapes' – low-maintenance design without sacrificing beauty. Open 10am to 5pm (or dusk if earlier) Tuesday to Sunday (May to October) and Wednesday to Sunday (November to April).

GRASSES FOR SMALL GARDENS

AS RECOMMENDED BY PENNARD PLANTS

Carex brunnea 'Jenneke'

Pennisetum thunbergii 'Red Buttons'

Calamagrostis x acutiflora 'Overdam'

Pennisetum setaceum 'Rubrum'

G rasses – you either love them or hate them. We couldn't live without them, though, for they provide much of our staple diet; the grains and cereals we eat belong to their family. In some countries, they provide building materials in the form of bamboo, they give us our golf courses and, of course, our gardens wouldn't be the same without that green sward. Here is a selection of those which are the most beautiful and decorative in our borders.

1 *Carex brunnea* 'Jenneke'
Recently introduced from Germany, this is an evergreen mound of fine gold and green variegated leaves. This is just such a stunning grass it had to be included, although it needs a little protection in winter, so is best grown in a container. Height and spread 45cm (18in).

2 *Stipa tenuissima*
Known as Mexican feather grass or pony tails. Very fine leaves and clouds of green 'flowers' fading to beige. Great when planted in drifts, as it moves around in the slightest breeze. It likes sun and good drainage. Height 60cm (24in), spread 30cm (12in).

3 *Imperata cylindrica* 'Rubra'
The blood grass, with flat leaves which turn reddish-purple as the season progresses, finally dying down in autumn. Not the

easiest grass but there is nothing quite like it, particularly in a sunny spot. Good in pots, too. It prefers a well-drained site. Height 75cm (30in), spread 60cm (24in). H3

4 *Hakonechloa macra*
The variegated version is often planted but this, the green form, seems little known. It is a slowly increasing clump of leaves on stalks, like a mini bamboo but without the problems. It grows well in partial shade and looks stunning beneath white-stemmed birch. Height 45cm (18in), spread 60cm (24in).

5 *Uncinia rubra*
A must-have grass. Originating in New Zealand and known as the black hooked sedge, this evergreen foliage is red-brown year round, and black flower spikes appear in summer. For the best colour, plant in a sunny

but moist position. Also good in patio pots. Height and spread 45cm (18in).

6 *Pennisetum setaceum* 'Rubrum' 🏆

For sheer impact, this plant has it all. Bronze-red foliage and long red plumes like a fox's tail make this a grass everyone wants. Best treated as an annual or brought into a heated greenhouse or conservatory in winter. Height 1m (3ft), spread 60cm (24in). H3

7 *Calamagrostis emodensis* 'Nepal'

A great plant, although a little large for the small garden. Bluish-green leaves with white, feathery, arching flower plumes in July and August. Will stand drought conditions and self-seeds around, but not menacingly so. Height 90cm (35in), spread 75cm (30in).

8 *Calamagrostis* x *acutiflora* 'Overdam'

A cool-season grass with thin, arching leaves, edged yellow, fading to white, followed by purplish flower plumes that age to brown. Invaluable for spring borders when its display is at its best, but still looks good in autumn. Height 90cm (35in), spread 60cm (24in).

9 *Carex oshimensis* 'Evergold' 🏆

Another evergreen clump-forming grass. The leaves have a broad central yellow stripe and

CULTIVATION

Most grasses prefer an open, sunny position in well-drained soil. The evergreen varieties require a little more water and should not be pruned - just trimmed of brown foliage. The deciduous types should be hard pruned to ground level in early spring. Feeding is not generally necessary - grasses grow better in poor soil - but plants grown in pots will benefit from liquid feeding during summer. If growing in pots, use a John Innes potting compost mixed with some horticultural grit to improve drainage. Grasses are, on the whole, easy-care plants, which thrive on neglect.

grow in an arching mound of bright foliage. Best in a pot, as the foliage gets mud-spattered in the ground. Prefers a slightly sheltered spot in light shade. Height 30cm (12in), spread 45cm (18in). H4

10 *Pennisetum thunbergii* 'Red Buttons'

This has everything; it is hardy, flowers for ages and is easy to grow. The foliage is a semi-evergreen clump of bright green, tinted red when it turns cold, with dark-red plumes aloft airy stems from June until frosts. Likes sun and well-drained soil. Height 90cm (35in), spread 75cm (30in). H3

PENNARD PLANTS
The Walled Gardens, East Pennard,
Somerset BA4 6TU
T: 01749 860039 E: sales@pennardplants.com
W: www.pennardplants.com

Established in 2001 in a derelict Victorian walled garden in Somerset, **Pennard Plants** started by growing grasses. The range has increased and it now produces 90 varieties of agapanthus, 100 types of irises, and a myriad of other plants, but grasses are still a very important part of its business. It grows around 250 varieties, with summer and autumn flowering types, such as *Miscanthus* and *Pennisetum*, taking up a large proportion of sales. The nursery is open on Wednesdays, 10am to 3pm. Call first to check on availability of plants.

HELENIUMS AND COMPANION PLANTS

AS RECOMMENDED BY SAMPFORD SHRUBS NURSERY AND HOLBROOK GARDENS

H. 'Ragamuffin'

I t would be easy to be tempted by the glories of camellias in March or the stunning colours of maples in October, but the single factor uniting our choice of plants is a long period of interest and a lasting contribution to the colour, structure and wildlife of the garden. Heleniums and their companion plants fulfil these criteria and extend the gardening season into spring and autumn. Another factor is their ability to thrive in most garden habitats.

TOP FOUR HELENIUMS

Most Heleniums found in gardens are derived from two wild parents. *Helenium bigelovii* blooms from late June on shorter plants and regularly repeats well. *H. autumnale* flowers during August and September and repeats, but has less time to do so. For our top four, we've picked some from each group.

1 *H.* 'Waltraut' 🏆
'Waltraut' has big, relaxed tawny-orange single daisies from late June, on a short plant, growing to 90cm (35in). It has amazing persistence and is often still blooming away in late October.

2 *H.* 'Flammenrad'
This *Helenium* is the essence of a Karl Foerster (a German designer) plant. Open and generous spoon-shaped individual petals, unevenly marked red on yellow,

open from early August. The plant is of medium height, at 1.2m (4ft), but may need a few pea sticks to retain its shape.

3 H. 'Rauchtopas'

Unlike some tall daisies which have tatty leaves down the stem, this has almost glossy leaves, but the flowers are the plant's appeal. The dished petals are straw-yellow on top and dark amber below. Height can be 1.1m (3ft 7in).

4 H. 'Ragamuffin'

One of our own introductions. Predominantly orange from mid-August, on plants of medium height of 1.2m (4ft), the slightly uneven flowers retain some of that Foerster character, but in an urchin-like direction.

PLANTS TO GO WITH HELENIUMS

1 *Malus* x *zumi* 'Golden Hornet' ♉

This never fails to flower profusely in April and May, and has yellow crab apples from August to October. The trunk is host to lichens, where birds search for food.

2 *Astrantia major*

Amazingly robust and equally happily in both full sun and light woodland. The domes of creamy flowers are surrounded by papery bracts with green markings. They are honey-scented and a favourite with bees and hoverflies. Grows to 60cm (24in).

3 *Buddleja davidii* cultivars

Think of buddlejas and you tend to think of butterflies. They're colourful for a few weeks in summer, and give structure at the back of a border. Reaches 2m (6ft 7in).

4 *Dipsacus inermis*

A superb plant. The lemon flowerheads last many weeks from late August and are a magnet for hoverflies, bees and butterflies. They remain all winter, providing seed for birds. Height reaches 1.5m (5ft).

5 *Salvia uliginosa* ♉

A plant that forms an open, airy and self-supporting structure with *Verbena bonariensis*, *Ratibida pinnata* and *Rudbeckia subtomentosa*. Fresh green aromatic foliage complements the succession of Cambridge blue flowers from July to November. Grows to 2m (6ft 7in).

6 *Stipa gigantea* ♉

S. gigantea starts early and finishes late. It's open, airy, and takes up little space. The golden heads give a third dimension to flat borders. Good with Heleniums, Echinaceas or Eupatoriums. Reaches 2.5m (8ft 3in).

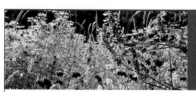

SAMPFORD SHRUBS AND HOLBROOK GARDENS
Sampford Peverell, Holbrook, Tiverton,
Devon EX16 7EN
T: 01884 821164 W: www.samshrub.co.uk

✿ NCCPG National Collection holder of *Helenium*
Sampford Shrubs Nursery and Holbrook Gardens is in east Devon. The nursery was established in 1982 by Martin Hughes-Jones and Susan Proud. They grow the plants they like and the ones that do well for them. Rainfall is something over 1m (3ft). The nursery has been peat-free since 1995. Open Tuesday to Saturday, 9am to 5pm.

HELLEBORES

AS RECOMMENDED BY PHILIP BAULK AND JOHN MASSEY OF ASHWOOD NURSERIES

H. Ashwood Garden hybrid, double form

Hellebores – genus *Helleborus* – are superb early-flowering perennials. Some start to bloom at about Christmas time, when flowers are very precious. Possibly 18 species are distributed throughout central and southern Europe, Turkey, Russia and China. *Helleborus foetidus* and *H. occidentalis* are scattered throughout Great Britain, but not in Ireland. Hellebores are very hardy, long-lived, free-flowering, easy to grow and deserve a home in every garden. Whether you require dazzling whites, pure yellows or the darkest of blacks, there's every colour except a true blue. Here are the top 10.

1 *H.* x *hybridus* Ashwood Garden hybrids
It's very difficult to choose only one garden hybrid, because they all offer such excellent value. There's a wonderful contrast between the Ashwood pure white sepals and chocolate nectaries. At Ashwood, they are grown on a slope sheltered by deciduous shrubs. It's a good idea to dig mushroom compost into the soil before you plant.

2 *H.* x *sternii*
We always had difficulty growing this hellebore, before it was seen planted under pine trees. *H.* x *sternii* seems happy under any needle-bearing conifer. Ashwood grows it under a *Cedrus deodara*, lifting the canopy when it flowers each year. *H.* x *sternii* starts to flower in mid December and lasts until the end of May.

3 *H. foetidus* Wester Flisk Group
An architecturally striking evergreen plant. The greyish green, almost lead-like, foliage is supported by deep purple-red stems and leaf stalks. They contrast beautifully with the clusters of pendant-green flowers, edged purple-red, which last from January to June. Excellent for structure and winter interest in a shady position in the garden.

4 *H. orientalis* subsp. *abchasicus* Early Purple Group
A real old favourite. I remember it growing under a Portugese laurel in my parents' garden. Very long-lived, and one of the earliest to flower, usually before Christmas. The plum-coloured flowers fade a little at the edges. This cultivar is over 100 years old, but is still very vigorous.

5 *H.* x *ericsmithii*
A very beautiful inter-species hybrid forming an evergreen bushy plant with grey-green, occasionally marbled, foliage. The clusters of large ivory-white flowers are flushed pinkish bronze and deepen with age. It

H. Ashwood Garden hybrids

H. Ashwood Garden hybrid, double form

CULTIVATION

Hellebores will grow in most soils, acid or alkaline – but not poor, peaty ones. They prefer rich, moist free-draining soil in semi-shade. Dense shade can reduce flowering. Planting hellebores on a sloping bed will improve the drainage and make it easier to look up into the flowers. A sheltered position away from strong winds is important. Remove faded flower stems by late May unless the seed is required. In late December remove all foliage from the garden hybrids and deciduous species, then mulch with spent mushroom compost or well-rotted manure. Garden hybrids are hungry and dislike being moved once established.

H. x *hybridus* Wester Flisk Group

H. dumetorum

seems to be happy in a sunnier position, but is definitely best away from strong winds.

6 *H. dumetorum*

A deciduous hellebore of great charm. The small cone-shaped, greenish-white flowers are very frost hardy. They appear in early spring, with lots of leaf bracts. The true foliage appears later and is often bronzy to begin with. I plant it under a witch hazel, with snowdrops and winter aconites.

7 *H.* x *nigercors* ♆

The large ivory, flattish flowers have a hint of green. The long-lasting clusters are so profuse that you may well need to trim off a few leaves to see all the flowers. You will need to remove the old flowering stems by late May to aid recovery.

8 *H. torquatus*

Slow to establish but worth the wait, this is a variable deciduous species. The flowers can be saucer-shaped and outward-facing, or somewhat nodding and rather conical, and vary in colour from green to violet-black, sometimes with a charming greyish bloom.

9 *H. argutifolius* (syn. *H. corsicus*) ♈

A handsome, evergreen hellebore forming an upright clump. The leathery leaves are mid-green and sharply toothed, and these are topped off by large terminal clusters of apple-green cup-shaped flowers. Remove the old flowering stems at the end of May if the seed is not required.

10 *H. purpurascens*

This is a hellebore with so much subtle charm; the cup-shaped flowers are generally lilac-mauve and often green within, opening in very early spring as soon as they emerge through the soil. The deciduous foliage is also very attractive, being deeply divided and palmate.

H. Ashwood Garden hybrid, white

H. x *ericsmithii*

HEMEROCALLIS

AS RECOMMENDED BY JAN AND ANDY WYERS OF A LA CARTE DAYLILIES

H. 'Apache Uprising'

Hemerocallis, known as the daylily, is a clump-forming, fibrous-rooted perennial, native to Asia and Siberia. From 20 species of yellow or tawny-orange trumpet-shaped flowers, intensive breeding work has resulted in more than 40,000 registered cultivars in an astonishing array of shapes, sizes and colours. Individual flowers last for just one day, but a succession of buds ensures their replacement over a period of at least three or four weeks. The main bloom time is during the midsummer season, but early- and late-flowering varieties can extend this period from May until August. We have chosen plants that have stood the test of time rather than the more recent introductions.

H. 'American Revolution'

Spider blooms

H. 'Bellini'

1 *H.* 'American Revolution'

This has a dark, wine-red flower, with a small yellow throat and small green heart. Bred in America, this older-style daylily has narrow petals. One of the best black-reds for our climate and still very popular. The height of the scape (flower stem) is 70cm (28in). It flowers mid-season.

2 *H.* 'Joan Senior'

This was the plant that led to our interest, resulting in our large collection of daylilies. A legendary near white, which has 15cm-(6in) wide flowers and grows to 63cm (25in) in height. It would look good in a black-and-white themed border with 'American Revolution'.

3 *H.* 'Siloam French Marble'

A little-known, small-flowered plant from Pauline Henry, who bred and registered many beautiful daylilies. The flower is 10cm (4in) in diameter and is a delicate shade of pale ivory, with a stunning cherry-red eyezone, the central area surrounding the throat. The throat itself is green. Height is 39cm (15in).

4 *H.* 'Bellini'

A beautifully formed, small-flowered daylily in shades of soft lilac-mauve, complemented by a deep-green throat. This is the sort of shade that many people do not expect in daylilies. It reaches at least 58cm (23in) in height and tends to make big plants.

5 *H.* 'Barbara Mitchell'

This is an award-winning buff-pink daylily, with superbly formed flowers with overlapping petals and darker veins. Its growth can be slow, but well worth the wait. It's one of the most popular daylilies ever raised; the large flowers are 15cm (6in) in diameter and the height is about 50cm (20in).

6 H. 'Apache Uprising'

This cultivar has large 15cm (6in) ruffled flowers of bright red. There are many excellent red daylilies, from black-reds to orange-reds, but 'Apache Uprising' is a stunning scarlet red. The ruffled flowers are carried high, 85cm (34in), on sturdy stems, giving a wonderful late-season display.

CULTIVATION

Daylilies are easy to grow and will thrive given a sunny spot and fertile soil. The best times to plant are in the spring and early autumn. Dig a planting hole big enough for the root system. Mix in some compost or well-rotted manure. Make a mound and spread the roots over it, then fill in the hole so the crown of the plant is about 2.5cm (1in) below the surface. Firm gently to ensure there are no air pockets under the plant, and water well. Allow about 60cm (24in) between plants. Mulching will help to conserve moisture.

H. 'Barbara Mitchell'

H. 'El Desperado'

H. 'Siloam French Marble'

7 H. 'Betty Warren Woods'

This is a truly excellent performer, with a succession of bright lemon-cream yellow flowers. The petal edges are ruffled, with a gold edging in warmer weather. As a bonus, it often re-blooms, thus extending the season even further. This evergreen daylily is 60cm (24in) tall and has medium-sized flowers of 12cm (5in) in diameter.

8 H. 'Green Widow'

The 'Green Widow' is one of an increasingly popular category of daylilies known as spiders. The colour is a green-infused yellow with a remarkably vivid green throat. It is rather a slow grower but it blooms well when established. It has a height of 65cm (26in), with flowers measuring 16cm (6in) across.

H. 'Green Widow'

9 H. 'Edgar Brown'

A fine, pale-pink daylily notable for its heavy-gold ruffled edging, a feature of many modern daylily cultivars. It grows to around 70cm (28in) in height, with flowers 12cm (5in) across. Foliage is semi-evergreen, which means there is partial die-back in winter, with new growth produced in the spring.

10 H. 'El Desperado'

This cultivar illustrates another relatively recent trend in daylily hybridising, namely the matching eye (this is the central area surrounding the throat) and picotee edge. Here, the background is yellow and the eye and edge are wine-purple. This is an excellent plant in the late season, growing to 70cm (28in) tall, with a flower diameter of approximately 11cm (4in).

A LA CARTE DAYLILIES
Little Hermitage, St Catherine's Down,
nr Ventnor, Isle of Wight PO38 2PD
T: 01983 730512 E: andy@alacartedaylilies.co.uk
W: www.alacartedaylilies.co.uk

Jan Wyers started collecting daylilies in the 1980s and founded **A La Carte Daylilies** in 1994. Two years later, her husband Andy left his job to help run the mail-order business, specialising in daylilies. Jan was really enchanted by the small-flowered and miniature cultivars and has a National Collection of them. Andy holds a National Collection of Large Flowered (post-1960 award-winning) daylilies. Jan and Andy grow in excess of 1,200 daylily cultivars. Visits by appointment only.

HEUCHERAS, TIARELLAS AND HEUCHERELLAS

AS RECOMMENDED BY CAIRNSMORE NURSERY

Heuchera 'Obsidian'

Heuchera 'Caramel'

x Heucherella 'Stoplight'

Heucheras and Tiarellas are members of the saxifrage family, and Heucherellas are the hybrid offspring genus between *Heuchera* and *Tiarella*. Heucheras and Tiarellas exhibit diverse forms according to their habitats. These are being harnessed by breeders to produce cultivars for our gardens. They are invaluable evergreen plants with their neat, mounded habit, wide range of leaf colours and patterns, and long-lasting flower spikes.

1 *Heuchera* 'Caramel'

'Caramel' has sensual, soft matt leaves and, in the centre of the plant, the newer leaves are red-orange, fading to light orange-yellow as they age, with red undersides. In winter, red tints develop and deepen. It can grow up to 20cm (8in) high with a spread of 75cm (30in).

2 *Heuchera* 'Lime Rickey'

This is a very neat *Heuchera*, 20cm (8in) high and 30cm (12in) wide. It has attractive ruffled, chartreuse-coloured leaves, for which it does require a good deal of shade. It produces pure white flowers.

3 *Heuchera* 'Marmalade'

A vigorous plant that grows to 40cm (16in) high and 60cm (24in) wide. Leaf colour develops according to sun exposure, being apricot in semi-shade and sienna in sun. The ruffled leaves are purplish beneath. It looks good with orange and apricot pansies in spring, and purple petunis in summer.

4 *Heuchera* 'Midnight Rose'

Choose this *Heuchera* for its unique dark leaves speckled with marks of shocking pink, turning cream as the season progresses. It grows to 25cm (10in) high and 40cm (16in) wide. To highlight the colouring, position it near the dark-leaved *Physocarpus opulifolius* 'Diabolo' or *Cercis canadensis* 'Forest Pansy'.

5 *Heuchera* 'Obsidian'

An outstanding, dark-leaved *Heuchera* that grows reliably in a range of conditions, to

25cm (10in) high and 40cm (16in) wide. The leaves appear to have been cut from black satin. In shade it makes an attractive partnership with the fern *Athyrium niponicum* var. *pictum*.

6 Heuchera 'Peppermint Spice'

This plant has well-marked foliage of central dark veins, and profuse spires of rose-pink flowers. It reaches 20cm (8in) high and 30cm (12in) wide, and exhibits good winter colour. Underplant with *Tulipa* 'Queen of Night' for a stunning spring display.

7 Heuchera 'Plum Pudding'

Deservedly popular, this common cultivar grows robustly in sun or shade with its silver-patterned, shiny burgundy foliage. It has a compact habit and can be up to 20cm (8in) high and 40cm (16in) wide.

8 Tiarella 'Spring Symphony'

Cairnsmore's number one choice of *Tiarella*. It is compact, being up to 20cm (8in) high and 30cm (12in) wide, with bright green, fingered leaves marked with dark centres. Pink buds open to lightly fragranced, white flowers in spring.

9 x Heucherella 'Kimono' ♛

A most reliable, large x *Heucherella*, which can be 45cm (18in) high and 45cm (18in) wide, for semi-shade or full sun. The leaves are deeply dissected and light green, with dark chocolate veining overlaid with a silver sheen. Its leaves overlap, like feathers on a bird's breast.

10 x Heucherella 'Stoplight'

A broad, mounding plant, which can grow to 15 x 40cm (6 x 16in), with bright yellow-green leaves, centrally marked with red. In summer shade the colour intensifies to acid-yellow, while cold winter weather infuses the leaves with red. In spring there are airy white flowers. Teams well with a red-flowered *Astrantia* like 'Ruby Wedding'.

CULTIVATION

These plants hate cold, wet soils and require good drainage. Tiarellas tolerate full shade, while x Heucherellas thrive in shade or semi-shade, and Heucheras take shade or full sun. Replant Heucheras every three to four years, or they grow out of the ground on ugly, woody stems.

CAIRNSMORE NURSERY
Chapmanton Road, Castle Douglas,
Kirkcudbrightshire DG7 2NU
T: 01556 504819 M: 0798 017 6458
E: info@cairnsmorenursery.co.uk
W: www.cairnsmorenursery.co.uk

Cairnsmore Nursery was set up in Castle Douglas, Dumfries and Galloway, Scotland in 2001. As the range of Heucheras has developed, so has its interest in them. It now specialises in Heucheras, importing the latest cultivars directly from the US and Europe. All its Heucheras, Tiarellas and x Heucherellas are grown at the nursery in peat-free compost. Wildlife is encouraged and, although not totally organic, the use of inorganic chemicals is minimal. It regularly exhibits at RHS and other major flower shows. It is open 10am to 5pm, Tuesday to Saturday between March and October.

HOSTAS

AS RECOMMENDED BY TIM PENROSE OF BOWDEN HOSTAS

H. 'Popcorn'

H. 'Striptease'

H. 'Gold Standard'

Hostas – genus *Hosta* – are natives of the Far East with their centre of distribution being Japan. Hostas in the wild are typically clump-forming perennial plants growing in open glades or in the forest. They were formerly known by the title *Funkia* (after the little-known botanist Heinrich Funk). Initially only 20-25 species were available but more recently, with the advent of tissue culturing, many plants were introduced and many sports and seedlings that are striking, garden worthy plants have become firm British favourites.

1 *H.* 'June' 🏆
There is room in every garden for a 'June' – fascinatingly, found in tissue culture in a laboratory and almost forgotten. It has a bright golden centre if grown in sun, dusky blue if grown in shade.

2 *H.* 'Fire Island'
There's a current fad for hostas with red stems and this is at the forefront of all the red-stemmed varieties. It is particularly special since the red flecks continue up the stems into the leaf and look stunning. Grow in sun to appreciate its bright golden leaves.

3 *H.* 'Striptease'
The best moment of any show is when a client asks me to identify a plant, and if it's this one, it is easy to identify. A subtle white strip on a darker green centre with a light green border, it will always have a place in my heart.

4 *H.* 'Cracker Crumbs'
This bright golden-leaved miniature makes a gorgeous mound and is attractive. It also bulks up very quickly, which is a good reason to purchase one. Ideal in a rockery or a mini trough, this is one that will run and run.

5 *H.* 'Devon Green'

This, sported from 'Halcyon' (the most wonderful of all blues) is a classic all of its own. With a dark green lustre, it will tolerate as much sun as can be thrown at it.

6 *H.* 'Blue Mouse Ears'

There are some hostas that are destined to become classics and this is certainly one of them. So popular since coming onto the market a couple of years ago, this tight mound of thick blue leaves looks just like mouse ears. Wonderful in a small rockery.

7 *H.* 'Gold Standard'

This has been available for many years but, for me, it never loses its appeal. It emerges green, then turns bright gold with a narrow green border. A classic that bulks up well and makes an excellent mound in a pot or in the ground. It grows to a height of 75cm (30in).

8 *H.* 'War Paint'

We knew this would be a hit and how right we were. It has splashes of white and pale green, with an enormous leaf that holds a rippled edge. Although it greens up later in the season, it is still no less stunning.

H. 'Blue Mouse Ears'

CULTIVATION

Generally, hostas can be planted at any time of the year when the soil is workable, although thorough preparation of the ground will ensure fine specimens. A mulch will assist the plant's growth, as will any good garden compost. Their main enemy is the slug and snail population, particularly in inner-city gardens. They are widely thought of as shade-tolerant, but many hostas will grow and thrive in sunlight providing the roots are well-watered.

9 *H.* 'Touch of Class'

'June', mentioned earlier, has sported some super garden-worthy plants and this is the latest and probably one of the finest. Thick blue leaves with a yellow centre, topped with lavender flowers make it a superb specimen.

10 *H.* 'Popcorn'

I was wrong about this hosta – I thought it would sell like hot cakes and it hasn't. But I still love it, with its exciting, yellow-white leaves with a wide green border making it stand out from so many other hostas.

BOWDEN HOSTAS
Cleave House, Sticklepath, Okehampton, Devon EX20 2NL
T: 01837 840989
E: info@bowdenhostas.com
W: www.bowdenhostas.com

❀ NCCPG National Collection holder of *Hosta* (modern hybrids)
Started in 1987, with a collection of approximately 1,500 plants, **Bowden Hostas** is now owned and run by Ruth (daughter of founders Ann and Roger Bowden) who, with her husband Tim, deals with all the day-to-day issues of running the nursery and attending the many flower shows in the season. In 2007, they were proud to win their third RHS Chelsea Gold Medal in a row. Bowden Hostas welcomes visitors, but please call beforehand.

BEARDED IRIS

AS RECOMMENDED BY RICHARD CAYEUX OF CAYEUX IRIS

I. 'Feu de Ciel'

Bearded irises are hardy and can be left in the ground through hard winters. In summer, they provide a drought-resistant, low-maintenance solution to hosepipe bans and dry conditions. The smaller varieties of bearded iris flower first; thus, if you choose a selection of small, intermediate and tall bearded irises (and a range of early-, late- and mid-flowering varieties within each group), you can have irises flowering in the garden from mid April until early June.

I. 'Andalou'

I. 'Ambroisie'

1 *I.* 'Alizés' (Cayeux 1987) ♔
Although not one of the more recent
varieties, this is an excellent grower and
prolific flowerer. Its pure white standards
give a good contrast to the white falls
with their wide, mid-blue border. It's a
mid-season bloomer, growing to 85cm
(33in), with a sweet floral scent.

2 *I.* 'Ambroisie' (Cayeux 1997) ♔
This variety offers an excellent new colour,
between plain raspberry and rosy mulberry,
with beards of the same colour. Its redness
has been much used by hybridisers keen to
create a 'true' red – very difficult in irises.
It flowers late, grows to 85cm (33in) and
has a sweet, floral scent.

3 *I.* 'Andalou' (Cayeux 1995) ♔
A fast-multiplying variety with 16 or more
stalks from just one rhizome after three
years. Named 'Andalou' to evoke southern
Spain – an eye-catching combination of
rich yellow standards and deep-red velvety

falls. A prolific bloomer, it flowers early-
to mid-season and has excellent foliage.
Grows to 90cm (35in) tall.

4 *I.* 'Feu du Ciel' (Cayeux 1993) ♔
This is one of the deepest oranges we've
created and one of the most vigorous in this
colour category. Flowering mid-season, it
has won several prizes, including the French
Award of Courson in 1996. An orange that
brings a warm colour to the garden. Grows
to 90cm (35in) tall; has a chocolate scent.

IRIS MYTHOLOGY

In Greek mythology, when the gods
Zeus or Hera wanted to speak to mortals,
they summoned lovely Iris, goddess
of the rainbow, who hurried back to Earth
over her bridge of colours, bearing their
messages. She was the link between 'the
eye of heaven' and Earth – between the
soul and the body (thus 'iris' as the centre
of your eye, since on death the soul was
thought to exit through the eyes).

Always plant bearded iris in full sun and well-drained soil, with the top of the rhizome half out of the soil. Shade and not regularly dividing them are the two main causes of non flowering. Bearded Iris thrive in dry conditions; once established, you can water just twice a month in summer without any ill effects. Over-watering can lead to rhizomes rotting and dying. In three or four years, the rhizomes will have multiplied and must be split to form new clumps. In late autumn, the dying foliage and the other leaves should be cut back to about 15cm (6in).

I. 'Frison-roche'

5 *I.* 'Frison-roche' (Cayeux 1995)

A tall, pure white iris, flowering early- to mid-season. It's a useful addition to many planting schemes, because it draws the eye as it rises above surrounding plants to 1m (3ft 3in) tall. The robust stems often have four ruffled flowers blooming at the same time. Discreet ivory beards. Easy to grow.

6 *I.* 'Ghost Train'

Black irises are very much in vogue and look especially dramatic planted with whites, pale lavenders and light blues. This is possibly the best black iris – expensive, but top quality. It has perfectly ruffled flowers and is a prolific bloomer. Flowering mid-season, it grows to 95cm (37in).

I. 'Ghost Train'

7 *I.* 'Haut les Voiles' (Cayeux 2000)

Cayeux Iris crossed two Dykes Medal winners ('Edith Wolford' and 'Honky Tonk Blues') to achieve this magnificent ruffled bi-colour with its clear butter-yellow standards and bluish lavender falls, with almost invisible beards. People always remark on it. One of the best yellow-blue

I. 'Haut les Voiles'

I. 'Mer du Sud'

I. 'Provençal'

bi-colours. Mid- to late-season, it grows to 95cm (37in) tall.

8 *I.* 'La Vie en Rose' (Cayeux 2000)

This pretty variety was bred from another Cayeux iris, 'Hélène C'. It has deep flamingo-pink flowers, big and nicely ruffled, with a small white area under the eye-catching coral beards. The 90cm (35in) stems give between eight to 10 buds each in mid-season, and it's a vigorous grower.

9 *I.* 'Mer du Sud' (Cayeux 1997) ♔

One of our most successful irises, bred from the variety 'Dusky Challenger' to create a deep marine-blue, almost free of violet. It always attracts the eye and makes a real statement. It's extremely vigorous, with up to three flowers blooming simultaneously. Reaches 80cm (31in) in height.

10 *I.* 'Provençal' (Cayeux 1978)

A favourite iris, created by my father Jean Cayeux in 1978, and still a bestseller. It was recently chosen for many show gardens at Chelsea. A cheerful, reliable flower with garnet-red standards and yellow falls, edged with the same garnet red. Flowering early, it grows to 85cm (33in).

CAYEUX IRIS
La Carcaudière, 45500 POILLY-LES-GIEN, France
T: 0800 0964 8115 (freephone from the UK)
T: 0033 238 670 508 F: 0033 238 678 498
E: info@iris-cayeux.com W: www.iris-cayeux.com

The Cayeux family has been breeding irises in France since 1895. Richard Cayeux, the current director, selects and creates new varieties just as rigorously as his forbearers. Irises must be robust, resistant to wind, long-flowering and able to withstand minimal watering in summer. The 55-acre (22ha) nursery is open from early May until early June during the flowering season, with peak blooming around 20-27 May. Telephone at the beginning of May to check dates. English mail order catalogue available.

BEARDLESS IRIS

AS RECOMMENDED BY SUE MARSHALL OF IRIS OF SISSINGHURST

I. 'Goring Sunrise'

Although bearded irises automatically spring to mind whenever irises (genus *Iris*) are mentioned, the beardless varieties, or 'Apogons', cover a wide spectrum of colour and flowering times. As they originate from a wide area of the world, they're suitable for a range of growing conditions, from dry shade to boggy areas, sunny sites, rockeries and ponds. The main categories of beardless iris are Siberian iris, *ensatas*, Pacific Coast iris, Winter-flowering, 'Louisiana', Spuria iris, *laevigata* and some species iris. Of the beardless irises, Siberian irises are probably the best-known, growing in a variety of colours and generally flowering during June.

I. sibirica 'Coronation Anthem'

SIBERIAN IRISES (*I. SIBIRICA*)

Cultivation is easy for all Siberian irises. They grow in any garden soil, provided it isn't too acidic or alkaline and doesn't dry out. Once established, they will tolerate periods of drought and also some shade. Plants should be planted 5cm (2in) deep in spring or autumn, and water until established. Plants die down in winter and old foliage should be cleared away by spring when new shoots appear. A general fertiliser can be applied in spring. Plants can be divided in two to three years. Beware of slugs because of the potential damage to newly-emerging leaves.

1 *I. sibirica* 'Coronation Anthem'

Growing to nearly 1m (3ft 3in), this plant is a show stopper, with huge, ruffled deep-blue flowers with a violet tinge. The signals are cream and gold and the style arms are pale blue. The leaves are narrow. Visitors to the garden always comment on this plant.

2 *I. sibirica* 'Butter and Sugar' ♛

A delightful combination of yellow and white flowers, the standards are white and falls yellow. The plants grow to a height of 76cm (2ft 6in). Bred by Currier McEwen, this plant was the first non-fading yellow-white Siberian iris to be introduced.

I. sibirica 'Butter and Sugar'

3 *I. sibirica* 'Sutton Valence'

This iris was bred in Kent by local iris expert Olga Wells, and so has to be included in a list of favourites. It's named after a local village. Growth is luxuriant and the flowers are a clear, bright blue. A truly stunning plant. Grows to 30cm (12in.)

4 *I. pseudacorus* 'Ivory'

The yellow flag is the only native British iris to be found in ponds and ditches. As it is

I. pseudacorus 'Ivory'

PACIFIC COAST IRISES

These need acidic soil which doesn't dry out. In cooler areas they will grow in full sun; in hotter areas a little shade is beneficial. Planting is undertaken in autumn and divisions should not be too small, but comprising of several rhizomes. Keep well watered until established. You can mulch with bark chippings but anything will do, as long as it's not alkaline. If needed, plants can be grown in containers. As plants set seed easily, it's worth trying to grow from seed and, with a little luck, you may obtain plants of various colours.

I. 'Floating World'

extremely vigorous, you could choose to grow one of the paler varieties like 'Ivory' which are less invasive. The plant has thick rhizomes and pale lemon flowers with delicate brown markings. It grows to 1m (3ft 3in) tall.

5 *I. lazica* ♆

A species of winter-flowering iris, probably not as well-known as *I. unguicularis*. *I. lazica* is not as untidy in the garden as *unguicularis* and flowers as regularly, but perhaps a little later, in winter. The plant forms a neat, evergreen clump, around 30cm (12in) high, with violet flowers.

6 *I. ensata* 'Dace'

The ensatas are among the most spectacular of all the iris family, with large flowers from late June to early July. They prefer moist conditions but will not tolerate being immersed in water. 'Dace' is a pure white variety with large flowers. The flowers of ensatas appear flatter than some irises.

I. 'Black Gamecock'

I. x robusta 'Gerald Darby'

I. lazica

7 I. x *robusta* 'Gerald Darby' ♔

The wide leaves emerge in spring and are tinged with purple at the base. The plant grows to 26cm (10in) in height. The flowers emerge in May and June; they're violet-blue in colour, on long stems tinged with purple. These plants need minimal attention; just a general-purpose feed in both spring and autumn.

8 I. 'Floating World' ♔

One of the Pacific Coast irises from the US, which are all evergreen. This variety was bred by Norah Scopes, who has introduced several varieties over the last 10 years. It's a mix of violet, white and pink-blue tones. Grows to 26-30cm (10-12in).

9 I. 'Goring Sunrise'

Another beautiful Pacific Coast variety with evergreen foliage and flowers of yellow and almost gold. Height again reaches about 26-30cm (10-12in).

10 I. 'Black Gamecock'

This has large, almost black flowers with a deep yellow signal. It grows to about 60cm (24in) tall and is a real show stopper. This is also a Pacific Coast iris.

IRIS OF SISSINGHURST
Roughlands Farm, Goudhurst Road,
Marden, Kent TN12 9NH
T: 01622 831511
E: orders@irisofsissinghurst.com
W: www.irisofsissinghurst.com
Gardens open occasionally, by appointment only

The nursery is based in Kent and was originally located in the village of Sissinghurst, almost opposite the famous National Trust gardens, hence the nursery name. On the retirement of one partner, the nursery relocated to its current site at Marden in Kent just over five years ago. Plants are grown on site and sold either at shows, special selling weekends that coincide with flowering of plants, or by mail order. It grows all types of iris.

JAPANESE IRIS

AS RECOMMENDED BY MARWOOD HILL GARDENS

I. ensata 'Moonlight Waves'

I n its native Japan, *Iris ensata* has been cultivated for centuries. It was considered very important and sacred and is always found growing near temples. It is easy to imagine how the wild iris, typically with purple flowers, began to be given a place in gardens, and how this sparked a desire to grow any *Iris ensata* that was slightly different. Collectors in Japan searched for new colours in the wild, and breeders brought the Japanese iris to its present array of exquisite forms and colours. Here are 10 which grow well and are readily available.

1 *I. ensata* 'Moonlight Waves'
One of the most popular cultivars, with pure white flowers that lighten up an early summer border. It produces spikes, 1m (3ft) high, in late June and early July, giving a stunning display every year.

2 *I. ensata* 'Ocean Mist'
Raised in 1952 at the famous Oregon nursery of Walter Marx, the six-petalled flowers of light and medium blue with a white centre are a stunning addition to any border.

I. ensata 'Ocean Mist'

CULTIVATION

A rich, moist, slightly acid soil is ideal
for the cultivation of these irises. They
are not plants to put in ponds or for
sitting in waterlogged soils; equally they
do not like dry, well-drained areas. An
open, sunny site is ideal and will result
in a more vigorous plant which produces
an abundance of flowers from late June
through to July. The best time to plant
is in the spring when growth is starting
and this is also the best time to divide old
clumps. However, *Iris ensata* do not need
dividing too often and are best left to
develop themselves.

I. ensata 'Reveille'

3 *I. ensata* **'Kumo-no-obi'**
A typically-shaped Japanese iris, with three petals recalling the simple true shape of the original iris, before the hybridisers created their flamboyant cultivars. A dark, glowing shade of purple makes this cultivar a must for naturalising with vibrant-coloured candelabra primulas.

4 *I. ensata* **'Light at Dawn'**
Another cultivar from the Marx nursery, raised in 1957. This one has a unique border of pinkish-blue around the edge of the white petals.

5 *I. ensata* **'Reveille'**
Pale violet with lavender-blue veins. Reliable, no problems in growing and gives a good display each year.

6 *I. ensata* **'Sensation'**
Double rich violet-blue flowers with small yellow signals make this cultivar an ideal companion with 'Moonlight Waves' or any of the other paler-coloured forms.

7 *I. ensata* **'Rose Queen'** ♆
A simple, six-petalled flower typical of the early Japanese iris, a rose-pink colour with darker veins and produced in abundance. Raised in 1915, this is a very popular cultivar, which has received the Award of Garden Merit from the Royal Horticultural Society after trials. It is widely available.

8 *I. ensata* **'Caprician Butterfly'** ♆
A lovely flamboyant cultivar with a combination of colours. Its dark purple base is heavily veined with white, and the petals have a white fringe at the edges. A relatively recent American introduction from 1986, which is very popular and obtainable.

9 *I. ensata* **'Gusto'**
Another six-petalled double cultivar of dark blue with a large white centre. Slightly taller than most forms, it carries its beautiful flowers well and will often have a repeat flowering in late July and August.

10 *I. ensata* **'Pink Frost'**
Also from the Marx nursery, this cultivar produces its sumptuous, very ruffled orchid-pink flowers on 1m (3ft) stems. It has a dusting of white irregular spotting on the flowers.

MARWOOD HILL GARDENS
Marwood, Barnstaple, North Devon EX31 4EB
T: 01271 342528 (visitor information)
or 01271 342577 (nursery/plant sales)
E: info@marwoodhillgarden.co.uk
W: www.marwoodhillgarden.co.uk

❀ NCCPG National Collection holder of *Astilbe*, *Iris ensata* and *Tulbaghia*
Started in the 1970s, the nursery is part of **Marwood Hill Gardens** in North Devon – a 20-acre privately-owned garden created by Dr Jimmy Smart. A great proportion of the plants sold to visitors are propagated from plants growing in the gardens. A wide range of unusual, as well as usual, shrubs and herbaceous plants is grown. The gardens are open to the public daily, except Christmas Day. The Plant Centre and Garden Tea Room are open March to October. Opening times vary, so it is always wise to check before a visit.

LILIES

AS RECOMMENDED BY HW HYDE AND SON

L. 'Pink Heaven'

Lilies are one of the easiest summer flowering bulbs to grow. They can be planted either in pots or indeed direct into the border. They are totally hardy and with a minimum of attention the bulbs will increase year after year. For the purpose of this article we have selected some of the best varieties from each group of hybrids – these are all tried and tested varieties.

L. 'Black Beauty'

OTs in Europe and Orienpets in the US, and it is still one of the best, producing huge, strongly scented flowers from mid-July, to a height of between 80cm-1.2m (32in-4ft).

4 *L.* 'Salmon Star'

One of the most unusual-coloured Oriental hybrids available. Its sweetly scented flowers are produced from late July onwards. Because this variety only grows about 60cm (24in) tall, it is probably best grown in large containers filled with ericaceous compost.

5 *L. speciosum* var. *rubrum*

Once widely used as a cut flower, this has been superseded by modern hybrids, but is still a very useful addition to any garden, as its sweetly scented flowers open from mid-August into September, well after most lilies have finished. It must be planted in well-drained acid soil.

1 *L.* 'Pink Heaven'

'Pink Heaven' is in our top 10 because it is the best of a new group of hybrids called LOs (*L. longiflorum* x Oriental). In general hybrids from this group are easy to grow and produce huge, scented flowers in early July. However, due to the size of the flowers they can get damaged by rain. A bit of a specialist item but spectacular nonetheless.

2 *L.* 'Black Beauty'

One of our all-time favourites, 'Black Beauty' is best planted in the back of a border; established plants can attain a height of 2m (6ft 6in). It often produces upwards of 30 sweetly scented flowers on a stem mid-July to August, and grows best in a well-drained, neutral to alkaline soil.

3 *L.* 'Conca d'Or'

'Conca d'Or' is one of the original varieties from a group of hybrids that are known as

L. speciosum var. *rubrum*

6 L. 'Courier'

'Courier' is from a group of hybrids that are the result of hybridising longiflorums with Asiatic hybrids, and the benefits that these hybrids have over Asiatics is that the flowers have a slight perfume, the bulbs increase quickly and they are very easy to grow in any good soil, flowering late June to July.

7 L. 'Black Out'

'Black Out' is an outstanding Asiatic hybrid, which produces masses of unscented flowers from about the middle of June. In general Asiatic hybrids are some of the easiest to

CULTIVATION

Lily bulbs are best planted with about 12-16cm (5-6in) of soil above the bulb. A well-drained, moist soil is a must; they will not grow in heavy clay as the bulbs will rot in the winter. We find the best time to plant them is in spring. When they have finished flowering, the stems must be allowed to die back naturally. The bulbs are totally hardy and are best when left outside for the winter; under no circumstances must they be dug up and dried off. Oriental hybrids need an acidic soil, whereas Asiatic hybrids need an alkaline soil.

L. 'Courier'

grow; they need an alkaline soil and are all unscented, making them the perfect choice for hayfever sufferers.

8 *L.* 'African Queen'

Another lily best suited to the back of a border, as it can grow very tall – 1.5-2m (5ft-6ft 6in). Its large, trumpet-shaped orange flowers are produced from about the middle of July onwards. It is extremely scented and needs a neutral-to-alkaline soil.

9 *L.* 'Casa Blanca' 🏆

Many Oriental hybrids have been released since 'Casa Blanca', but few can rival its elegant white flowers or perfume. Easy to grow, but as with all Oriental hybrids it must have an acid soil. It flowers late July to mid-August and can grow to 1.5m (5ft), but is normally shorter.

10 *L. duchartrei*

No top 10 would be complete without at least one species lily. *L.duchartrei* produces exquisitely scented, white flowers with deep maroon spots. It's not easy to grow: if it likes its position, it will do well, if it doesn't, it will disappear. A challenge, even for the more experienced gardener.

L. 'African Queen'

L. 'Black Out'

HW HYDE AND SON
The Nursery, New Road, Ruscombe, nr Twyford, Berkshire RG10 9LN
T: 0118 934 0011 E: info@hwhyde.co.uk
W: www.hwhyde.co.uk

The nursery was founded in 1926 by Herbert William Hyde when he returned from World War I. Before that he was the head gardener at a local estate. His passion was growing and showing chrysanthemums and dahlias. In the 1940s his son, David William, joined the business. Currently **HW Hyde and Son** is owned and run by David's three children, Sarah, Richard and Elizabeth. They specialise in growing both species and hybrid lilies. The nursery is available to visit when not at shows - please phone for more information.

LUPINS

AS RECOMMENDED BY WESTCOUNTRY LUPINS

A plethora of Lupins

The Latin name for lupin, *Lupinus*, is derived from *Lupus*, meaning wolf or destroyer. Because lupins will grow in poor soil they have also attracted the misleading idea that they can destroy the fertility of the soil. This isn't true; lupins make their own nitrogen, enabling them to grow in poorer soils, but not chalk. Ideally a well-drained, neutral to slightly acidic soil will ensure 100% success, but most soils will be fine. These are 10 of our best varieties, protected by EU PBR (Plant Breeder's Rights) and US Plant Patent law; commercial propagation is illegal without a licence. The flower in late spring and summer.

L. 'Ivory Chiffon'

L. 'Chameleon'

L. 'Blossom'

1 *L.* 'Blossom'
This lupin has white-flushed pink bells. It flowers in mid-season and grows to a height of 75cm (30in).

2 *L.* 'Chameleon'
This has yellow bells, with a raspberry picotee edge. It's a mid-season flowering plant and grows to 75cm (30in) tall.

3 *L.* 'Ivory Chiffon'
This is a cream self-coloured cultivar with a compact habit, growing to 60cm (24in) tall. It flowers late in the season.

LUPINS INSIDE AND OUT

Buy lupins from a good source, keep hoeing to retain moisture in the soil, spray at first signs of insect attack and feed with bonemeal or seaweed, before and during the growing season. You'll be rewarded with great spires in every colour, the humming of bumblebees as they go about their quest for nectar, and flowers that look great in the borders and fantastic in a vase. Their perfume fills the air with a peppery, mossy scent which is more noticeable indoors. Strip foliage and side shoots first, plunge into water and enjoy a colourful display for a good week.

A SUCESSION OF FLOWER

With the earliest of our new varieties forming flower buds by early April, the first bells and standards start to open by mid May. A week later, the whole flower stem is opened out like the wings of a butterfly. 'Masterpiece', 'Redhead', 'Imperial Robe', 'Red Arrow', 'Bubblegum', 'Bishop's Tipple', 'Sparky' and 'Terracotta' are among the first out, quickly followed by 'Blossom', 'Persian Slipper', 'Manhattan Lights', 'Desert Sun', 'Avalon', 'Red Rum', 'Saffron' and 'Salmon Star'. Last to arrive on the scene for their catwalk appearance are 'Storm', 'Polar Princess', 'Ivory Chiffon', 'Tequila Flame', 'Snowgoose', 'Gladiator', 'Bruiser' and 'Blueberry Pie'.

4 *L.* 'Manhattan Lights'

This is a mauve and yellow bi-colour, with a strong habit. It flowers mid-season and grows to a height of 75cm (30in).

5 *L.* 'Masterpiece'

This is a very much awaited new purple lupin, with a distinct orange fleck in the standards. 'Masterpiece' flowers early in the season and grows to a height of approximately 75cm (30in).

6 *L.* 'Persian Slipper'

A mid-season flowering lupin, with lagoon-blue flowers and white fleck standards. It grows to a height of 75cm (30in).

L. 'Persian Slipper'

L. 'Masterpiece'

L. 'Manhattan Lights'

L. 'Red Rum'

L. 'Saffron'

L. 'Salmon Star'

7 L. 'Red Rum'

This is a superb red, with white flecks. It begins early and has a long flowering season. Grows to 90cm (35in) tall.

8 L. 'Saffron'

This is a rich, lemony yellow self-coloured variety of lupin, with slender flower spikes. It flowers mid-season and reaches a height of around 90cm (35in).

9 L. 'Salmon Star'

A lovely coppery orange self-coloured cultivar. This is a vigorous grower, flowering early in the season and growing to a height of 90cm (35in).

10 L. 'Tequila Flame'

A red and yellow bi-colour. This is a good focal-point plant, flowering late in the season. It grows to a height of 90cm (35in).

WESTCOUNTRY LUPINS
Westcountry Nurseries, Donkey Meadow, Woolsey, Devon EX39 5QH
T/F: 01237 431111 E: info@westcountry-nurseries.co.uk
W: www.westcountrylupins.co.uk
Open daily, 10am to 4pm, all year

❀ NCCPG National Collection holder of *Lupin*
Westcountry Lupins started back in 1996, growing lupins in a field to select the best forms. If the exotic beauty of these magnificent plants has not yet captured you, take a chance and have a go, even if it's just a packet of seed; each seedling will be unique. It also has vegetatively propagated plants of the very best strains available.

PENSTEMONS

AS RECOMMENDED BY TERESA AND DAVID RYDER OF GARDEN PLANTS

P. 'Abbotsmerry'

P. hartwegii 'Albus'

P. 'Woodpecker'

There cannot be a more typical cottage garden sight than Penstemons in full bloom. Their characteristics range from low-growing alpines to shrubs well over 2m (6ft 7in). Broadly divided into North and Central American native species, and larger-flowered European hybrids, they provide a wide variety of colours. All share the characteristic heads of tubular flowers, with foliage ranging from small and needle-like to oval and glossy. There are more than 270 species and around 2,000 cultivars!

1 *P.* 'Abbotsmerry'

A personal-favourite colour combination. The large flowers are deep carmine with dark brown stripes in the throat, merging to form a prominent broad band on the lower lobes. It has broad, dark-green foliage and grows to around 75cm (30in) tall.

2 *P.* 'Alice Hindley' ♔

A large-flowered cultivar growing to around 1.2m (4ft) tall, producing long inflorescences of lilac-mauve flowers, the undersides of which are white, with a clear white throat. Wonderfully subtle, it blends in with almost any colour scheme. May need support if grown as a single specimen. H3

3 *P.* 'Andenken an Friedrich Hähn' ♔

Often referred to as 'Garnet', this is probably the easiest to grow and one of the hardiest cultivars. The wine-red flowers on burgundy stems are more slender than some, but this is more than compensated for by its stubborn refusal to stop flowering! Grows to 90cm (35in). H4

4 *P.* 'Burgundy'

The bold, deep-magenta flowers have a white throat, heavily marked with darker purple and with a conspicuous white staminode. Although growing to 1.5m (5ft), its bushy habit makes it a spectacular specimen in a large container. H3

5 P. 'Connie's Pink' ♔
An early-flowering cultivar of strong bushy habit, growing to around 1.2m (4ft) tall, and almost as wide. Bearing massed heads of slender-tubed, rose-pink flowers with a white throat, streaked reddish-pink. By deadheading, we've had this one in bloom until after Christmas! H3

6 P. hartwegii 'Albus'
One of the most simple and elegant Penstemons. It produces long, slender-tubed, ivory-white flowers over a very long period. With slender, bright-green foliage, it grows to around 75cm (30in). It has a slightly lax habit, so needs some support.

7 P. ovatus
A species that makes up for its small flower size, 2.5cm (1in), with vibrant electric-blue flowers and glossy, predominantly oval, serrated leaves. It can grow up to 1m (3ft 3in), but is probably nearer 75cm (30in).

8 P. 'Souvenir d'Adrian Regnier'
There are many pink and white cultivars, but this one presents each individual flower on a longer peduncle than usual. It quickly forms a substantial plant covered with candy-pink flowers, with a broad white throat, speckled and streaked. Growing to around 1.2m (4ft). Large, glossy foliage.

9 P. 'White Bedder' ♔
Probably one of the best-known white cultivars. Under close inspection, its flowers are often suffused with the palest hint of pink, and yet the overall impression is one of pure white. Grows to around 70cm (28in) tall, with bright-green foliage. H3

10 P. 'Woodpecker'
The best large-flowered blue cultivar to date, thought to be a chance seedling of 'Stapleford Gem'. The flowers, held in distinct whorls, are purple-blue with a reddish blush on the underside of the tube and the lower lobes. The throat is white, strongly marked with purple streaks. Grows to 1m (3ft 3in) tall.

CULTIVATION

Larger cultivars should be grown in moist, well-drained soil in full sun or partial shade. Some species need drier, sharply-drained conditions. Deadhead regularly to maintain a good display. Feed and prune in spring.

GARDEN PLANTS
Windy Ridge, Victory Road, St Margaret's-at-Cliffe, Dover, Kent CT15 6HF T: 01304 853225
E: gardenplants@gardenplants-nursery.co.uk
W: www.gardenplants-nursery.co.uk
Open daily (except Tuesday), 10am to 5.30pm, all year (closed during December)

Garden Plants is an enthusiast's nursery on the hills outside St Margaret's-at-Cliffe, between Dover and Deal. Accessed via unmade tracks, it's been built up by Teresa and David Ryder over many years, from a derelict site acquired in 1983. With an eye for the rare or unusual, they provide an ever-increasing range of perennials, shrubs and climbers, with an emphasis on alkaline- and maritime-tolerant plants, and a special interest in *Penstemon*.

POPPIES

AS RECOMMENDED BY SANDY WORTH OF WATER MEADOW NURSERY

P. 'Medallion' (Super Poppy Series)

Joseph Pitton de Tournefort brought the poppy – genus *Papaver* – to France in 1702, from his 'Journey through Levant'. Since this date, the poppy has been one of Europe and Britain's favourite plants, and it has undergone many changes. The latest in this new breeding is the Super Poppy Series from California, where the oriental poppy only lasts one day because of the heat. After trialling this new poppy at the nursery, we found it to tolerate extreme temperatures. It also has thicker petals that last longer in flower and give a second flowering. Listed here are my 10 favourite poppies.

1 *P. orientale* 'Big Jim'

Introduced and bred by Siebenthaler Nursery in Ohio, USA, 1935. A superb poppy, deserving to be better known. It has strong, upright stems and unusual, shallow bowl-shaped flowers in a bright, clear-red colour. Easy to grow, it looks fantastic with *Iris sibirica*. Grows to 90cm (35in) tall.

2 *P. orientale* 'Erste Zuneigung'

Meaning 'first tender moment', it's a double-flowering form, very soft pink. With multiple petals, it's an almost 'pompom' type of poppy, for the front of borders. Grows to 60cm (24in).

3 *P. orientale* 'The Promise'

Our first-named cultivar (2000). With inner petals held semi-upright and outer petals arranged as support, it has 'pinking shear' cutting to the petal edge. In pale, warm pink, with almost a cream base to the petals, dark blotches contrast and accentuate its colouring. Height reaches 81cm (32in).

4 *P. orientale* 'Perry's White'

The first cross or colour break recorded by Amos Perry of Perry's of Enfield, in the early 1900s. Once the plant is mature it throws out an abundance of flower buds. Grows to 60cm (24in). I wouldn't be without it.

5 *P. orientale* 'Mrs H. G. Stobart'

Introduced before 1930, this is beautiful in both colour and form; even the foliage is well-defined. A lower-growing type, in a deep, cerise-raspberry pink, with petals overlapping and a large, black blotch at the base of each petal. Grows to 71cm (28in).

P. orientale 'The Promise'

P. orientale 'Mrs H. G. Stobart'

FLOWER POWER

To prolong the flowering time of your poppies, it's recommended that as soon as the flower fades and falls, cut back the flowering stem before the poppy has a chance to set any seed. Keep doing this and you should get a lot more flowers. Your poppies will then go into summer dormancy and will rest. This is usually timed to the soil drying out. New leaves appear once the moisture's back in the soil. This leads to a second flowering period (if you deadheaded your plants earlier!) through late August, September and into October, frosts permitting.

6 *P.* 'Heartbeat' (Super Poppy Series)
Named for Basingstoke and Alton Cardiac
Rehabilitation Centre, this must be the best
poppy we have ever seen. The plant is tall –
90cm (35in) – with straight stems. It's a
delectable dark maroon-red. The petals have
'show-off' frilly edges and a dark blotch to
the centres. Completely breathtaking when
in flower.

7 *P.* 'Shasta' (Super Poppy Series)
This shorter-growing plant for the front
of the border produces an abundance of
flowers. It has a pale lime-white base
to the flowers and, depending on the
temperature, this picotee-style plant has
pale- to medium-pink colour to the edges
of the petals. Grows to 60cm (24in) tall.

P. 'Tequila Sunrise'
(Super Poppy Series)

P. 'Bright Star'
(Super Poppy Series)

CULTIVATION

Poppies should be positioned in full sun
for at least half the day. Mauve and purple
colours prefer an east or west border, as
the flowers last longer if out of the hot
sun. Soil should be well drained but not
dry. If your soil's heavy or poor-draining,
introduce sharp sand and grit mixed
together. Poppies will not tolerate wet
soils and rot very fast. Contrary to what
you may think, poppies are quite hungry
feeders. Use a good soil conditioner, like
Vitex Q4, worked deep into the soil, as
P. orientale plants are deep rooting.

P. 'Heartbeat' (Super Poppy Series)

8 P. 'Bright Star' (Super Poppy Series)
The newest addition to our range – and seeing is believing! A new colour break, in a glorious, glowing blue-pinky red; it really is star-shaped. Nature has outlined the petals' edges with a slightly deeper tone in the same shade. Good enough to eat! Reaches 65-70cm (26-28in) in height.

9 P. 'Tequila Sunrise' (Super Poppy Series)
This 'white' picotee poppy arrived from America with the suggested name of 'Atlantis'. Because of the difference in temperature in this country, it produces flowers with a creamy-orange base and salmon pinky-orange petals, with slightly cut edges. We love it. Height reaches 75cm (30in).

10 P. 'Medallion' (Super Poppy Series)
Large, upward-facing, plum-coloured purple-toned blooms, borne above glossy green foliage. An in-vogue shade that fades very prettily to old tapestry rose if planted in bright sunlight. It holds the record for staying in flower the longest. Cut back after flowering for a second crop. Height reaches 90cm (35in).

WATER MEADOW NURSERY
Water Meadows, Cheriton, nr Alresford, Hampshire SO24 0QB
T: 01962 771895 E: plantaholic@onetel.com
W: www.plantaholic.co.uk or www.newplants.co.uk
Open Mar to July, 10am to 5pm, Wed to Sat; Aug to Oct, Fri and Sat only; other times by appointment only

❀ NCCPG National Collection holder of *Papaver orientale*
Water Meadow Nursery is situated on the outskirts of Cheriton, near Alresford in Hampshire. The Nursery opened in 1991 and has extended its services from beyond the South of England to overseas countries such as France, Holland, Germany, Greece, Italy, Sweden and the US. This is due partly to the NCCPG National Collection of *P. orientale* Poppies and the new Super Poppy Series. Our collection is the largest in the world, numbering over 200 different varieties.

PRIMULAS

AS RECOMMENDED BY SUMMERDALE GARDEN NURSERY

P. pulverulenta Bartley hybrids

Described as one of the great garden genera, the primula has, over the years, earned a well-deserved spot in the hearts of generations of gardeners. There are about 425 species in the Himalayas and western China, with a scattering in Europe and North America. Breeding from a tiny proportion has created a rich array of garden hybrids. There is a primula to suit everybody and almost any spot in the garden.

1 *P.* Barnhaven hybrids
Available in colour strains from 'Tartan Red' to 'Butterscotch', with flowers in copper, bronze, barley sugar and champagne, how could anybody resist? With a habit similar to the wild primrose, these primulas throw up flower after flower in early spring.

2 *P. juliae* white-flowered
Covered in tiny white flowers, it looks like a little patch of snow on the ground. The creeping rootstock ensures it will increase each year. *P. juliae* 'Groenekans Glorie' is a free-flowering lavender-pink version worthy of space alongside its white counterpart.

3 *P.* Gold-laced Group
These exquisite miniature polyanthus have the darkest petals, with a yellow 'lace' edge. Flowering around March to April, they are a beautiful addition to the Easter garden. The best are those with a compact habit, reaching about 10-15cm (4-6in). They are happy in the ground, and look fabulous in a terracotta pot.

4 *P. sieboldii* ♕
Known as the Japanese primrose, its creeping rootstock throws up many flowers on sturdy stems in early summer. The petals vary from smooth and rounded to fringed, snowflake-like patterns in pure white to pale

pink, lavender blues and carmine-rose. Look out for the barnhaven strains.

5 *P. alpicola* ♈

This moisture-loving species from south-east Tibet never fails to impress. The sweetly-scented delicate bells hang off sturdy stems in umbels of pale yellow and violet. Can grow to 40cm (16in).

6 *P. chionantha* subsp. *chionantha*

This species hails from the mountains of western China. The almost star-shaped creamy flowers can grow to 60cm (24in)

If grown in a moisture-retentive soil it can clump and be divided in the spring.

7 *P. pulverulenta* Bartley hybrids ♈

The species forms a long-lasting candelabra of carmine red flowers in summer. Even better is the mixture 'Bartley Strain' with shades of pink and rose. It is fantastic when grown *en masse*.

8 *P.* 'Sue Jervis'

It's almost impossible to choose a favourite double primrose as they come in such a range of colours. 'Sue Jervis' has fully double, dusky-pink blooms, with a similar habit to the garden primrose.

9 *P.* 'Johanna'

The delicately-lobed leaves produce clusters of clear pale pink flowers growing up to 10-15cm (4-6in). Can be grown in a pot or a moist corner of the garden.

10 *P. waltonii*

Although difficult to obtain, it is worth making the effort to find. It throws up heads about 50cm (20in) high of nodding, bell-shaped flowers in dusky plum-red. Best grown in a shady, moist well-drained spot.

SALVIAS

AS RECOMMENDED BY WILLIAM DYSON OF DYSONS SALVIA NURSERIES

S. x jamensis 'Pat Vlasto'

S. guaranitica 'Blue Enigma'

S. x jamensis 'Peter Vidgeon'

The genus *Salvia* contains a staggering 900 species, some of those being the most highly ornamental in the entire plant kingdom. At Dysons Salvia Nurseries our main interest lies in the New World species and cultivars – those from Mexico and the southernmost states of the US. These plants are notable for their often considerable flowering period and a diversity and intensity of flower colour.

1 *S. greggii* 'Peach'

The most popular cultivar of *S. greggii*. The sheer profusion of its clear, deep peachy-coral flowers May to November is awesome. Clothed with shiny, dark green foliage, it has a bushy habit to around 60cm (2ft) tall. A very drought-tolerant plant which performs well sun and freely-draining soil. H3

2 *S. guaranitica* 'Blue Enigma' ♛

Herbaceous, clump-forming perennial. Although *S. guaranitica* is native to South America, this form is surprisingly hardy. Although late to emerge, it rises to 1.7m (5ft 7in) by July and produces deep blue flowers on bolt-upright stems from then until around October. H2

3 *S. involucrata* ♛

This plant behaves as a herbaceous perennial in Britain, but is closer to an evergreen in warmer climates. It produces long inflorescences of large, deep pink flowers from July to November and once established reaches a height of 1.5m (5ft). Hardy to at least -10°C, *S. involucrata* will tolerate partial shade. H3

4 *S. x jamensis* 'Pat Vlasto'

A shrubby perennial with aromatic leaves and peachy-pink flowers from May into November. There is a notable group growing in the RHS's garden at Wisley in Surrey. It grows to a height of 70cm (28in) and is very drought-tolerant. H2

5 *S.* x *jamensis* 'Peter Vidgeon'

Raised by plantsman Robin Middleton of Bagshot, its flowers are of good substance and a pleasing shade of lilac-pink with a ruffled edge. It grows to 70cm (28in) tall. We have only recently acquired this plant, but are already sufficiently impressed to recommend it. H2

6 *S. leucantha* 'Purple Velvet'

S. leucantha is best suited to a sheltered situation or a container that can be brought inside in late autumn, where it will continue its display well into the spring. It is floriferous and colourful, with deep purple flowers emerging from conspicuously furry, violet purple calyces. It can grow to a height of 1m (3ft 3in). H2

7 *S. microphylla* 'Cerro Potosi'

This excellent shrubby perennial produces flowers that are held well above its foliage. Drought-tolerant, tough, and reaching 65cm (26in), we recommend it for exposed sites due to its dense, bushy habit. H3

8 *S. microphylla* 'Hot Lips'.

It has extremely striking red- and white-bicoloured flowers, although they can emerge pure red early in the season and pure white in the autumn months. A very hardy plant, 'Hot Lips' will reach a height of 75cm (30in) and is very drought-tolerant. H3

9 *S.* 'Silas Dyson'

We raised this stunning hybrid, launching it at Chelsea in 2004. A very drought-tolerant shrubby perennial, its floral display begins in May, continuing until November. Wine-purple in bud, the blooms are crimson, maturing to deep pinkish-red with purple calyces. A very floriferous plant, growing to 80cm (31in). H3

10 *S.* 'Silke's Dream'

This shrubby perennial produces long inflorescences of pale, orangey-red flowers from July to November and grows to a height of 90cm (35in). H3

SEMPERVIVUMS

AS RECOMMENDED BY FERNWOOD NURSERY

S. atlanticum

S. 'Gallivarda'

S. 'Kramer's Spinrad'

Sempervivums are succulent, rosette-forming, alpine plants that come from mountain areas ranging from Morocco to across most of southern and central Europe and into Iran. The name means 'always alive', a reflection of their ability to survive harsh conditions. They were commonly grown on house roofs where, it was believed, they provided protection from lightning and thunderbolts. The juice from their leaves was used medicinally.

1 *S. arachnoideum* ♔

The species 'Cobweb Houseleek' is easily recognised by the dense cobweb of hairs that connect the rosette leaves to each other. During the winter the cobweb disappears, but forms again when growth commences in the spring. Most forms have pinkish-red flowers.

2 *S. atlanticum*

This is the only *Sempervivum* species from Africa. The plain yellowish-green rosettes contrast well with darker-leaved varieties and keep their brightness throughout the year. Under good growing conditions large numbers of offsets are produced.

3 *S. calcareum*

This species is characterised by greyish-green leaves marked with dark brown tips. The flowers are usually shades of cream and pink. Most forms produce many offsets so they soon develop into large attractive mounds.

4 *S. ciliosum* ♔

All forms of the species have dense hairs around the leaf margins. These give the rosettes a cactus-like appearance, although they are not at all prickly. Over winter the plants in a coldframe or unheated greenhouse.

5 S. 'Reinhardt'
The leaves of this cultivar are rich emerald-green and each leaf has a blackish-brown tip. The leaf surfaces and margins have minute silvery hairs that give a slightly frosted appearance to the rosettes.

6 S. 'Gallivarda'
The rosettes of the cultivar 'Gallivarda' are relatively large, open and strongly growing. The leaves range from bright carmine red through various shades of purplish-red, to dark brownish-purple.

7 S. 'Lilac Time'
A number of cultivars have greyish-blue or bluish-green leaves, but 'Lilac Time' is one of the best. The rosette leaves are smooth, elegantly shaped, pale bluish-green and often with neat red tips. In summer the leaves are tinged with beautiful shades of lilac and pink.

8 S. 'Dyke'
In the winter the leaves of this cultivar are dark green, but in the spring, they change to deep red. This colour gets more intense through the summer, but in the autumn the red fades and the rosettes turn back to green.

9 S. 'Kramer's Spinrad'
This is one of the best cultivars derived from S. arachnoideum. The rosettes are large and the leaves flush dark red in the summer, contrasting well with the bright white cobweb of connecting hairs. The flowers are also very spectacular, with wide, pinkish red petals.

10 S. 'Virgil'
The rosettes of this cultivar show a range of colours through the year. In winter they are greyish-purple, but in spring the colour darkens to intense violet. The leaves are often marked with shadows of purplish-black.

SNOWDROPS

AS RECOMMENDED BY IVYCROFT PLANTS

Galanthus nivalis

Snowdrops are principally late-winter plants, seen as sheets of white in country churchyards, around cottages and in woodlands. These are generally *Galanthus nivalis*, probably introduced by the Romans. Now it is possible to have flowers from September to April, showing many different characteristics. Not all snowdrops have green and white flowers; some are yellow and white, others have no green at all. Doubles and those with weirdly-shaped petals add to the variety. We have chosen those which are not difficult to source, not horrendously expensive and are good garden plants.

1 G. 'Dionysus'

This is one of the Greatorex doubles, bred in Norfolk in the 1950s. It is one of the earliest to flower, in February to March, with a tall, bold bloom with rounded petals, and increases well, though it seems to resent disturbance.

2 G. *elwesii* 'Barnes'

This is one of the earliest; emerging when most of the other plants have retired for the winter, it gives promise of all the other snowdrops to come and of spring. Early snowdrops generally need a warmer, less shady position than the mid-season varieties. Combines wonderfully with *Cyclamen coum*.

3 G. x *hybridus* 'Merlin'

'Merlin' appears to be a hybrid of *G. elwesii* and *G. plicatus* and is a big, bold plant with well-channelled leaves. The inner segment is all green. This is the most commonly grown snowdrop of this type. It was raised by James Allen in the late 1800s.

4 G. *nivalis* 'Lady Elphinstone'

'Lady Elphinstone' is one of the most beautiful snowdrops, small and neat, usually with uniform double yellow flowers. Sometimes she may have a few aberrant petals and can go green if unhappy or disturbed the previous year. She reverts to her proper hue when settled.

5 *G. nivalis* 'Walrus'

This double snowdrop is obviously different. It has thin greenish outer segments, which look like a walrus's tusks. The inner segments are beautifully uniform. The spathe above the flower is tall and can be split into two, similar to the 'Scharlockii' variety.

6 *G. nivalis* Snowdersii Group

Yellow snowdrops hold an enormous fascination. This particular variety was found in Northumberland in 1877 and has been admired ever since. It may not increase as fast as its green relations, but produces a wonderful show in a shady winter garden.

7 *G. nivalis* 'Viridapice'

This is a nice, large *nivalis*. It has green tips on each of the outer petals and is sometimes surmounted by a larger than usual spathe. It is a fine, strong grower, and flowers February to March.

8 *G. plicatus* 'Augustus'

This was one of our early acquisitions. It is very easy to recognise and grows and increases well. The leaves are broad, dark green and the flowers well rounded with

---

CULTIVATION

Snowdrops are easy to grow and increase well, preferring a moist, part-shaded position. Plant bulbs 4-5cm deep. As clumps develop, they may be lifted after three or four years and spread out. Leaving clumps can cause congestion and may force bulbs out of the ground, when they will dry out in summer and may die.

---

seersuckering on the outer petals. Named after the famous plantsman AE Bowles.

9 *G. plicatus* 'Trym'

This arose in a garden in Westbury-on-Trym around 2000 and has been on everyone's wishlist ever since. The outers mature into the shape of the eaves of a pagoda and display a strong green mark. It is a superb plant, vigorous and increases well.

10 'S. Arnott'

Known as one of the finest snowdrops. It is tall with well-rounded, scented flowers and increases well. Samuel Arnott was a Scottish businessman and plantsman. The plant probably occurred in his garden. It became a cornerstone of the Giant Snowdrops Company's business.

IVYCROFT PLANTS
Sue and Roger Norman, Ivington Green, Leominster, Herefordshire HR6 0JN
T: 01568 720344
E: roger&sue@ivycroft.freeserve.co.uk
W: www.ivycroft.freeserve.co.uk

Ivycroft Plants is a small nursery largely concentrating on plants it grows in its garden, and is full of a large range of beautiful and uncommon plants. The main groups it stocks are herbaceous perennials, bulbs, cyclamen, sempervivums, ferns and snowdrops. The garden and nursery are open Thursdays in February and April to September. It is willing to open by appointment year round for groups and individuals.

SWEET PEAS
SPENCER VARIETIES

AS RECOMMENDED BY MATTHEWMAN'S SWEETPEAS

Lathyrus odoratus

The Spencer sweet pea varieties originated in 1899 on the Althorp Estate in Northamptonshire, home of the Earls of Spencer and home of Princess Diana. The Earl's gardener at the time, Silas Cole, spotted one plant of a distinct sport in a row of grandiflora sweet peas. The sport was much more vigorous than the original plant. It had bigger flowers, which were more frilly, with longer stems. He seeded the plant and grew it the following year. The characteristics came through, and he named it 'Countess Spencer'. Today, many seed houses breed Spencer varieties. The strain was developed by Henry Eckford (1823–1905). The grandifloras are often referred to as 'heirloom', 'antique', or 'old-fashioned' varieties to avoid confusion with larger flowered modern strains. These are our top five.

Lathyrus odoratus

1 *L. odoratus* 'Richard and Judy'

This variety has an unusual two-tone mauve colour combination. The base of the petals is dark, and becomes lighter towards the edge, which produces a two-tone effect. It has a neat arrangement of florets on a good stem. This variety of sweet pea is recommended for gardens and exhibitions. 'Richard and Judy' was bred by David Matthewman and has an exceptional scent.

2 *L. odoratus* 'Charlie's Angel' ♛

Superb, frilly blooms are produced on long stems. 'Charlie's Angel' was raised by the late Charles Hanmer of Doncaster. It rates as one of the best pale blues ever produced, and was the first Spencer variety to receive an AGM from the RHS. 'Charlie's Angel' has a good scent.

3 *L. odoratus* 'Jilly' ♛

Arguably the best cream ever. The young flowers are so intense in colour they appear to be yellow. They develop into good-sized blooms with excellent stems. To me this is one of best varieties ever raised. It has a very good scent.

4 *L. odoratus* 'Anniversary'

Picotee varieties do not often make it to the top of the show bench, but this is an outstanding variety in every respect. It produces large, frilly blooms with clear pink edging. It has a very good scent.

5 *L. odoratus* 'Mrs Bernard Jones' ♛

This plant has stood the test of time, and is a consistent winner. It has very large flowers with ideal form and placement. Bernard Jones was something of a guru in the sweet pea world and this is arguably his best. It has been around for about 25 to 30 years.

SWEET PEAS – GRANDIFLORAS

AS RECOMMENDED BY MARK ROWLAND OF OWL'S ACRE SWEET PEAS

L. odoratus 'Black Knight'

L. odoratus 'Fire & Ice'

The grandiflora sweet peas had their heyday between 1880 and 1910 and were instrumental in making sweet peas one of the world's favourite garden flowers. Temporarily eclipsed by the large-flowered Spencer strain, they are once again captivating the gardening public with their elegant blooms and almost legendary fragrance. Their informal nature makes them ideal cottage garden plants, available in a bewildering array of colours and patterns.

1 *L. odoratus* 'Black Knight'

An Eckford variety dating from 1898 and widely regarded as the finest of the very dark grandifloras. The deep maroon flowers are not particularly fragrant, but the well-shaped petals have a rich sheen which makes them seem to glow. 'Black Knight' can grow up to a height of 1.5m (5ft).

2 *L. odoratus* 'Dorothy Eckford'

Introduced by Eckford in 1901, this variety was pirated by several other seedsmen in 1902 under numerous names, and it took the involvement of the National Sweet Pea Society to suppress these. An outstanding white grandiflora which was considered superior to the early Spencer varieties of the same colour, it can reach heights of 1.5m (5ft).

L. odoratus 'Lady Grisel Hamilton'

3 *L. odoratus* 'Fire & Ice'

This vigorous modern grandiflora was produced by Owl's Acre in 2005 and featured in the RHS Gold Medal-winning display of the same year. The outstandingly fragrant flowers have a crimson flare on the standard, while the wings have a blue picotee edge which suffuses the petals as the flower matures. It grows up to 1.5m (5ft).

4 *L. odoratus* 'Lady Grisel Hamilton'

A lovely pale heliotrope sweet pea, released by Eckford in 1899. The flowers are highly scented and have the somewhat hooded standard which was a characteristic of so many grandiflora varieties. The elegance of form and purity of colour are as seductive today as they were in 1899. 'Lady Grisel Hamilton' can reach heights of up to 1.5m (5ft).

5 *L. odoratus* 'Lord Nelson'

This deep navy-blue sweet pea was developed by House and Son of Westbury and released in 1907. The variety was released simultaneously in America by W Atlee Burpee & Co under the name 'Brilliant Blue'. Often reaching 1.5m (5ft), 'Lord Nelson' is outstanding for its richness of colour and quality of bloom

CULTIVATION

Sweet peas – genus *Lathyrus odoratus* – are generally easy to grow, and grandifloras are easier than most. Being annuals, they need to be raised from seed each year, but fortunately the seeds are large and produce vigorous seedlings. For best results seeds can be sown in pots in the autumn, and the young plants overwintered in a cold frame or greenhouse for planting out in spring. Spring sowing is also popular, but a temperature of 18-20°C is needed to ensure rapid, even germination. Alternatively, treat as a hardy annual and direct sow in March where the plants to flower.

OWL'S ACRE SWEET PEAS
Kellett Gate, Low Fulney, Spalding PE12 6EJ
T: 01775 723284 F: 01775 762694
E: mrowland@lathyrus.com
W: www.lathyrus.com

Owl's Acre is a family-run specialist sweet pea nursery on the outskirts of Spalding. Seed from our modern computer-controlled greenhouses is sent to gardeners and commercial growers worldwide. Among the output of our active breeding and development programme are the Cherub™ strain of dwarf sweet peas and the Winter Sunshine™ and Spring Sunshine™ series of early-flowering sweet peas for the commercial cut-flower grower. Mail order only.

TULIPS

AS RECOMMENDED BY RONALD BLOM OF BLOMS BULBS

T. humilis
Albocaerulea Oculata Group

T. 'Burning Heart'

T. 'Shirley'

Tulips are among the most versatile of all spring bulbs. They are ideal for planting in large formal beds, pockets in the border and containers, and make a lovely sight planted in groups in the rockery. The range is enormous and they can provide a fine display from as early as February until the end of May. As with all bulbs, the tulip already contains within itself all the essential ingredients to provide next year's flowers: the better the bulb, the better the flower.

1 *T. humilis* Albocaerulea Oculata Group

This is one of the delightful species tulips. Flowering in April, it only grows to a height of 10cm (4in) and if left undisturbed will naturalise easily, seeding itself freely. A beautiful variety with glistening white, pointed petals and a bold steel-blue base.

2 *T.* 'Burning Heart'

From the Darwin hybrid class, these tulips have impressive flower heads, which open out like saucers in the sunshine. They are creamy-yellow, turning creamy-white with age. The outer petals have a blood-red stripe at the centre, while the inner petals have a broader feathering.

3 *T.* 'Shirley'

One of the mid-season tulips, and one of the most fascinating to watch. At first it opens ivory-white with only the narrowest edge of soft purplish-blue, lightly spotted with the same colour on the petals. However, as the flower ages, it becomes suffused with purple.

4 *T.* 'Jane Packer'

These lily-flowering tulips tend to prove the most popular. The elegant blooms with pointed petals are borne on strong stems. 'Jane Packer' is one of the best available. The neat head is shining, signal-red complemented by the bright green foliage. Unusually, it has a deliciously sweet scent.

5 *T.* 'Antoinette'

'Antoinette' is a superb multi-flowered variety, carrying up to 10 flowers on each stem. They are soft yellow, with creamy-white edges, which take on a pinkish tone, suffusing the flower as it ages. Growing to a height of 40cm (16in), they are lovely in tubs or pots.

6 *T.* 'Rococo'

This strikingly beautiful variety can be found in the parrot tulips class. The waved petals are rich velvet-red with a dusky bloom on the outside petals that are crested with green. Growing to a height of 35cm (14in), they give a fantastic ornamental effect in the garden.

7 *T.* 'China Town' ♉

A strong, long-lasting variety, they make ideal flowers for exposed positions due to their short, sturdy habit, 30cm (12in) tall. The sculptured petals of phlox pink have a flame of moss green, but the real attraction is their foliage, which is edged silvery-white.

8 *T.* 'Queen of Night'

The blackest tulip, 'Queen of Night' is velvety maroon-black throughout. Growing to a height of 60cm (24in), it is extremely sturdy and long lasting. Looks fabulous in the border planted with the white tulip 'Snowpeak'.

CULTIVATION

Tulips can be planted any time from the middle of October until late December, 8-10cm (3-4in) deep and about 10cm (4in) apart in reasonably drained soil. Apply a slug repellent immediately after planting and repeat at monthly intervals until the stems stand well above the foliage. Tulip failures are mostly due to damage by slugs and snails.

9 *T.* 'Angélique' ♉

The double tulips flower from late April to May. They are extremely robust, at 45cm (18in), and produce wonderful, long-lasting flowers. The outside petals are blush-pink, becoming appleblossom at the petal edges. As the flower opens, it displays soft pink inner petals with a cream and yellow base.

10 *T.* 'Union Jack' ♉

We now know that the broken colours in Rembrandt tulips were caused by a virus. However, there are quite a few modern, virus-free, Rembrandt 'look-alikes' available, such as 'Union Jack'. It is May-flowering and has extremely beautiful colouring. The rich raspberry-red markings are on ivory ground with a cobalt-blue centre.

BLOMS BULBS
Primrose Nurseries, Melchbourne, Bedfordshire MK44 1ZZ
T: 01234 709099
E: help@blomsbulbs.com
W: www.blomsbulbs.com
Contact: Chris Blom

Bloms Bulbs was established in 1860 by Walter Blom. Five generations on, it is still a family-owned business, with nurseries in England and the Netherlands. It is headed by Ronald Blom and working alongside him are his sons, Paul and Christopher, and his daughter, Marie. In addition to the resources available within the family businesses, its owners have also built extensive relationships with all the major bulb growers both in the Netherlands and the UK.

TULIP – SPECIES

AS RECOMMENDED BY IVOR FOX OF MINIATURE BULBS

T. clusiana

T. ferganica

T. clusiana 'Sheila'

Access to the unique beauty of species tulips has been restricted until the last five years to specialist collectors and botanical gardens. However, new propagation methods now make these exciting spring bulbs available to discerning gardeners. Originating from the mountains and high meadows of Europe, Central Asia and the Middle East, they are robust and flower year after year with just a little attention. Covering a wide range of exciting colours and flower shapes, they grow happily in pots, borders and rockeries, and many naturalise.

1 *T. clusiana*

This species has long, slender pointed white petals with the back of the outer tepals deep raspberry-pink, complemented by an eye-catching purple blotch inside with matching stamens. It grows to a height of 20cm (8in) and flowers at the end of March to early April.

2 *T. clusiana* 'Cynthia' ♔

A form of *T. clusiana*, and very similar in shape and cultivar to its parent. The petals are creamy yellow with a touch of green and the outer tepals are carmine rose. Inside is a feathering of red with a purple blotch. It flowers early April and grows to 20cm (8in).

3 *T. clusiana* 'Sheila'

Another stunning member of the *clusiana* family, but rarely offered for sale. A long-lasting flower intensifying in colour. The petals are a striking apricot with a cardinal-red flame from the base to the top of its outer tepals. It can reach 20cm (8in) and flowers mid to late April.

4 *T. ferganica*

Eye-catching, fluted, deep-lemon flowers with the outer tepals flushed orange on a green base. The colour becomes deeper as the flower matures and opens in the sun. It grows well in pots and borders and likes a sunny position. Worth seeking out, it can grow to 25cm (10in).

5 *T. heweri*

Only collected in northern Afghanistan in 1971 and still rare in cultivation, this outstanding species tulips is multi-headed, frequently with three or more flowers per stem. The petals are an attractive, glowing yellow with a red flush on outer tepals. Its flowers are long-lasting, it is good in pots and it flowers mid-April.

6 *T. humilis*
Albocaerulea Oculata Group

The *T. humilis* family are outstanding and those from the Albocaerulea Oculata Group are the most sought-after. The flowers are spectacular and sweetly fragrant. The glistening white flowers have an eye-catching, large, steel-blue centre. Increases well and enjoys a sunny position. It flowers in April and grows to 10cm (4in) in height.

7 *T. humilis* 'Zephyr'

An outstanding member of the *humilis* family, only recently released, 'Zephyr' is multi-headed, low-growing and has attractive pointed petals. When the scarlet flowers open in full sun the stunning jet-black centre is revealed. A more vigorous cultivar from *T. humilis*, it flowers from the end of March to early April and can grow to 12cm (5in).

8 *T. julia*

Not yet widely available in cultivation. The outer petals are scarlet with an orange hue and are slightly bigger than the inner tepals. It has a very attractive black basal blotch edged with yellow. It needs a well-drained position. It flowers mid April and the height can be variable, usually around 22cm (9in).

9 *T. schrenkii*

A popular species tulips, for pots and the rockery, with orange-red flowers with a thin orange-to-yellow margin on the outer tepals. Very hardy and easy to grow in well-drained soil. Likes to be baked in the summer. It flowers mid-April and the height is variable, but dwarf selections are around 12cm (5in).

10 *T. orphanidea* Whittallii Group ♔

Absolutely stunning, this is a strong grower and long-lasting. The outer tepals start greenish-yellow, maturing to burnt orange-caramel flushed with buff. The central base is an unusual deep olive-green with a paler margin. It flowers mid-April and reaches a height of 20cm (8in).

MINIATURE BULBS
The Warren Estate, 9 Greengate Drive, Knaresborough, North Yorkshire HG5 9EN
T/F: 01423 542819 E: sales@miniaturebulbs.co.uk
W: www.miniaturebulbs.co.uk

Miniature Bulbs specialises in rare and unusual spring bulbs. It has been growing and exhibiting spring bulbs at the RHS and other major spring shows for over 35 years. It supplies bulbs to botanical gardens and specialist and discerning gardeners via catalogue, mail order and online, using its secure ordering facility, throughout the EU. It obtains new bulbs from around the world and utilises the latest bulb propagation methods with its associates. As a result, its range of bulbs is increasing every year with new and rare introductions.

VIOLETS

AS RECOMMENDED BY CLIVE GROVES OF CW GROVES & SON LTD

V. 'Köningin Charlotte' *V.* 'Lydia's Legacy' *V.* 'John Raddenbury'

The purple splash of the sweet violet (*Viola odorata*) can be seen alongside primroses in British hedgerows and woodlands during the spring. The violet has been enjoyed for centuries all over the world. Violets were one of the first flowering plants to be grown commercially and have been grown for flower markets and the perfume, wine and confectionary industries. While the distinctive purple of the violet is well known, the sweet violet can occur in a rainbow of colours for your garden.

1 *V.* 'Countess of Shaftsbury'
In the 1960s 'Countess of Shaftsbury' and 'Mrs David Lloyd George' were extremely popular as cut flowers. The flower is semi-double with mid-blue outer petals and a rose-pink rosette in the centre. It is one of the most beautiful violets in cultivation in recent years and is Clive Groves' favourite cultivar.

2 *V.* 'Princess de Galles'
The flowers are large and violet-blue with particularly long stems and are perfumed, ideal for posies and cut flowers. It was this perfume that attracted the red spider mite and caused devastation on the fields where they were grown. Also known as 'Princess of Wales', it grows well in summer shade.

3 *V.* 'Mrs David Lloyd George'
This rare violet is also called the 'Dorset Violet'. Bred in 1915 by JJ Kettle of Corfe

Mullen, Dorset, the parents of this cultivar were 'John Raddenbury' x 'Cyclope'. It resulted in a semi-double flower, with blue outer petals and white inner petals.

4 *V.* 'Köningin Charlotte'
The flowers of this violet unusually look skywards. It has a long flowering season from August to May. The flowers are blue-purple and extremely scented. This is a good cultivar for novice growers, which sets seeds readily.

5 *V.* 'Lydia's Legacy'
This was bred by Clive Groves and originated from the parent plant 'Lydia Groves', named after Clive's mother. Shortly after Lydia died, Clive found a sport growing from 'Lydia Groves', which he named 'Lydia's Legacy'. The new cultivar has bright cerise flowers, which are sometimes splashed with purple and a delicate scent.

6 V. 'Mrs R. Barton'

Bred by Mr George and Mrs Zambra in the Windward Violet Nurseries in Devon, this violet was a seedling from 'Princess of Wales'. Mr Barton was the nursery foreman and Mrs Barton the family cook. It is a free-flowering plant with long stems which bear single flowers – white with amethyst splashes.

7 V. 'The Czar'

This cultivar has stems long enough for cutting, is free-flowering, and its deep purple flowers have a strong scent. This historic violet has been used to hybridise many of the finest violet cultivars. As a result, many of the best have 'The Czar' in their ancestry.

8 V. 'John Raddenbury'

Introduced in 1895 from Australia, this violet is thought to be named after the curator of the Geelong Botanical Gardens in Victoria. It was grown by JJ Kettle, who helped to popularise it for the cut flower market. Flowers are mid-blue with a strong scent.

9 V. 'Lees Peachy Pink'

Named after George Lee, a market gardener who produced some important violet cultivars, this was rediscovered on the former nursery site of George Lee in Clevedon, Somerset, 50 years after it closed. The violet is vigorous in growth and has large, peachy-pink flowers with a delicate perfume.

10. V. 'Parme de Toulouse'

This Parma violet is still extensively grown around Toulouse, France, where micro-propagation has enabled nurseries to grow disease-free violets. As with most Parma violets, it has a double flower, which is mauve and strongly scented. It is used for making liqueur, confectionery and perfume.

CULTIVATION

As in the wild, *Viola odorata* cultivars favour areas of your garden that can provide winter sun and summer shade. This may be in a hedge bank, under a deciduous tree or in a herbaceous flower bed. These situations allow good light levels to encourage winter flowering and provide a cooler climate in summer, helping protect the violets from pests and disease, such as red spider mite. They also favour well-drained soil. Unlike Parma violets, the sweet violet is hardy. Parma violets can be grown in pots, so they can be moved indoors during the winter or covered with a cloche.

CW GROVES & SON LTD
The Nurseries, West Bay Road, Bridport, Dorset DT6 4BA
T: 01308 422654
F: 01308 420888
E: garden@grovesnurseries.co.uk

CW Groves and Son is a family nursery, established in 1866 by Charles William Groves, in Piddletrenthide near Dorchester, Dorset. Today the nursery and garden centre is based in Bridport and run by fifth-generation managing director Clive W Groves. Clive's father, Charles William Groves, began the collection of violets. The enthusiasm and love for violets has continued through the generations with Clive, and he has been successful in hybridising many new cultivars.

WATER LILIES
AS RECOMMENDED BY BENNETTS WATER GARDENS

N. 'Perry's Baby Red'

I n the late 19th century Latour Marliac pioneered the hybridisation of hardy water lilies producing shades of pinks and reds when there were only whites or yellows. These new cultivars were eagerly snapped up by Claude Monet whose paintings have immortalised the magic of water lilies in bloom. Hardy *Nymphaea* consist of either a tough black Marliac rhizome or softer tuber of the Odorata type. Both root stock types are whitish inside with fibrous roots that grow into the mud to anchor and nourish the plant. Leaves lie on the water from April until October and the plant blooms from May.

1 N. 'Perry's Baby Red'
This is one of the hybrids produced by the late Perry Slocum. It is easy to control and would suit the average garden pond with a depth between 15-30cm (6-12in).

2 N. 'Pink Sensation'
Perry Slocum selected and named this variety in 1947. It is a reliable all-rounder.

'Pink Sensation' is great for pond depths between 20-50cm (8-20in). It delivers stunning cerise-pink blooms.

3 N. 'James Brydon' ♆
This is an excellent variety with cup-shaped deep-pink flowers. This is not the first to bloom, but when it does the quantity of flowers are spectacular and contrast well

with its burgundy-coloured leaves. Plants should be planted between 25-50cm deep (10-20in) and can prosper in minimum sun where many lilies would fail.

4 N. 'Escarboucle' ♔

A tried and tested variety of nearly 100 years, this is one of the most outstanding species of all water lilies. It is a slow-growing blood red that can eventually grow into a large plant. Yellow-tipped red stamens and leaves range from burgundy to dark green. Water depth should be 30-70cm (12-28in) over the plant. It reproduces very slowly and could take years to over-colonise a garden pond.

5 N. 'Gonnère' ♔

Produced by Marliac, this one produces stunning large white double petalled blooms. The rhizome of these plants is an Odorata type and better suited to larger ponds with depths ranging from 25-60cm (10-24in). It is aptly known as 'Snowball' in the US.

6 N. 'Colorado'

Another excellent Odorata rooted water lily produced by Kirk Strawn in 1994. This has spectacular flowers. They are peach blended with salmon pink with a deepening shade towards the base of the petals and the stamens. It is free flowering in full sun with variegated leaves and performs well in depths of 25-50cm (10-20in).

7 N. 'Joey Tomocik'

Produced in 1993, this is another hybrid from Kirk Strawn. 'Joey Tomocik' is a large flowering plant and produces blooms in deep yellow. To grow successfully, it requires a mud bottom pond or frequent

N. 'Colorado'

N. 'Gloire du Temple-sur-Lot'

N. 'Marliacea chromatella'

CULTIVATION

Hardy water lilies can be grown in ponds and lakes that warm up in the summer and need at least half a day of full sunshine to produce a decent succession of flowers. Varieties should be selected for their vigour to suit your pond depth and temperature. Planting is a process of pushing them into the mud or compost at an angle of about 45° with the growing point within 7.2cm (3in) of the surface of the mud. Bare roots float, so be sure to firm them well and even put gravel over the top of the compost when planting into a container. Pot grown plants should be lifted, pruned and re-potted when the rhizome has spread out of the container. Odorata type roots 'crawl' quickly and are therefore suited to mud-bottomed ponds.

repotting into a large container. For depths of 30-90cm (12-35in) this lily can produce a 2m (7ft) diameter leaf spread in one season.

8 N. 'Marliacea Chromatella' ♆

Commonly known as golden cup, this is one of the most reliable yellows. It is also one of the most popular water lilies, regardless of colour. Released in 1877 it is a slow growing variety, but sometimes grows to an enormous size. It is a prolific producer and can rapidly over-colonise a pond that it takes a liking to. 'Marliacea Chromatella' is a suitable lily for depths ranging from 30-75cm (12-30in). However, it can sometimes rot in anaerobic and acidic conditions.

9 N. 'Gloire du Temple-sur-Lot'

This stunning variety produces large double pale pink blooms. Each flower contains a huge number of slightly crimpled petals. This is another bloody Odorata type that loves to crawl and is best suited to a mud-bottomed pond. Suits depths of 30-75cm (12-30in).

10 N. 'Fabiola'

This is another of Marliac's produced in 1910. It is a good free-flowering pink variety, with large pale rose flowers that darken with age to a deep satin pink. It is slow growing, but can eventually become quite a large plant even in the colder depths of 40-80cm (16-31in). Planted at a 45cm (18in) depth, 'Fabiola' should flower in the first season. However, at 80cm (31in) deep it may take two years or more before it becomes established enough to produce blooms. This lily variety is synonymous with 'Mrs Richmond'.

BENNETTS WATER GARDENS
Putton Lane, Chickerell, Weymouth, Dorset DT3 4AF
T: 01305 785150
E: enquiries@waterlily.co.uk W: www.waterlily.co.uk
Open 10am to 5pm (Last admission 4pm) Closed Monday and Saturday April to September

✿ NCCPG National Collection holder of *Nymphaea*
Norman Bennett started growing water lilies in 1959 in the disused clay pits of Chickerell Brickworks near Weymouth. Those original plants were supplied from the very same nursery in France that supplied Claude Monet's water lily garden in Giverny. These varieties that Monet painted now form part of the National Collection held here today. Since then Jonathon Bennett has overseen the landscaping of this eight-acre (3ha) site to create a unique attraction. The Replica Monet Bridge was commissioned in 1999 to commemorate 100 years since Monet's painting of his Japanese Bridge called 'Water Lily pond 1899'.

Grow greener with
Genie™
Genie is a peat-free, loam-free compost made from recycled garden waste. Not only does it grow great plants, it is protecting the wildlife of our natural peat bogs and preserving our native meadows and woodlands. And because it's made from garden waste, it provides a perfect circle of sustainability! Genie is literally the greenest growing medium around.
The Evolution of Compost
Genie
Sowing & Cuttings
Potting
MULTI PURPOSE
General Use

PHOTOGRAPHS

Unless otherwise specified, copyright for the photographs used in this book belongs to the garden nurseries. We would like to thank the following people and nurseries for providing images:

Adrian and Richard Bloom, Bloom Pictures (Bressingham Gardens), Alisdair Aird (Tilebarn Nursery), Andrea Jones and the Garden Exposures Photo Library (Crûg Farm Plants), Ashwood Nurseries, Blackboys Nursery, Brian Fidler (Pure Plants), Brian Warrington (Evergreen Conifer Centre), Chris Ireland-Jones (Avon Bulbs), Chris Link (Gobbett Nursery), Clive Watt Groves (Groves Nursery), Collin Varndell (Groves Nursery), David Ward (Beth Chatto Gardens), De Jong Lelies (Harts Nursery), Fibrex Nurseries Ltd, Fiona Lanc (Welsh Holly), Fiona Mcleod (Pure Plants), Graham Titchmarsh/RHS Herbarium, Great Western Gladiolus, Hardy's Cottage Garden Plants, Howard Wills (Fernwood Nursery), Jim Stephens (Duchy of Cornwall Nursery), John Amand and Debbie Joliff (Jacques Amand International), John Eddy (Trevena Cross Nurseries), June Haddow (Kenwith Nursery), Junkers Nursery Ltd, Kenneth Cox (Glendoick Gardens), Kingfisher Nursery, Martin Gibbons (The Palm Centre), Martyn Denney (Tilebarn Nursery), Michael Shuttleworth (Broadleigh Bulbs), Neil Timm (The Fern Nursery), Nicola Browne (Stone Lane Gardens Arboretum & Tree Nursery), Notcutts Nurseries, Peter Manfield (Village Nurseries), Ruth Penrose (Bowden Hostas), Sandy Worth (Water Meadow Nursery), Sarah Merry and Phil Corbett (Cool Temperate), Simon Charlesworth (Downderry Nursery), Sonja and Dave Root (Kelways Ltd), Spring Reach Nursery, Stephen Rogers (Dove Cottage Nursery), The Harry Smith Collection, The RHS Herbarium, The World of Ferns, Tim Sandall (The Wisley Plant Centre), Trehane Nursery, Trevor Fawcett (British Gladiolus Society), Trevor Nicholson-Christie (Dove Cottage Nursery), www.davidaustinroses.com, Zebrina Rendall/RHS Herbarium.

INDEX